Editorial Address and Orders:
P.O. Box 660725
Birmingham, AL 35266-0725
Fax: 205-822-0463

Language, Culture, and Hegemony in Modern France

(1539 to the Millennium)

Language, Culture, and Hegemony in Modern France
(1539 to the Millennium)

Freeman G. Henry

SUMMA PUBLICATIONS, INC.
Birmingham, Alabama
2008

Copyright 2008
Summa Publications, Inc.
ISBN 978-1-883479-59-6
(1-883479-59-2)

Library of Congress Control Number 2007942246

Printed in the United States of America on acid-free paper

Cover design by Susan Dendy

Set in Adobe Garamond
UB Communications, Parsippany, NJ

For Jane
For the children
For the grandchildren

Table of Contents

Acknowledgments

THIS BOOK HAS BEEN YEARS in the making. It is in a very real sense the product of a career. Numerous individuals and institutions have contributed directly or indirectly along the way. Whereas it is impossible to thank them all here, it is fitting that I express sincere gratitude to those that have been the most instrumental to the process. Research for the project at major libraries in France was supported by a CLASS travel grant from the College of Liberal Arts of the University of South Carolina (which has since become the College of Arts and Sciences) and by release time for research approved by the Department of Languages, Literatures, and Cultures. The Bibliothèque Nationale de France, the Bibliothèque de l'Arsenal, and the Bibliothèque de l'Institut National de Jeunes Sourds de Paris all deserve special praise for facilitating on-site consultation of rare documents and for their photocopy services that permitted viewing from afar. Several university libraries in this country welcomed my investigations and provided special assistance: the University of North Carolina Library, the University of Georgia Library, the Gallaudet University Library, and the integrated libraries the University of South Carolina and their superb Interlibrary Loan Department. Certain materials were also made available on-site by the University of Leicester Library in the UK.

My gratitude extends most especially to Howard Bloch of Yale University, who took time out from a very busy schedule to read the manuscript and to write a thoughtful and moving preface, to Jacques-Philippe Saint-Gérand of the Université Blaise Pascal for reading the manuscript and offering counsel and critical commentary, as well as to Madame Michelle Balle-Stinckwich, the INJS librarian who made researching the origins and development of French Sign Language so rewarding. At the University of South Carolina Jo Cottingham of the Interlibrary Loan Department cut through Gordian knots to arrange for the acquisition of materials from abroad. I thank her for her efforts.

On a more personal note, I am truly indebted to four close friends—Don Rosick, Pat Mason, Roy Thomas, and Dann Thomas—who followed the project from beginning to end and who were unfailing in their support. Finally, without complaint even when complaint was due, my wife Jane has provided both inspiration and encouragement over the many months. Her abiding strength has been a godsend. It is to her that I dedicate this book.

Preface

Language, Culture, and Hegemony in Modern France

SOME FIFTEEN YEARS AGO I attended a ceremony under the cupola of the Institut de France where the Académie Française bestows its annual book awards. I had been taken to the event by an old friend, Bernard Cerquiglini, whose title was then the Delegate at Large to the French Language. A linguist who specializes in the history of the language, and Chomsky's French translator, Bernard entered cities in France in the back seat of a car with flags on its fenders, like the recorded royal entries of the fourteenth and fifteenth centuries. I arrived at the Delegate's office on the Rue de Bellechasse in time to overhear a conversation between Bernard and an official in the Prime Minister's office about the government's policy towards the circumflex and the political fallout over spelling reform. Both were to take part in a live debate that night on national television. Minister of Culture Jacques Toubon, perhaps in anticipation of the internet age, had sought by decree to eliminate some of the accents that had been part of the French language since the spelling reforms of the seventeenth century. As is well known, the effort failed. A ruling by the Constitutional Council declared illegal any attempt to impose language by statute, though the government did have the right to require civil servants to use French. Bernard Cerquiglini eventually returned to civilian life as a professor at the University of Paris at Jussieu, and from the cool perspective of a veteran general of a heated verbal war, he wrote a very amusing book, *L'Accent du souvenir*. Cerquiglini maintains that the circumflex, introduced only in the nineteenth century as the sign of an unpronounced "s," sits like a crown on the head of certain vowels. To eliminate this reminder of royalty was, for François Mitterand's socialist government, to complete the work of the Revolution. In the very year of the appearance of *L'Accent du souvenir* Bernard Cerquiglini was inducted not into the Académie française, but into the language poets group known as "Oulipo."

The ceremony at the Institut de France featured trumpets and the stiff-as-sticks Garde Républicaine, a mixture of democracy and the trappings of royalty that impressed this observer with just how deep the roots run between modern France and the Ancien Régime. The awards were bestowed with great rhetorical fanfare. While fully a third of the "académiciens" slept, some with chin on sword, Jacqueline de Romilly, then one of only two women in the Académie, delivered a wickedly erudite talk on the history of the word "vertu," as it evolved from the idea of masculine strength in Augustan Rome to designate the feminine capacity to resist masculine strength in the eighteenth century. Maurice Druon, Secrétaire Perpétuel de l'Académie Française, presented a global census of the speakers of French. Like the Chief Executive Officer of a great corporation, he rehearsed the rising and falling numbers of French speakers within the hexagon and in the DOM's and TOM's of the Francophone world. It was then that I realized for the first time that French is not simply the language of the country of France, but that French is an element of what makes France France, that French is a country in its own right, and that Bernard Cerquiglini was indeed the ambassador to a not so foreign land.

Language, Culture, and Hegemony in Modern France, an integrated history of the French language and its culture, addresses the ways that language and nation have been entwined since François I signed the Ordinance of Villers-Cotterêts in 1539 declaring that French and not Latin shall be used in all judicial edicts. This relation, in the terms that Freeman Henry judiciously frames it, is a dynamic one. Extra-linguistic factors—be they cultural, historic, legal, psychological, or ideological—determine the internal content and form of French; content and form—phonemics, lexicology, lexicography, orthography, semantics, syntax—in turn shape the surrounding environment. Thus, Freeman Henry, the author of books on Charles Baudelaire and Théophile Gautier, strings a series of pearls on the woven threads of language and nation in his treatment of Joachim Du Bellay's *Deffence et illustration de la langue françoyse*; of Malherbe and the founding of the Académie Française with its *Dictionnaire*; of French as a language of civility; of Descartes and French as the language most suited to logical thought, an idea embodied in the *Logic* and *Grammar* of Port-Royal. Henry deftly draws our attention to the royalist Antoine de Rivarol's famous dictum—"Ce qui n'est pas clair n'est pas français" ("What is not clear is not French")—to the growth of French as a universal language and to France's place in the "Republic of Letters" of the

Ancien Régime. His chapters on Rousseau, Condillac, the *Encyclopédie* and the Philosophes, Voltaire's language in the context of France's place in the Europe of the second half of the eighteenth and early nineteenth centuries, and the rise of French as an international language of diplomacy are woven into the story of how the French, more than any other people, managed to capitalize upon language as a principle of social and political cohesion. Even after the upheavals, including linguistic, of the Revolution, France managed to consolidate socially by consolidating linguistically throughout the nineteenth century. Language, as Freeman Henry shows with imagination and flair, embodied the newly defined construct of the nation. The Abbé Grégoire's campaign against patois, which is part of the story told by Eugen Weber in *Peasants into Frenchmen*, and the extension of the universalism of French into the equivalent of linguistic republicanism produced a seeming equality among people of different race and ethnicity who speak a common tongue. With this paradox: that linguistic egalitarianism erased "minor" languages, dialects, patois, and regional differences. "It is not surprising, then, that standardization and universalization of the French language, in the name of national unity, would become a permanent plank in the platforms of the various forms of governments to follow—empire, monarchy, or republic." And this, to the present. "Indeed, it is clear that France's initial refusal to sign the Charter of Regional or Minority Languages (adopted by the European Council in 1992 and ratified in 1997) and subsequent refusal to ratify it represent a continuation of a language policy two centuries old that finds its justification in article 2 of the present French Constitution: 'La langue de la République est le français.'" The French language works to produce "a socio-semantic homogeneity capable of conveying linguistically a uniform (or standard) image of France as a nation." Language is thus formative not only of civility and manners, but of citizenship.

Language, Culture, and Hegemony in Modern France makes use of a myriad of wonderful sources—primary literary texts, literary histories, official and legal documents, linguistic studies and scientific literature, grammar books and conduct manuals, proverbs, scholarly books and journals. Henry strikes just the right balance between the great sweeps of history and a zeroing in upon well chosen examples: DuBellay' *Deffence*, Port-Royal's *Grammaire*, Rivarol's *Discours sur l'universalité de la langue française*, various linguistic self-help manuals containing the secrets of social ascension after the Revolution, such as the 1808 *Dictionnaire du bas-langage ou des manières de parler usitées parmi le peuple; ouvrage dans lequel on a réuni les expressions proverbiales, figurées et triviales; les sobriquets, termes ironiques et facétieux; les barbarismes, solécismes; et généralement les locutions basses et vicieuses que l'on doit rejeter de la bonne conversation*; or brothers Louis-Nicolas and Henri-Honoré Bescherelle's *Grammaire Nationale ou Grammaire de Voltaire, de Racine, de Fénélon, de J.-J. Rousseau, de Buffon, de Bernardin de Saint-Pierre, de Chateaubriand, de Lamartine, et de tous les écrivains les plus distingués de la France; Renfermant plus de mille exemples qui servent à fonder LE CODE DE LA LANGUE FRANÇAISE. Ouvrage éminemment classique, publié sous les auspices de MM. Casimir Delavigne, De Jouy, Villemain, Tissot, Nodier, de Gérande, E. Johanneau, Boniface Levi et Satabie* (1835–6). These are books, titled à l'ancienne, whose titles are their thesis!

    Language, Culture, and Hegemony in Modern France is not the first external history of the French language. But, in distinction to Erich Auerbach's *Introduction to Romance Languages and Literature* (English translation 1961), it focuses intensely upon French and upon the relation of language to nation. In distinction to Walther von Wartburg's *Structure et évolution de la langue française*, it carries us through the twentieth century, beginning with a discussion of Bédier's edition of *La Chanson de Roland*, Lanson's *Histoire de la littérature française*, and Ferdinand de Saussure's structural linguistics in the *Cours de linguistique générale*, and ending with the language debates of the 1990s and first years of the new millennium. Freeman Henry takes seriously the semantic and phonetic evolution of Modern French. He has an outsider's canny eye upon the wars against English and Franglais, which, he notes, is a peculiarly French phenomenon and did not occur in other European countries where the incursion of English was even greater. We learn from *Language, Culture, and Hegemony in Modern France* about the issues and stakes surrounding the establishment in 1966 of the Haut Comité pour la Défense et l'Expansion de la Langue Française and the creation in 1972 of individual ministerial committees, each with oversight over a particular lexical corpus. All of which will culminate in 1994 with the "Loi Toubon," affirming the French government's policy of vigilance to "guarantee the primacy of French on national soil" and whose first article, "Langue de la République en vertu de la Constitution," reads: "la langue française est un élément de la personnalité et du patrimoine de la France. Elle est la langue de l'enseignement, du travail, des échanges et des services publics. Elle est le lien privilégié des Etats constituant la communauté de la francophonie." The French government prosecuted thousands of cases of linguistic infraction against the "Loi Toubon." The year 2000, for example, brought 6584 investigations, 826 infractions, 608 warning citations, 218 adjudications, and 80 convictions, with a total of 40,540 Euros in fines, or approximately 500 Euros per disloyal speech act.

Freeman Henry does not limit himself to instances of spoken or written French, or even discourse or writings about French. In his consideration of French as a universal language of culture, diplomacy, and logic, he raises the issue of utopic linguistic thought as a way of understanding the nature of language in the here and now. He moves broadly and interestingly through universal language schemes both in France and elsewhere. He considers music and sign language for the deaf as a universal language. He elucidates the debate between the French Langue des Signes and American Sign Language. *Language, Culture, and Hegemony in Modern France* contains a wonderful chapter on Louis Braille and pre-Braille writing systems for the blind; on the French-inflected origins of the Gallaudet School for the Deaf in Washington, D.C.; and on the founding linguistic civilizing mission carried out worldwide by the Alliance Française.

Language, Culture, and Hegemony in Modern France ends with a highly original and fascinating chapter on gender and definite and indefinite articles in late twentieth-century French and the creation of the Commission Générale de Terminologie et de la Néologie under Jacques Chirac. Freeman Henry addresses the question of why the feminization of some French nouns and titles of address takes on such importance in France and not in other French-speaking countries, certain cantons of Switzerland, for example, or Quebec. He offers a sophisticated answer in what he terms a "psycho-phonological phenomenon"—a delicate interplay of syllables that fall into gender specific paradigms that are very hard for the non-native speaker to master, and that somehow make you French because you have heard the right distinctions from early childhood. Here we get as close as possible to the equation of a proper mastery of the French language with birth. Finally, the official suppression of titles such as "Madame la ministre" puts the French language up against the Republican model, but also serves to mark its specific difference from Anglo-American culture and its identity politics. "Anglo-Saxons define themselves," the Commission states, as "a juxtaposition of individuals or communities, each of which claims, in the name of its particularity, a differential treatment." In contrast, France is, was, and, however much it may be at a linguistic crossroads at present, will always be defined by French.

"The grammar that runs in their veins," to adapt the famous phrase of Max Müller, "is French."

Commenting upon Bernard Pivot's Preface to Yves Laroche-Claire's 2004 *Evitez le franglais, parlez français*, Freeman Henry states that "To write a preface for another author is to accept a measure of complicity...." *Language, Culture, and Hegemony in Modern France* is a book with which it is easy to be complicit. A pleasure to read, an imaginative journey beyond mere language, a deep and historically inflected meditation upon the relation of language to social and state formation, it will carry you, dear reader, to a realm where words border on thought, thought on identity, and identity on a world larger than ourselves.

R. Howard Bloch
Yale University

1

Introduction

1.1 Background

THE FOLLOWING PAGES ARE THE PRODUCT of a prolonged personal and professional relationship with the French language and French culture. The formative years of the relationship date back to the 1960s when as an undergraduate student I fell under the spell of the French mystique: the beauty of the language, first and foremost, but also the history, the literature, the visual arts, the architecture, the fashion, the viticulture, the culinary arts. I was not alone. The attraction seemed endemic, courses overflowed, touring artists and entertainers were met by sellout crowds: Le Tréteau de Paris with its classical fare, usually a play by Molière; Pierre Fournier and his marvelous cello; folk groups who sang songs from out of a distant Middle Ages that nurtured visions of a simpler, more wholesome life, long before Dylan. *Jules et Jim, L'année dernière à Marienbad,* and Bardot brought images of a society whose passion and intellectualism challenged norms and made Sartre and Camus all the more indispensable and Ionesco comprehensible.

A Kiwanis International project sent me to France in 1962 as an intern in the accounting and inventory departments of a leading textile firm in Lyon. I returned enthralled. My fate was sealed. Selecting a Ph.D. venue proved a straightforward task: Boulder, the University of Colorado. Its reputation drew on names readily recognizable in the field—Wallace Fowlie, Pierre Delattre, Richard Chadbourne, Andrée Kail, Jacques Barchilon, and visiting professors such as Alice Coléno, author of *Les portes d'ivoire,* and Jean-Marie Domenach, editor of *L'Esprit.* But it was the linguistic environment that attracted me more than the faculty. Ph.D. candidates there were immersed in a program that prioritized French language usage at every turn, from instruction and exams to the ubiquitous exposés and research papers and even conversations in the corridors and at social functions. The majority of the students came from France. Several others had been drawn to Boulder from Francophone countries such as Belgium or Switzerland. Others still were not native speakers of English: Poles, Italians, Latin Americans. Only the English of administrative officialdom—schedules and course descriptions, grade reports and the like—found its way into the French sector of Old Main, the oldest building on campus, a linguistically and culturally Gallicized enclave amidst the sandstone structures and tile roofs. It was a French-speaking island; and the French spoken had to be correct, expressive French. If Pierre Delattre, the famous phonetician, had recently departed to accept a position elsewhere, his influence and courses remained intact. As teaching assistants, everyone was expected to learn and internalize his "principles" and to be able to utilize the lessons provided in his "difficulties" guide.

The program required two courses in Old French. They were taught by Frede Jensen, a Dane with a Germanic penchant for historical linguistics that knew no compromise. He led us exactingly through the maze of etymologies and sound shifts and introduced us to the language and literature of medieval France. Some of the students of a non-linguistic bent agonized, especially the native speakers who believed that their mastery of the modern vernacular should suffice. Others, those who truly appreciated language as a phenomenon, were delighted. Whereas in many very good Ph.D. programs in the United States and the United Kingdom such courses might include translations into English, Jensen mandated that his students translate Old French into modern French. If the challenge was particularly daunting for "non-natives," it proved to be an unanticipated benefit for some of us; it provided the opportunity to experience the development of the French language from its incipience to its maturity, an opportunity to acquire an innate feeling for the language akin to that of the "native speaker." Linguistically, henceforth, a stylistic appreciation of the language no longer seemed beyond us. Professionally, moreover, that experience—plus the usual year abroad as *assistant(e) d'anglais* in a French lycée (mine spent at Lycée Janson de Sailly in Paris amidst the foment of 1968)—fostered the confidence to speak, write, and publish in French.

1.2 A return to sources

After many years spent publishing and editing mainly literary studies in both English and French, I returned to my first calling in 2005 with the publication of *Le grand concours*, a critical edition of Denis Robelot's French translation (1803) of Johann Christoph Schwab's *Dissertation sur les causes de l'universalité de la langue françoise et la durée vraisemblable de son empire.* Schwab's Dissertation was awarded first place in the Berlin Academy's essay contest of 1782–1784, only to be eclipsed for political reasons by Antoine de Rivarol's famous essay. It was particularly gratifying to be able to help set the record straight and to make a salient text available to readers of French after two centuries of undue obscurity.

As gratifying as that return to sources was, it was an outgrowth of the current study, which has been in preparation for more than a decade. *Language, Culture, and Hegemony in Modern France (1539 to the Millennium)* is an integrated history of the French language and its culture. It addresses historically aspects germane to the origin, development, and features of the language (etymology, lexicology, lexicography, neology, semantics, phonology, phonemics, phonetics, syntax, orthography, and so on) while, at the same time, providing systematically a social, intellectual, and political framework within which the language functions and in response to which features endure or mutations occur. This framework is thus composed of extra-linguistic factors that may be termed—in a non-formulaic sense—"metalinguistic" or "epilinguistic." "Metalinguistic" here does not mean the science relating to metalanguage, nor the complex (controversial) theory produced in the 1920s and 1930s by Edward Sapir and Benjamin Lee Whorf (elucidated in 1996 by Penny Lee in her study *The Whorf Theory Complex*). It does mean the concept as defined by Mario Pei in his reference to George L. Trager's understanding of "metalinguistics": "The relations of language to other patterned systems of society, or to the rest of culture-determined behavior; the study of what people talk or write about and why, how they react to it, covering those aspects of linguistics which deal with the relation of language to the rest of the culture" (Pei 1966: 160). The term "epilinguistic" is to be understood in much the same way as Cécile Canut defines it in her article "Subjectivité, imaginaires et fantasmes des langues: la mise en discours 'épilinguistique.'" Canut emphasizes the subjectivity of individual discourse in relation to language, the attitude toward language determined by non-linguistic factors, be they psychological, sociological, epistemological, or ideological, in other words what people believe, sense, expect, theorize, or imagine language to be rather than what it is in a scientifically verifiable sense. (Justification for such an approach is not difficult to establish: historically, over the centuries, is there a people that has been more actively involved in the life of its language than the French?)

This holistic approach to the history of language increases dynamics and broadens parameters to correspond to the "language culture spectrum" of modern France. In addition to the national idiom and the identity it confers, the "language culture spectrum" accommodates interrelated rubrics that affect attitudes up and down the intellectual and social scale: the theory and philosophy of language, the theory of cognition, language origins, ethics, aesthetics and taste, gender, language institutions and learned societies, economics. Among the "patterned systems" surveyed are competing language-related sub-cultures, identities that promote a sense of self outside the national norm and beyond register and code switching as a sociolinguistic phenomenon: France's numerous regional languages, dialects, and patois; the collective identity of the blind fostered by Louis Braille and his marvelous scripting invention; the rise of deaf culture thanks to pioneering work in sign language by abbé de L'Epée, abbé Sicard, and Laurent Clerc and leading, ultimately, to Langue des Signes Française (LSF) and American Sign Language (ASL). Efforts to promote universal communication also have their place: the myriad attempts to create planned artificial languages culminating in Esperanto and Volapük but also including the very successful Solrésol, the universal musical language devised by Jean-François Sudre and savored by kings and emperors.

Especially prominent in this language history are the strategies of state intervention that date from the Renaissance and persist to this day. François I's decision to issue the Villers-Cotterêts Ordinance in 1539 initiated a policy and set in motion a chain of events destined to span more than four centuries. Henceforth government would become increasingly involved in promoting and controlling language within France and beyond its borders. The intentions of the French king foreshadow the expansion of hegemonic imperatives undertaken more or less systematically by ensuing regimes. The goal of displacing Latin and disempowering regional languages and dialects by mandating the exclusive use of the French language in administrative and judicial proceedings was a matter of political and economic expediency. The king sought to shore up monarchical authority and nurture national identity/ cohesion by cultivating a national idiom that would serve as official vehicle of commerce and law and allow French poets to compete aesthetically with Italian masters. The die had been cast; the country would respond accordingly; its policies would evolve relative to evolving exigencies, but the primary principle would remain intact. From that point on, language in France was to be an affair of state subject to the ideology of those in power. The study outlines and analyzes the "political" history of the French language from the Renaissance to the present and devotes separate chapters to the most recent issues: Anglicization and the Loi Toubon, feminization and *Femme, j'écris ton nom*.

1.3 An overview

The chapter following this introduction, "The Making of the Republic of Letters: Voltaire's Europe, Voltaire's Language," chronicles concepts and occurrences which, from the late-fifteenth century to the end of the eighteenth century, establish French as the universal language of Europe and its diplomatic medium, French culture as paragon, and the written language as ideal. Following the lead of François I, Charles IX, Henri IV, Richelieu, and Louis XIV all forged policies designed to promote the national idiom. Milestones were established along the way: the Academy, a national theater, the Dictionary, the Encyclopedia. Major contributors to the success were numerous: Du Bellay, Ronsard, Malherbe, Vaugelas, Descartes, the grammarians and logicians of Port-Royal, Condillac, Rousseau, Diderot, Voltaire. The language itself underwent a series of expansions and contractions. Sixteenth-century exuberance gave way to seventeenth-century regularization and refinement. Direct syntax, theorized as none other than the cognitive paradigm itself, the lexical fixity of a logocentric epistemology, the euphony of the superior aesthetic sensibility, all contributed to the aura of France as the very center of Western civilization. Lexically, if the neologism came to be disdained theoretically as a deterrent to clarity, terms of all sorts were drawn into the vernacular nevertheless. As early as the sixteenth century medical texts were translated from Latin to French, thus making for a burgeoning lexical corpus in medicine. Descartes removed the final obstacles: thanks to his writings in French, philosophy and mathematics no longer needed to depend on the languages of Antiquity. Descartes liberated both thought and language, that is to say the

French language. The many scientific papers produced (in French) by the Academy would soon find their way to intellectual centers as distant as Russia, Sweden, and the New World. Moreover, other modern languages contributed along the way: borrowings from Italian, German, and English enriched the corpus—Italian for the arts, German for mineralogy and geology, English for popular culture, and so on. The sound system changed gradually, underwent a process of reduction that brought it closer to today's norms. Orthography remained resistant: even Voltaire who championed reform took little care in his own works.

Chapter Three, "Revolution, Restoration, Language for Profit," depicts 1) the Revolution's struggle with conflicting ideologies: how to democratize the French language and yet retain its elitist heritage, on the one hand, and how to impose it "patriotically" yet "fraternally" upon speakers of regional languages and dialects, on the other hand; 2) the Restoration's restorative language policies which, beyond lexis and grammar, sought to strengthen the country's moral fiber; and 3) the rush of grammarians and lexicographers to "capitalize" on an expanding language market in which fortunes were to be made. Abbé Grégoire's sobering report jolted Revolutionaries: if French was the universal language of Europe, it was a minority language in France. From 1794 on, a primary goal would be to bring the peasantry under linguistic (and therefore political) control. As Revolution gave way to Empire and Restoration, language replaced lineage as social marker. Upward mobility depended increasingly on linguistic prowess. As a consequence of expanding literacy and greater accessibility to the reformed educational institutions, the market for self-help grammars, school textbooks, and dictionaries exploded. Free enterprise vied with government monopolies for the spoils. Platitudes and patriotic slogans hyped the products; fortunes were made.

Chapter Five, "From Jones to Martinet: Language, Science, Nation," stretches into the twentieth century. It outlines the myriad intellectual, social, and political manifestations relevant to language in France: the linguistic narcissism following the Revolution (in blatant contrast to Germany's linguistic dynamism), the drive for standardization, the role of the Linguistic Society of Paris in the rise of philology and the transition to modern linguistics; the competition of universal language schemes and Sudre's Solrésol; the Alliance Française as national curative; the development of Old French studies and the theory of national literary history, the emergence of phonocentrism in the media era. It is during this period that the French language becomes the idiom as we know it today. The phonetic reductionism stemming from standardization/leveling and based on the Parisian model was widespread by the end of World War II. At the millennium's end, despite increased demographic fluidity and significant variations whose future is impossible to predict, both vowels and consonants seem relatively stable. Verb tenses such as the *passé surcomposé* and the *passé simple* appear endangered, however; and lexis and syntax (to a lesser degree) are a matter of concern, given inroads made by the English language (Chapter Six). Orthographic reform, beyond the standardized norms that have now been in place for decades, has met with resistance. Only minor headway has been made. A truly simplified system of orthographic representation is not likely to win favor in the near future, either with the public at large or with the majority of editors of France's major dictionaries.

Chapters Four, Six, and Seven are devoted to more limited themes. Chapter Four, "Overcoming Impairments: Braille, LSF, ASL," details the history and philosophy of linguistic philanthropy (which owes a large debt to Diderot) from the Ancien Régime to the present. The aforementioned Braille, L'Epée, Sicard, and their successors had to overcome formidable obstacles in their endeavors (notably oralism in the case of the deaf). Their efforts are visible yet today in the institutions for the blind and deaf that have been supported by the French government since the Revolution and have influenced institutions throughout Europe and North America. Sign language theory and pragmatics owe a great deal to the French. Much more than a calque, these languages are now viewed as holistic entities, indeed as natural languages. Educators soon realized that any deaf community, left to its own devices, will develop its own manual code and that expression will not be limited to hand gesture alone. As they learned more about the process, they began to use that indigenous code as a foundation. Today's "manual languages" are dynamic, indeed; both LSF and ASL rely on body posture, facial expression, hand gesture, and more recently cued speech. Deaf communities have a cultural identity no less viable than that of any other language community, a reality the European Union has only begun to recognize.

Chapters Six, "Enemy at the Gates," and Seven, "A House Divided," treat recent controversial measures undertaken by the French government to control language to a greater extent than ever before. The "enemy at the gates" is the English language and the measure is the 1994 "Loi Toubon" under whose authority thousands of cases of language infractions are investigated each year. The chapter takes into account the most recent information on the purview of the law and the extent to which France's neighbors are affected by the proliferation of Anglicisms. The French, for reasons that should be obvious to readers of this history, have developed national language sensibilities beyond the norm. The notion that the English language manifestations that find their way into the national idiom constitute a form of imperialism every bit as threatening as commercial and cultural imperialism has existed since the 1960s. Etiemble published his book on *franglais* in 1964. Forty years later the theme is rampant. What is the reality of the underlying concern? Is it a matter of the atavistic aversion to neologisms in general, or is there more at stake? The chapter considers these questions and concludes that there is evidence the French language is responding creatively to the challenge.

Chapter Seven covers the inflammatory feminization project that placed the Academy, government, and feminists at odds and that resulted in the publication of the 1999 government gender guide. What is there about genders in French that stirs emotions in both males and females to such an extent? Despite related grammatical gender systems, speakers of other Romance languages have not experienced anything like the discord encountered in France over the last quarter century. The fact is that the French grammatical gender system does differ significantly from those of its language cousins. The chapter contextualizes the project, situates it within current feminist theories of language, examines the gender system historically, and offers a novel psycho-phonological explanation for the emotionalism on both sides of the question.

The concluding chapter looks to the four and a half centuries of history recorded in the previous chapters in an attempt to respond to claims that France is currently in a state of social, political, and economic crisis that spells misfortune for its culture and its language.

2

The Making of the Republic of Letters:
Voltaire's Europe, Voltaire's Language

THE SYSTEMATIC MODERNIZATION, standardization, and institutionalization of the Hebrew language in Israel's drive to statehood constitute a linguistic accomplishment of the first magnitude. Indeed, early efforts undertaken by Eliezer Ben-Yehuda and embraced by the Academy of the Hebrew Language in the mid-twentieth century have forged within a contracted time frame a refurbished national vernacular of the sort that had taken most nations centuries to develop. Internationally competitive, diplomatically competent, scientifically and technically sophisticated, socially and dialectically diverse, modern Hebrew has taken its place alongside the world's major languages. The task of turning Biblical Hebrew into a common idiom required a number of specialized procedures supported of course by requisite hegemonic imperatives. Semantics were expanded through neologisms drawn from the ancient language, borrowings from various foreign languages (predominantly Arabic, German, Russian, and English), agglutinations of various kinds, and so on. Syntax, grammar, and pronunciation, based principally on Sephardic Hebrew, underwent an intricate process of regularization resulting from consensus-wrenching debate, all of which was followed by codification, publication in the form of *The Complete Dictionary of Ancient and Modern Hebrew*, and finally the adoption and implementation of said standards by the public education system.

As unparalleled as this phenomenon may seem, it is not without precedent. Esperanto and Volapük come to mind, but these are artificial languages with no particular national prerogative. Swahili, adapted from its Bantu roots and adopted as national idiom by Tanzania and Kenya, serves also as lingua franca to large populations in Zambia, Malawi, and Uganda. In reality, what Israelis have been able to accomplish systematically, efficaciously, with both political complicity and the overriding support of an aggregate society, does have a more compelling predecessor whose history provided a protracted model.[1] The French language of the early sixteenth century, viewed inside the realm as culturally and linguistically inferior to Latin and Greek and outside the realm as deficient and aesthetically inferior to Italian and Spanish, in less than two hundred years, by dint of similar national resolve and sustained collective impetus, ascended to the status of "universal language of Europe." What is more, within that period France became recognized as the prime mover within the so-called "Republic of Letters": an ideological, cosmopolitan construct whose geographic domain extended across Europe from Russia and Sweden to England and southward to the Mediterranean, whose capital lay in Paris, whose aesthetics derived from the French classical frame, and whose recognized medium of cultural, commercial, and diplomatic exchange was the French language.

2.1 Beginnings: culture and politics

Such is not to say that the French language of François I's early reign was little known outside his kingdom. France had long been a major player in European politics and culture. The French language had established footholds in England, Germany, Holland, and elsewhere, and the University of Paris continued to attract foreign scholars from principal European venues. In fact if the sixteenth century would spawn the formalization of French grammar as such within France, it would also witness the publication of important French grammars in each of the aforementioned countries, John Palsgrave's *L'esclarissement de la langue françoyse* (London: Haukyns, 1530) for instance, the most heralded among them, predates the Frenchman Jacques Dubois's *In linguam gallicam Isagoge* by a year (Paris: R. Estienne, 1531).[2]

---

[1] The French-Israeli language/culture connection has its formal beginnings in the nineteenth century. The formation of the Alliance Israélite Universelle in 1860, the publication of its broadly disseminated *Bulletin*, its network of French-speaking schools located around the Mediterranean Basin, and the establishment of the Ecole Normale Israélite orientale have been amply chronicled. See Spaëth (especially 110–15).

[2] Palsgrave's work holds a special place in the history of the French language. It was the most complete overview of the French language published in the sixteenth century. In

Cultural momentum had been seized by Italy, however. The Italian Renaissance inspired both envy and imitation. François I would respond by importing its artists and artisans. The influence and results are discernable yet today, from the genteel lines of the pleasure palaces of the Loire Valley to the many works of period art in French museums and the myriad sonnets of the numerous volumes. In the area of language the king had other ideas and other goals in mind. His target was Latin, the language of the Church and European officialdom for centuries. His goals were not new. As early as 1490 (during the reign of Charles VIII) the ordinance of 28 December of that year stated that henceforth in order to avoid abuse and confusion all documents relating to judicial matters administered by the courts and in the entirety of Languedoc "seront mis et redigez par ecrit en langage François ou maternel." Latin was thus to be excluded from the proceedings, although regional languages and dialects were not. If the intent is clear, the effect fell short; for twenty years later (1510) a similar ordinance, worded with greater precision, took its place. Its need was occasioned by the persistence of Latin in the courts, as the opening sentence reveals: "Pour obvier aux abus et inconveniens qui sont par ci-devant advenus au moïen de ce que les juges desdits païs de droit escrit ont fait les procés criminels desdits païs en latin" (Ordonnance de juin 1510). Twenty-five years later (1535) the practice was cited once again, this time within a particular geographic realm: "[. . .] les juges de nostre païs de Provence ont fait les procés criminels dudit païs en Latin" (qtd. in Brunot 2: 549–50 ["Additions" by Hélène Naïs]).

By 1539 François I felt compelled to seek broader remedy: the exclusive use of the French language in judicial and official administrative matters throughout the country as a means of fostering political cohesion on the one hand and as an inducement for writers and poets to craft their works in a national idiom rivaling Italian on the other. These concepts did not originate with the king either. The distinction appears to belong in part to Claude de Seyssel, counselor to Louis XII, whose translations of several of the classics into the vernacular following his return from Italy provided access

---

spite of the French title, it was written in English to serve as a guide for teaching French to English speakers. Its publication plus the appearance of numerous manuals in London indicate a revival of interest in the French language which had declined significantly since the thirteenth century when it was widespread among the aristocracy and was used in parliamentary procedure and debate (Rickard 1968: 24).

to readers of French and whose opinion that by means of a program of enrichment and magnification the French language could become the equal of Latin and Greek.[3] It was François I who enacted the measure, nevertheless. The Villers-Cotterêts Ordinance of 1539 required that all judicial decrees

> [. . .] soient faits et escrits si clairement, qu'il n'y ait ne puisse auoir aucune ambiguïté ou incertitude, ne lieu à demander interpretation. Et pour ce que de telles choses sont souuent aduenues sur l'intelligence des mots latins contenus esdits arrests, nous voulons d'ores en auant que tous arrests, ensemble toutes autres procedures, soient de nos cours souueraines et autres subalternes et inferieures, soient de regeistres, enquestes, contrats, commissions, sentences, testaments, et autres quelconques actes et exploicts de justice, ou qui en dependent, soient prononcez, enregistrez et deliurez aux parties en langaige maternel françois et non autrement. (qtd. in Brunot 2: 30)

"Et non autrement." The king intentionally excluded from such proceedings for the first time all regional languages and dialects as well as Latin. The magnitude of this decision cannot be overestimated. In addition to the eight languages officially recognized within the Hexagon of the present day (Alsacian, Basque, Breton, Catalan, Corsican, Flemish, French, Occitan), linguistic geographers have identified two others as emerging from medieval France (Franco-Provençal and North-Occitan) alongside nineteen "major dialects" (from north to south): Picard, Norman, Champenois, Gallo, Lorrain, Angevin, Francien, Burgundian, Franc-Comtois, Poitevin, Berrichon, Crescent, Limousin, Auvergnat, Provençal Alpin, Gascon, Mid-Occitan, Languedocian, Provençal (Lodge 72). Linguistic reality entailed greater complexity still, for prolonged isolation and local initiatives had created idiosyncratic diversities difficult to document today but which impeded communication beyond certain boundaries. (As shall be discussed in Chapter Five [5.4.2], the problem of dialect and regionalism was of such willful character that it would not be resolved definitively until World War I.)

The goals of the Ordinance, it is clear, were political and cultural rather than philanthropic or egalitarian. Should the primary goal have been

---

[3] The reigns of the three monarchs in question are as follows: Charles VIII (1483–1498), Louis XII (1498–1515), François I (1515–1547). It was Charles VIII who brought back the first seeds of the Italian Renaissance, following incursions that took him and his troops to Florence, Naples, and Rome.

to eliminate confusion, abuse, and ambiguity for participants in legal proceedings, regional languages and dialects (the sole means of communication for the vast majority) would have been encouraged. Establishment of an overarching supraregional language was deemed to be in the interest of the State, a means of nurturing a cohesive national identity and progress in the arts and commerce. Implementation remained a challenge. Fortunately, a solution stood ready-made, in the form of an institution that had existed since the Capetians: the "parlement." If resistance might be encountered in universities and elsewhere, the Crown could enforce its mandate in the high courts of the land, the Parlement de Paris and its various regional counterparts: the king's justice rendered in "une langue d'Etat," writes Brunot, an "official French" that was already in use:

> C'est en français que l'administration parla, délibéra, écrivit, en français que furent rédigées les Coutumes. [. . .] Dans cette vie d'affaires quotidiennes, de débats, de plaidoyers, où tous étaient mêlés, s'élabora un français nouveau, un peu pédant, un peu lourd et gauche, mais solide, grave, exact. Je l'appellerais volontiers le dialecte administratif et judiciaire. (Brunot 2: 31–32)

That accomplishment was not easily achieved, however. The magistrates of the Parlement de Paris and Catholic theologians had great interest in maintaining the predominance of Latin. Not only did its use isolate them linguistically from the public and ensure the established hierarchy, it was also seen as a safeguard in the face of a mounting religious reform movement that relied on populism and the vernacular. The Villers-Cotterêts Ordinance mandated that the French language be used in the courts. The matter of the Sorbonne proved more complex; in fact, chronologically, it received the king's early attention. In 1530 Guillaume Budé sought permission to create a "college" for the teaching of Latin, Greek, and Hebrew similar to those in Alcala and Louvain. When Erasmus declined to come to Paris to direct the school, the king imposed his own priorities. He created a corps of "lecteurs royaux," a parauniversity, so to speak, where parallel, independent courses could be offered in the vernacular—the distant ancestor of the Collège de France (so named during the Restoration). Similarly, in 1536 François I joined his sister, Marguerite de Navarre, in supporting Clément Marot's right to translate the Psalms. That decision increased concern for the integrity of the Holy Writ in the eyes of those who viewed Saint Jerome's work as divinely inspired. The fact that Calvin wrote alternately in Latin and in

French in order to appeal both to scholars and the "common folk" intensified their concern. Later, in 1555, Olivétan's translation of the Bible fueled increased opposition. In his preface he wrote that his attempts to bring the Good News to "simples gens" incapable of deciphering the Latin texts were compounded by the limitations of the French language itself, "si diverse en soy [...] qu'il est bien dificile de pouvoir satisfaire à toutes aureilles et de parler à tous intelligiblement" (qtd. in Clerico 162). Adversaries decried the use of such a defective language for rendering Christendom's holiest texts. Those who believed in the future of the vernacular, to the contrary, found further reason to work to develop it and pointed to the program proposed by Joachim Du Bellay.

2.1.1 Du Bellay's *Deffence*

By the year 1549 the Renaissance had come full-fledged to France. The year stands out owing to the publication of Du Bellay's *La deffence et illustration de la langue françoyse*. François I had died two years earlier. His son Henri II ascended to the throne bent on consolidating his father's political and cultural gains. Around him the movement assumed an increasingly decided French character. Earlier enchantment with Italian models gave way progressively to other designs and other imperatives drawing on the vision of France as cultural (and aspirant political) heir to the Roman Empire and bearer of the newly lighted torch of humanism. Dictated by the prestige factors associated with Antiquity, language and letters rose to the fore as markers to establish in this energized environment. The new generation was already being formed in the Collège de Coqueret where Dorat (Jean Dinemandi) extolled Greco-Roman civilization and the need to perpetuate it before enthusiastic youths anxious to take their place in the French pantheon: Pierre de Ronsard, Jean Antoine de Baïf, and Joachim Du Bellay himself. In the coming years these core members would be joined by Pontus de Tyard, Etienne Jodelle, Jean Bastier de La Péruse, Rémi Belleau, Guillaume Des Autles, and belatedly Jacques Peletier du Mans to constitute a group that has come to be celebrated as France's founding school of letters: La Pléiade.

Within that context Du Bellay's *Deffence et illustration de la langue françoyse* has been canonized not only as manifesto but also as founding document of "modern" (read post-medieval) French culture. As important as it was to become in the reconstruction of cultural identity, the text proves less than innovative in historical terms. In matters concerning the adoption of Greco-Roman literary models and the need to elevate the French language to a higher plane in order to "nationalize" them, Jacques Pelletier du Mans had preceded him by four years. The foreword to his translation *L'art poetique d'Horace* (1545) contains these precepts and more, many of which seem to have been borrowed wholesale by Du Bellay. Likewise, Thomas Sebillet's *L'art poëtique François*, first published anonymously in 1548, called for adoption of the epigram and the sonnet (introduced by Marot) as a means of bringing to the French language the innovations perfected by the Italians (Morçay and Müller 229–30). Further, in the composition of the *Deffence*, Du Bellay pillaged page after page of the Italian Sperone Speroni's *Dialogo* (1542), translated into French and published in Lyon in 1546 (Villey 19). Speroni proposed for Tuscan the very enrichment program Du Bellay would present for French. Of course history would lead in another direction in Italy. Factioning there would delay both political and linguistic unification for three centuries.

The *Deffence* had a rallying effect in France. Du Bellay followed all the right procedures, paid all the right tributes. The work is dedicated to Cardinal Jean Du Bellay (first cousin of Joachim's father), a diplomat and influential supporter of French letters whose personal physician was none other than François Rabelais. It is depicted as an act of patriotism ("à l'entreprise de laquelle rien ne m'a induyt, que l'affection naturelle envers ma patrie"). The dedication thus draws into its midst Church, State, and the administration of French cultural affairs. The work itself was published "avec privilege," that is to say with official sanction of the Crown, in tandem with (as "illustration") "Cinquante Sonnetz à la louange de l'Oliue, l'Anterotique de la vieille & de la ieune amye, & vers Lyriques nouvellement composez" (Du Bellay, "Extrait de privilege"). Along the way, of course, Du Bellay would be careful to pay proper homage to both François I and Henri II.

Both politically and religiously correct, the text recognizes biblical origins; the world's innumerable "manieres de parler" derive from the "diuersité, & confusion" of the "Tour de Babel" episode and subsequently from "l'inconstance humaine" (Livre 1, Chapitre 1). From that point, however, humanistic prerogatives take over. Dynamics that would become increasingly prevalent in Western thought control the fate of individual languages; for they are presented as the product of human culture, each language being innate at incipience and subject to perfectibility (progress) or neglect. The

French language thus has every right and potential to ascendance as Greek and Latin before it and every possibility of being the primary medium in Europe to greater attainment in both the arts and the sciences. The language of the French nation has especially earned that right in his age, Du Bellay argues, because French civilization, in terms of laws and civility, had either equaled or surpassed the attainments of its antique forebears. Such is the mandate of the "Modernes" (Livre 1, Chapitre 2), in opposition to the "Anciens," a recurrent theme destined to survive into the nineteenth century and the early days of French romanticism.

Du Bellay's literary vision proves to be composite, however. As in anticipation of grammarians who would pose France's "meilleurs auteurs" as models for instituting language standards following the Revolution, Du Bellay looks to proven sources for guidance and inspiration. Whereas the French language must obtain as "natural" medium of expression for the realm, he recognizes that

> d'autant que l'Amplification de nostre Langue (qui est ce, que ie traite) ne
> se peut faire sans Doctrine, & sans Erudition, ie veux bien auertir, ceux,
> qui aspirent à ceste gloire, d'imiter les bons Aucteurs Grecz, & Romains,
> voyre bien Italiens, Hespagnolz, & autres. (Livre 2, Chapitre 3)

That agenda excludes, however, genres that had been mainstays for the medieval "jeux floraux": "Rondeaux, Ballades, Vyrlaiz, Chātz Royaulx, Chansons, & autres telles episseries, qui corrūpent nostre Lāngue" (Livre 2, Chapitre 4). Odes, elegies, the pseudo-classical sonnet, eclogues, the epigram, and epic poems (Homeric or Virgilian but with a French national character) are all cited as viable means to the enhancement of French poetry, the Poet of that day being the consummate purveyor of cultural prestige.

As for the French language itself, Du Bellay blames a lack of institutional control for its paucity. He writes of it in Livre 2, Chapitre 2: "[. . .] ie ne le puis mieux defendre, qu'atribuant la Pauureté d'iceluy non à son propre, & naturel, mais à la negligence de ceux, qui en ont pris le gouuernement." Such is of course a distant appeal for a national "academy," a regulating body to take charge. In the interim Du Bellay calls upon compatriots to answer the challenge by expanding the language through the judicious creation of neologisms (Livre 2, Chapitre 6), by perfecting the art of rhyming according to the natural beauty of the French language (Livre 2, Chapitre 7), by mastering the natural rhythms of the language (Livre 2, Chapitre 8), and by regularizing expression according to the natural (unforced) interplay of "oreille" and "sens" (Livre 2, Chapitres 9, 10). The work culminates in an exhortation to "patriots" to write in French and a panegyric extolling the topographical beauty of the country and its mission relative to the arts, the sciences, and commerce (Livre 2, Chapitre 12). The terms of the conclusion vibrate with a zeal that leaves little doubt as to the messianic character of that mission and its place in the history of Western civilization: Greece and Rome have seen their day. With the lessons of their accomplishments in tow and its own language liberated from their past, the future belongs to France.

If Du Bellay's proposals were short on specifics and long on platitudes, a combination of inspiration, determination, and patronage produced impressive results. Gone was the facile verse of Clément Marot and his followers.[4] In the coming years Rabelais's humanism and Maurice Scève's idealism would find new voices—French voices—and new or regenerated forms within and beyond the Pléiade. Dates and titles document the fecundity of this "renascence." Pléiade members contributed the following works, among others: Du Bellay (*L'Olive*, 1549; *Les antiquités de Rome, Les regrets*, 1558), Ronsard (*Odes, Amours, Hymnes, La Franciade* [a national epic], 1550–1578), Jodelle (*Cléopâtre captive* [tragedy], *Eugène* [comedy], 1552), Belleau (*La bergerie*, 1565; *Amours*, 1576), Baïf (*Amours de Méline*, 1552; *Amours de Francine*, 1555). Indeed, the prestige of the group was such that Ronsard had become Charles IX's official poet as early as 1560 and in 1570 Baïf would be able to persuade the monarch both to form an Academy of Poetry and Music and to support orthographic reforms.[5] Outside the Pléiade writers of various bents voiced harmony or counterpoint: Louise Labé (*Elégies, Sonnets*, 1555), Agrippa D'Aubigné (*Le printemps*, 1572–1575; *Les tragiques* [in the service of Protestantism], 1577–1616); the neo-Italianists Philippe Desportes (*Amours de Diane*, 1573), Jean de Sponde *Sonnets*; *Stances*, 1598 [posthumous]), and Jean Bertaut (*Oeuvres poétiques*, 1601); the dramatists Robert Garnier (*Antigone*, 1580; *Bradamente*, 1582; *Les Juives*, 1583 [tragedies]) and Pierre de Larivey (imitations, transpositions, and translations of nine comedies in

---

[4] Marot (1496–1544) would again find favor in the seventeenth century. Both Boileau and La Fontaine would praise the clarity, grace, and charm of his poetry, in contrast to the unruliness they attributed to other Renaissance writers.

[5] For the full breadth of the sixteenth-century academy movement, especially as it concerns Charles IX and Henri III, see Chapter II ("The External History of Sixteenth-Century French Academies") of Frances A. Yates's *The French Academies of the Sixteenth Century*.

the Italian style); and of course Michel de Montaigne whose *Essais* would appear in various editions beginning in 1580.

2.1.2 Early challenges: lexis nexus

The French language proved thus able to support a wide variety of non-medieval literary genres, in both prose and poetry, from those of the classical and Italian frames to the innovative essay.

Such says nothing of the language itself, however. How had it evolved in order to respond to the exigencies of a reinvigorated intellectual climate that included the sciences, commerce, contact with the New World, and new directions in philosophical inquiry? Sixteenth-century France had none of the media advantages and few of the institutional advantages of modern-day Israel. A succession of monarchs from François I to Henri IV, the highly divisive wars of religion, a feudal system that resisted centralization, a citizenry largely illiterate and unsure of alliances, in brief the French nation-state as it is now known was yet to be formed. Yet the language did respond, grudgingly in some ways, inconsistently over the decades, but significantly, meaningfully, robustly, and most of all, pridefully.

An important aspect of that pride resided in the provinces. Poets were especially proud of their regional origins, and their verse reflected it. Du Bellay's call for neologisms corresponded to their bent for incorporating regionalisms in their works as a means of producing poetic effect and as tribute to their linguistic and cultural roots. Those who find Rabelais's French a particular challenge can point to his dogged use of words stemming from the various patois of his native Touraine. Ronsard defended vigorously the practice of inserting into his *Odes* (1550) words borrowed from the Vandômois of his childhood:

> Depuis l'achevement de mon livre, Lecteur, j'ai entendu que nos con-
> sciencieus poëtes ont trouvé mauvais de quoi je parle (comme ils disent)
> mon Vandomois, écrivant ores charlit, ores nuaus, ores ullent, et plusieurs
> autres mots que je confesse veritablement sentir mon terroi. Mais [...]
> tant s'en faut que je refuze les vocables Picards, Angevins, Tourangeaus,
> Mansseaus, lors qu'ils expriment un mot qui defaut en nostre François,
> que si j'avoi parlé le naïf dialecte de Vandomois, je ne m'estimeroi bani
> pour cela d'eloquence des Muses. (Ronsard 2: 977)

Baïf and others echoed Ronsard's thoughts. Peletier du Mans and Henri Estienne supported him in their theoretical writings as well. Of course such attitude ran the risk of rekindling linguistic feudalism. But this was a time of fervor; enthusiasm surged unbridled and would have to be curtailed in the interest of uniformity. That task, however, would belong primarily to the century to follow.

In the meanwhile the French lexis swelled with a multitude of creations, borrowings, and agglutinations emanating from the various intellectual, political, social, professional, commercial, and technical milieus within which the quest for knowledge, gain, and voice spurred language development. The burgeoning practice of forming neologisms (germane to the early development of both Greek and Latin and justified by supporting quotations drawn especially from Horace) attracted both endorsement and admonition from theorists such as Du Bellay, Sébillet, Peletier, and Pasquier. The overriding concern was that the resulting vocable be "naturalized" ("naturaliser" a fifteenth-century verb tapped by Peletier)—that is, acclimated to the unique "nature" of the French language and implicitly, as the term would evolve to signify, respectful of the nation itself (Clerico 206). Apart from the provincialisms cherished by certain poets or which found their way into the emerging vernacular for non-aesthetic reasons, numerous other resources were exploited in this frenzy. Archaic words that had fallen from favor were flogged back into use. Italianisms—drawn admiringly from the most advanced culture of the time—and Hispanisms—derived more reluctantly from a strained relationship—filled other voids. Ironically perhaps, despite the course of linguistic liberation on which France had embarked, Latin and Greek served as primary reservoirs (though not without contention), especially in rhetoric, medicine, and the sciences.

None of these disciplines has been more romanticized than medicine. An aspirant science bent on establishing its Gallic credentials at schools in Paris and Montpellier, a recalcitrant Church, stories of clandestine dissections in the bowels of cathedrals, medical science has come to embody the very polarizations that the Renaissance struggled to overcome. Language figured prominently in those efforts. The required knowledge of Latin was seen increasingly as an impediment to medical studies. J. Canappe (professor of surgery at Lyon) began translating into French important anatomical texts as early as 1538. Thanks largely to his endeavors, progress in medicine ceased to be seen as depending on the linguistic and scientific parameters of the

Ancients. Canappe was adamant; he concluded that "maladies are not cured by eloquence but by remedies"; his scope extended to include all languages capable of accommodating the exigencies and intricacies of medical science: "l'art de medecine et chirurgie ne gist pas du tout aux langues, car cest tout ung de lentendre en Grec ou Latin ou Arabic ou Francoys, ou (si tu veulx) en Breton Bretonnant, poureu qu'on lentende bien." (qtd. in Brunot 2: 40). If critics perceived danger in making medicine linguistically accessible to those not formally trained in the "art" (and therefore in Latin), other translations followed suit. Within a decade a significant corpus of medical works with increasingly uniform terminology formed new foundations for French readers. Similar strides can be noted for related quadrants such as semiotics (today's pathology), apothecary science (pharmacology), anatomy, and physiology (hygienics/epidemiology).

Of course sixteenth-century sciences were often a compendium of occultism (alchemy), fantasy, and practical elements. Some of them lent themselves to "linguistic acclimation" more readily than others. Astronomy, cosmography, and its next of kin geography, for instance, all attracted popularizing works in French, from the daring prognostications of a Nostradamus to maps and practical guides. Progress in other areas came more slowly. Mathematical works written in French remained rudimentary for decades. The same may be said for the natural sciences for which Latin served as a convenient international vehicle of communication and dissemination. As for philosophic discourse, Pontus de Tyard and a few others pushed for the use of the vernacular with little success. Descartes in the following century would find that presenting his theories in French would earn him the distinction of finally liberating that domain from the grips of Plato and Aristotle.

Thus as the century drew to a close a vast array of new words commingled heterogeneously within the expanded vernacular. Italianisms had found their way into social and cultural contexts: architecture (*arcade*, *balcon*, *cornice*), music (*cadence*, *concert*), courtly life (*altesse*, *courtiser*), war (*cavallerie*, *colonelle*, *infanterie*). Hispanisms accounted for a less sizable contribution: *bizarre*, *camarade*, *casque*, *mascarade*. Even German, not well known in France until the eighteenth century, added a few terms: *bière*, *chope*, *huguenot*. As for new creations, Du Bellay's formulas served as models. The several enriching practices drawing on the French language itself and listed in the *Deffence* (Livre 2, Chapitre 9) were adopted sporadically by contributors: infinitives and adjectives as nouns (*l'aller*, *le vide*) and adjectives as adverbs, ultimately less well received (*leger* in place of *legerement*). Common verb and noun suffixes were added to adjectives (*verve* › *verver*, *vervement*); adjectival suffixes abounded, most of them recognizable today: *al, an, é, er, ier, eux, in, u*. A decided taste for the diminutive (*et, ot, in, on, teau,* etc.) would be seen as an abuse in later years. Prefixes were used similarly: (*avant-jeu, contre-coeur, entretroublé*). Moreover, agglutinations of all sorts brought hybrids into the language. The traditional means of combining elements of Latin or Greek (*monologue, intercostal*) soon grew to include other types of agglutinates. Hyphenated epithetical juxtapositions, for example, became mainstays: *doux-aigre, jaune-rouge, aime-musique, front-cornu, divin-humain* (Huchon 72–80, Matoré 330–36). With such irrepressible forces at work it is hardly surprising that lexicography should emerge amidst the jumble. The founding effort belongs to Robert Estienne (*Dictionarium latinogallicum*, 1531–1538/*Dictionnaire Francoislatin*, 1539, 2nd edition [1549] augmented to 13,000 entries). The work would be expanded further in revised editions (1564, 1573) in which the many entries referencing judicial terminology and practices are of special interest. Its heir, the *Thesor de la langue françoyse tant ancienne que moderne* compiled by Jean Nicot, would appear soon after the turn of the century (1606).

The introduction of Peter Rickard's *La langue française au seizième siècle* offers in encapsulated form a wealth of information concerning the state of linguistic knowledge at the time and chronicles the attempts of grammarians to analyze the French language. The importance of the latter cannot be overemphasized. Heretofore, only ancient languages had been deemed worthy of analysis; "langues vulgaires" had been the subject of descriptive works, almost as curiosities. Several grammarians other than Palsgrave and Dubois joined in the effort: Jean Dorsai (*Gramatica quadrilingus partitiones, in gratiam puerorum* [partly in French], 1550; Louis Meigret (*Le Traicte de la grãmmere françoeze*), 1557; Pierre de La Ramée (*Gramere*), 1562 (2nd edition 1572); Henri Estienne (*Hypomneses de gallica lingua*), 1582; Charles Maupas (*Grammaire Françoise*), 1607, among others.

The results at this early stage are fledgling and unequal, as one might imagine. The only models on which grammarians could draw were based on Latin, a language that differed significantly both morphologically and syntactically from French. Rickard describes "typical grammars" (grammarians borrowed freely from each other) as containing primarily the following sections:

1. orthography and pronunciation;
2. "etymology," that which we understand today as morphology;
3. syntax, limited to agreement of subject and verb, adjective and noun, relative and antecedent.

Difficulties and inconsistencies were numerous: the definite article had no counterpart in Latin; substantive and adjective were viewed as a single entity; grammatical genders were ill-defined (Dubois listed as many as five of them, including the "uncertain"); Latin declensions led grammarians to invent declensions, cases composed of prepositions and definite articles: *le roi* (accusative and nominative), *du roi* (genitive and ablative), *au roi* (dative), *ô roi* (vocative), etc. (Rickard 1968: 28–31).

According to Georges Matoré the present state of French orthography and its lack of sight to sound correspondence dates from the late-thirteenth century when French began to be used in official capacities. The need for clearly presented hand-written documents led to certain orthographic alterations designed to eliminate calligraphic and semantic confusion: final *y* replaces *i* (icy, luy), an initial *h* is added to *uis* (porte) to distinguish it from *uis* (vis, meaning visage); a *g* is placed after a nasal (ung). Homonyms were differentiated in similar fashion: *c* is added to form *sceau* in order to distinguish it from *seau*. A lost letter from Latin could be reintroduced etymologically: Latin *viginti>* medieval *vint* but it becomes *vingt* in order to distinguish it from (il) *vint*. As time passed these alterations were generalized. By the early sixteenth century numerous rather far-fetched etymological forms had found their way into the language: *poicer* (*poisser*) to represent the Latin *picare* or *ligons* (*lisons*) to represent *legimus*, and so on. Sometimes a French equivalent letter or letters would even be written in superscript above the Latin counterpart (Brunot 2: 94).

Reform efforts began at an early date. In his 1529 *Champfleury*, Geoffroy Tory proposed the use of accents to distinguish open *e* and closed *e*, the use of the cedilla (borrowed from Spanish) to indicate phonetic *s*, as well as the separation of *j* and *i* and *v* and *u*. Dubois supported the return of final *i* where *y* had prevailed (lui/luy) and the elimination of the *g* after nasals. Louis Meigret, the most extreme of the reformers, recommended the simplifications *doibvent>doivent*, *umbre>ombre* and the suppression of *x* as the sign of the plural and the use of *z* for intervocalic *s* (Matoré 350–51).

Despite such efforts, the French language at the beginning of the seventeenth century was far from stable. If it is accessible to the twenty-first-century reader, morphological impediments, as well as aspects of orthography, grammar, and syntax make it a greater challenge than texts written only a few decades later. Genders were still in a state of flux, transitive and intransitive verbs were still exchanging functions, the use of articles and pronouns (especially subject pronouns and demonstratives) was yet to be regularized, stems of certain verbs could vary in form. Direct word order (subject, verb, object) prevailed generally, but inversions (many of them Latinizations common to the learned "style soutenu") constituted a much larger percentage of instances than would be the case forty years later. Grammarians (as well as the lexicographers previously cited) were often preoccupied with the relationship of the vernacular to Latin. As for usage in general, large gaps existed between the spoken language and the written language. Grammarians had not yet succeeded in establishing common ground. Claims and counter-claims left such matters unsettled within the context of a rapidly developing society whose political, economic, and cultural proclivities would place increasing demands on the vernacular (Clerico 211–17).

2.2 Malherbe, Marie de Gournay, and the founding of the Academy

Peter Rickard's companion volume, *The French Language in the Seventeenth Century: Contemporary Opinion in France*, provides an insightful means for measuring the enormously diverse interest "domestication" of the French language generated in the decades to follow. His superb anthology surveys opinions registered by some fifty commentators of varying backgrounds and perspectives, from Marie Le Jars de Gournay—the outspoken editor and companion of Montaigne—to François Charpentier's preface to the historic *Dictionnaire de l'Académie française* published in 1694. The seven sections into which the writings are divided establish parameters: 1) antecedents of the French language, 2) spelling and pronunciation, 3) grammar, 4) lexicography, 5) usage, 6) stylistics, 7) in praise of French. It is appropriate that the final section should be devoted to panegyrists, for at the century's end all of Europe would stand in admiration of France's culture and language.

It is also appropriate that Rickard's introduction should recognize in epigraph form "the earliest truly influential authority on the French language": "Enfin Malherbe vint" (Rickard 5). The recognition comes from the first canto of Boileau's *Art poétique* (1674, the so-called definitive expression of the aesthetic and linguistic doctrine the century struggled to mold). The breadth and depth of Malherbe's contribution have been measured most adeptly by Claude Abraham in his heralded *Enfin Malherbe: The Influence of Malherbe on French Lyric Prosody, 1605–1674*. Although Abraham brings to light numerous inaccuracies, misunderstandings, and exaggerations, it is clear that the immediate social and political environment provided a nurturing medium for reform. Henri IV brought a grudging peace to a land wracked by upheaval and religious strife. The Edict of Nantes of 1598 and the Treaty of Vervins (ending the war with Spain) of the same year set the political tone of his reign and facilitated consolidation of royal imperatives as well as economic and cultural development. It was in the context of this calm (as brief as it was, for Henri IV would be assassinated in 1610) that the king appointed François de Malherbe official poet at Court (1605), a position that would extend into the reign of Louis XIII.

If competing impetuses were already vying for prominence (and would continue to do so throughout the century),[6] it was Malherbe and the precepts of his *Commentaires sur Desportes* that became irrevocably associated with an ever-mounting drive toward the institutionalization and canonization of French language and culture. As would become increasingly the practice, success in such matters depended more on contacts at Court than the allure of doctrines or theories. Malherbe was an opportunist of the first order, a paragon of social and aesthetic decorum who, like Antoine de Rivarol more than a century and a half later, was able to shape a persona and gain title as master of the French language. His call for reform was consistent with the monarchy's political aspirations to attain greater regulation and control of society at large in what would prove to be a march toward making France the most centralized country in Europe.

> Malherbe stands for conformity with the mood of a forward-looking and already substantially "de-Gasconised" Court, for uniformity, for the rule of law and order in language, rather than free expression, which now seemed discreditably facile, breathless and slack. He repudiates the past, even to the extent of not seeing what was best in it; he rejects the intrusion of personal idiosyncrasy; he opposes the use of older words, of dialect terms, and even of many neologisms. [. . .] He appears to have been strongly opposed to

---

[6] Abraham, in his introduction (1–11), points to the existence of two competing trends from virtually the beginning of the seventeenth century: a movement toward purism, discipline, and control that was already underway prior to Malherbe and an inherited aesthetic that valued invention and inspiration over clarity and technical precision.

anything which savoured of a separate poetic vocabulary. He insists on the proper distinctions between pairs of synonyms, and condemns the unthinking exuberance of the older vocabulary, that uncritically *quantitative* attitude towards language which had been all too fashionable in the previous century. (Rickard 1992: 6)

It would be naïve to maintain that language reform could be imposed in any *ipso facto* fashion. The very notion is elitist, of course. Languages are living entities that exist in a variety of forms and in constant flux. Broadly accepted change requires cooperation at numerous socio-economic levels over a significant time period (all the lengthier prior to the media age). For the Ancien Régime of the seventeenth century (and for the foreseeable future) there was no means to that end, nor was such the goal. Major reformist characteristics did make an impact across the upper levels of society, however (and not exclusively among poets), thanks in part to Malherbe. Eloquence stands out most prominently: eloquence—controlled, decorous, precise, rational and yet pleasing expression—the mark of a superior mind and lineage, whether the medium be poetry or social discourse. Of course Malherbe had a great deal to say about prosody. His concerns constitute the very stuff that would compose the French "classical" model: regularity of stanza and line (especially the twelve-syllable *alexandrin*), homophony and appropriate rhyme words and schemes, syntactical restraint, the domains of sonnet and ode, and, overall, a measured systematization of language made to reflect the aspirations of a society on the move toward increased order, stability, and—therefore—greater attainment (Fromilhague, Parts One and Two).

The establishment of the Académie Française would come to be recognized as a pinnacle in these efforts to raise the vernacular to new heights. Officially, this would be Louis XIII's doing, given the royal sanction granted in 1635, a year after its founding (1634). In reality it was part of Richelieu's master plan to solidify central authority within the country and increase France's sway abroad. Agreement as to purpose and function stirred debate and rekindled opposition. Resistance to Malherbe's precepts had fomented discord from the very beginning. Opponents clung to the personalizations, exuberant metaphors, free-flowing syntax, and lexical color the Renaissance had nurtured and revered. A familiar refrain was sounded by Jean-Pierre Camus in his *Issue aux Censeurs* (1625). Reformers, he contended, constituted a "secte langagière," a coterie of "puristes" bent on attacking genuine style and purging the language of "mauvais mots." The measures, he warned, would result in an "appauvrissement" reducing the beauty and spontaneity of the French language to "une honteuse disette et mendicité" (qtd. in Brunot 3: 10). The following year (1626) *L'Ombre*, written by Mademoiselle Marie Le Jars de Gournay, appeared in Paris and (along with *Les Advis ou les Présens* published eight years later) quickly became championed as the sixteenth century's response to Malherbe.

Marie de Gournay, Montaigne's latter-day editor and confidant, is credited with compiling the 1595 posthumous edition of the *Essais*, as well as both the 1617 and 1635 (definitive) editions. Beyond extolling the virtues of the texts to which she devoted such a large part of her life, this "fille d'alliance" of the great writer (as she was known to contemporaries) rose by dint of will to defend vociferously Renaissance mores, taste, language, and philosophy against the "ravages" of reform. Indeed, she had every right to be indignant. After all, it was in her salon that the initial concept of the French Academy was first broached (Ilsley 12). Moreover, the institution, as it would be constituted, excluded women, all women: the consequence, she reasoned, of a pompous, patriarchal society become both draconian and oppressive. This turn, especially, struck hard; for not only had she toiled for years in the interest of French language and culture, she had published the essays *Egalité des hommes et des femmes* in 1622 and *Grief des dames* in 1626. Marie de Gournay thus entered the annals of early feminism, albeit in the restrained fashion attuned to the exigencies of the times (Ilsley 200-01, Hillman ["Introduction" to Gournay 13–17], Nakam 12–13).

Among other aspects of the reform, *L'Ombre* targets lexical restrictions pertaining to the neologisms, regionalisms, and diminutives that had found such favor over the years. "Les docteurs en l'art de parler, dont ce temps est fertile hors tout exemple," Marie wrote,

> nous accablent d'une nuée de considerations et de corrections. [. . .] L'ex-cellence et perfection du langage consiste, selon leur opinion, a fuir quelques mots ou phrases que les personnes vulgaires ne sçavent pas dire; mots derivez ou empruntez du latin (grand reproche à leur goust), vieillissans, ou tirez d'autres termes, ou particuliers à quelque province de la France; je dis fuir a quelque prix, circonspection et necessité qu'on les peust employer, parce qu'ils sont si jolis de croire que parler parfaitement et parler François pur et trivial sont mesme chose, ignorans que la pureté

n'est qu'une partie de la perfection d'une langue, et davantage mescog-
noissans en la nostre ceste pureté deuement qualifiée, d'autant qu'ils la
constituent à luy retrancher, à l'exemple de quelque language mort, le
droict d'emprunt et de propagation, comme si la faculté d'amemendement
n'estoit pas du nombre de ses proprietez et de ses appartenances tandis
qu'elle restera vive. (qtd. in Rickard 1992: 339)

In the eyes of detractors, passages such as this one served as self-refutations.
Whatever the aesthetic worth of the writing, the length and complexity of
sentences and the lack of lexical control (especially synonyms used repeti-
tiously as they had been since the *chansons de geste*) distorted the thought
and subverted the nascent logocentrism reformers believed to be the key to
optimizing the national idiom's potentials.

2.3 Vaugelas: language and civility

Malherbe's death in 1628 did not stem the surge. To the detriment of
the old style his disciples soon found increasing favor with the *libraires*
(printer-vendors): Jean Honorat de Bueil de Racan, Honoré d'Urfé, Jean
Louis Guez de Balzac, Claude Favre de Vaugelas, Jean Chapelain, among
others. In the jousting for favor, prominence, and authority within the Academy
itself and in the wings (especially in the celebrated luxury of the Hôtel de
Rambouillet's Chambre Bleue as early as 1620), the name of Vaugelas comes
to the fore. As grammarian charged with directing the functions of the Academy,
the views he expressed in his *Remarques sur la langue françoise* published in
1647 became instrumental in defining two major concepts germane to the
language and culture of the period: *le bon usage* and *l'honnête homme*.

Vaugelas (1585–1650), a Savoyard by birth, had the good fortune of
having grown up under the tutelage of his father Antoine, a distinguished
scholar/jurisconsult, who founded with François de Sales the Académie
Florimontane (an Italian-modeled ancestor of the French Academy) and who
introduced the lad at Court. As a young man he relocated to Paris where,
following intermittent peregrinations and hardships, he eventually made the
acquaintance of the prominent authors of the day and gained entry to the most
fashionable salons, among them the coterie that met at the home of Valentin
Conrart and that—under Richelieu's insistence—organized as the "Compagnie
Officielle" or Académie Française and attained instant prominence with the

decision to compile a dictionary of the French language. That decision—also at the insistence of Richelieu—a reluctant one for members who hesitated to accept such an arduous and protracted task, entailed in reality a much larger charge. The formal proposal, drafted by Chapelain, committed the group to four projects: a dictionary, a grammar, a rhetoric, and a poetics. The dictionary, nevertheless, took priority; the project was approved in 1638. The work was to be compiled alphabetically by gleaning systematically words (other than proper nouns) and phrases from writings deemed to be composed in "pure" French, by subjecting the findings to the group's collective scrutiny, and by making decisions in concert based on criteria and procedures established by the Compagnie. Work soon lagged, however, owing to lack of direction and a director. Richelieu intervened once more. This time Vaugelas was granted the position (with a stipend of "2000 livres"), and matters took a turn for the better.

As Wendy Ayers-Bennett has demonstrated in her *Vaugelas and the Development of the French Language*, Vaugelas used his position with the Academy to test and hone his theory of usage. The (Bibliothèque de l') Arsenal manuscript of *Remarques sur la langue françoise* is a jumble with marginalia, erasures, and variant passages. The 1647 published version, then, must have been produced over a lengthy period, an early draft of which may have been presented before the Academy as early as 1637 (Ayers-Bennett 3). It is essential to emphasize that the book was a bestseller of sorts in an age of rampant illiteracy. However unexpectedly, the grammar of the French language had suddenly become fashionable, both in Paris and in the provinces. If the phenomenon boded well for similar endeavors in the future, it was owed to a variety of factors. Vaugelas had struck a common socio-aesthetic chord within a supportive political milieu. Attitudes concerning dress, taste, conduct, and speech were already evolving toward the refinement that would become synonymous with the reign of Louis XIV. Moreover, French society itself, from top to bottom, benefited from the gradual shifts toward civility that had been underway for some time and that had also laid foundations for a broadened economic infrastructure (Elias 2: 229–333). The Fronde of the 1640s and 1650s, the aristocratic revolt stemming from resistance to Richelieu's centralizing designs (perpetuated by Mazarin) and to impending absolute monarchism, was but a hiccup. More than ever before, Paris, Vaugelas's Paris, would preside in both political and social spheres.

Vaugelas's role as recorder of proper usage served the Academy and the monarchy well. The interrelation of the concepts of *bon usage* and *honnête homme* derives from corresponding trends in linguistic and social propriety at Court. His stated goals in the *Remarques* leave little doubt as to sources:

> Mon dessein n'est pas de reformer nostre langue, ny d'abolir des mots, ny d'en faire, mais seulement de monstrer le bon vsage de ceux qui sont faits, & s'il est douteux ou inconnu, de l'esclaircir, & de le faire connoistre. [...] C'est la façon de parler de la plus saine partie de la Cour, conformément à la façon d'escrire de la plus saine partie des Auteurs du temps. (qtd. in Ayers-Bennett 13)

Vaugelas thus exercised discernment in the selection of models. The phrase "la plus saine partie" twice penned gives ample notice. He considered his charge, it is clear, to be that of esthete: hierarchically, superior manners (*politesse*), speech, and writing are all products of a refinement of taste not universally shared, not even at Court. Vaugelas's determinations may therefore be viewed as elitist in the extreme, an elitism that is not to be confused, however, with period pedantry whose Latinizations "foreignized" the vernacular lexically and syntactically. Linguistically, for guidance he turned to Malherbe and to the prose translations of Nicolas Coeffeteau. Yet he remained independently oriented, incorporating personal observations drawn from salon frequentations and the formal discourse he encountered within the Academy and in communication with officialdom. The results, as Ayers-Bennett states (66, 133), are less than consistent, owing to uncertain methodology. Overall, however, salient features cohere. Registers tend to merge: if the written language is depicted as being more demanding than the spoken language, careful speakers will speak as they write, exercising due care with regard to phraseology, lexical selection, and logic while prioritizing clarity and harmony/euphony. Grammar, rhetoric, and style thus cross-pollinate, create a cultural continuum in relation to which a performative impetus fuels a drive for perfection. Beyond the myriad purely linguistic prescriptive categorizations (neologisms, archaisms, solecisms to avoid, barbarisms, *netteté* of syntax, *pureté* of pronunciation, etc.), Vaugelas's *Remarques* posit an idealized social standard epitomized by *l'honnête homme*: refined, impeccably mannered, stylishly creative yet utterly controlled in his use of language and in his sense of decorum.

Vaugelas's shortcomings as a grammarian thus find ample compensation in matters of taste. Like most of his colleagues at the Academy, he knew little of the history of his own language, a fact that sometimes led him astray (Brunot 2: 54). But he did have a heightened sense of social discourse and a healthy respect for the freedom to be creative while maintaining the "purity" of the French language. The *Remarques* assumed the function of social guide in matters of language and became a companion to those who aspired to climb the ranks in a society that was becoming increasingly mobile. The book thus appealed to a broad spectrum of readers, in the provinces as well as in Paris, from the "bourgeois gentilshommes" of the day who found hope in its pages to Pierre Corneille who revised his plays with the *Remarques* at hand or Jean Racine who used the text as a means to pare the provincialisms from his speech (Ayers-Bennett 191).

2.4 Descartes: The art of living and the science of thinking

Louis XIV came to the throne in 1660. With him came absolutism, prosperity, and intrigue, a curious mixture combining a centralizing imperative that fed on the systematic subjugation of the aristocracy, a mercantile economy that multiplied options and fortunes (and therefore civic loyalties) for enterprising commoners, and a ceremonial opulence that both stimulated and dictated fashion in dress, manners, the arts, and language. W. H. Lewis's classic history, *The Splendid Century*, chronicles the propagation and codification of the "art of living"—a cultural construct that would become international vogue. Books treating all sorts of related matters soon appeared on the market: obligations to and proper conduct toward servants, appropriate attire (including wigs, powder, and headwear, advice on when and how to wear them and what part of a vestment may remain unbuttoned according to the occasion), menus and culinary etiquette, dinner conversation, after-dinner conversation, accompanying a lady to her carriage, handkerchief courtesy, appreciation of the fine arts, theater, opera, and sermons as well as the rules of decorum governing all of them (Lewis 195–213).

It was a time of disciplined invention and canonization. Quinault provided captivating librettos for Lully. Racine took French poetry to new heights before audiences moved to a cathartic silence, Molière made everybody laugh—sheepishly perhaps, for human frailty lay at the base of his jibes and mockery. France had become a stage on which Bossuet sermonized, La

Rochfoucauld minimized, Pascal asceticized, Boileau codified, La Bruyère and Saint Simon memorialized, Le Nôtre formalized, and La Fontaine modernized, the latter adeptly, cunningly, virtually unbeknownst to those who otherwise would have protested.

Eyes throughout Europe turned toward Paris and Versailles. Many came to see—and to hear—for themselves. At the same time the vernacular, the French national idiom, caused ears to perk and pages to turn across the Continent. In effect momentum outside France had been building for some time, thanks in no small way to the intellectual movement sparked earlier in the century by René Descartes and destined to be hailed by Hegel as the revolution with which the modern era truly begins (Bridoux 23). Indeed, Descartes freed scientific inquiry from the yoke of Aristotle, scholasticism, and the Church. He did so, generally speaking and despite sporadic opposition and accusations of atheism, without alienating authorities, religious or temporal. He had learned valuable lessons from Galileo and Théophile de Viau. Metaphorically, he depicted the "chemin" (path) of scientific inquiry (and progress) as passing harmlessly alongside the "maisons" of society, that is to say its institutions, namely the Monarchy and the Church. His theory of dualism, according to which the "material" aspect of the human body and its "mechanics" had been created prior to and separate from the creation of the soul, legitimized the disciplines of medicine and physics. His *Cogito*, "je pense donc je suis," accorded primacy to thought, the functioning of the mind; and his method brought order, rigor, and a means of independent verification. Writings on topics ranging from geometry, meteorites, and dioptrics to the principles of philosophy and the nature of passions constituted a universalism that quickly drew an international audience of stature. As early as 1642 Holland was already grappling with his ideas, professors and students unsure of common ground; Elizabeth of Bohemia, herself of worthy intellect, maintained a lengthy correspondence with the philosopher, much of it dealing with the intricacies of his thought; and Christina of Sweden was so taken with Descartes's thinking that in 1649 she extended an invitation to visit. He departed in early September. Once there he was called upon to tutor the monarch in her personal library each morning. The fifty-three-year old adapted poorly to the schedule and the climate. On February 11th, 1650 Descartes succumbed to pneumonia. By that time Cartesianism had already settled in and would go on to feed the rationalism of the following century.

Implicitly, Descartes's theory posits the need for the language of scientific inquiry to be self-sufficient and therefore semantically, syntactically, and logically attuned to cognition itself. It is thus important to recognize not only that he wrote persuasively and with style in his native tongue, not only that he broke with tradition and chose the vernacular over Latin, but also that in doing so he conferred special status on the French language. His eyes were clearly on the future, as the penultimate paragraph of *Discours de la méthode* attests:

> Et si j'écris en français, qui est la langue de mon pays, plutôt qu'en latin, qui est celle de mes précepteurs, c'est à cause que j'espère que ceux qui ne se servent que de leur raison naturelle toute pure jugeront mieux de mes opinions que ceux qui ne croient qu'aux livres anciens. Et pour ceux qui joignent le bon sens avec l'étude, lesquels seuls je souhaite pour mes juges, ils ne seront point, je m'assure, si partiaux pour le latin, qu'ils refusent d'entendre mes raisons pour ce que je les explique en langue vulgaire. (Descartes 179)

2.5 Port-Royal: the French language as universal

That status was destined to be reinforced a decade later when Antoine Arnauld and Claude Lancelot published *Grammaire générale et raisonnée* (1660) and Arnauld collaborated with Pierre Nicole to produce its sequel, *La logique ou l'art de penser* (1662). In a letter to Marin Mersenne (November 20, 1629) Descartes had lamented the lack of a universal language accessible to all and had called for a new grammar "laquelle on puisse rendre commune pour toutes les langues" (Descartes 913). The *Grammaire générale* addressed this need, as the extended title confirms: "contenant Les fondemens de l'art de parler; expliquez d'une manière claire & naturelle; Les raisons de ce qui est commun à toutes les langues [. . .]; Et plusieurs remarques nouvelles sur la Langue Françoise." The treatise is thus presented as a theory or philosophy of language born of Cartesian universalism and taking the form of a universal grammar written in French and pertaining particularly to the French language. As for praxis, the *Logique ou l'art de penser*, also written in French, provided method and modality: "les Regles communes [et] plusieurs observations nouvelles propres à former le iugement."

At first glance the source and context of these texts may seem strange: Port-Royal, the seat of Jansenism (so-called by adversaries), a movement of austere religious conviction whose teachings would cause conflict as late as the Revolution. Founded by Cornelius Jansen (1585–1638)—who had been rebuked by the Jesuits—and the Abbé St. Cyran (1581–1643), the community espoused "Augustinian" principles that included the requirement of a state of perfect contrition (perfect love toward God) in order to receive communion. Enter Antoine Arnauld, spokesman for the second generation of adepts, who published *De la fréquente communion* in 1643, a scathing indictment of the moral laxity attributed to Jesuit teachings. Controversy swirled, culminating in 1656 with the Sorbonne condemning Arnaud's doctrine of Grace and the issuance of a Papal Bull undermining Jansen's writings. Blaise Pascal's beautifully crafted rebuttal, eighteen letters titled the *Provinciales* (1656–57), led him to begin drafting *L'art de persuader*, a treatise merging aesthetics, language, and logic. Such was the immediate context in which the *Grammaire* and the *Logique* were composed. Of course the controversy would continue for the next half century; politics would exact its toll, leaning first this way and then that, until in 1710 communal buildings were razed and all traces (including the cemetery) were subsequently plowed under (Lewis 80–85).

Whatever its religious doctrines, Port-Royal was also a seat of respect for learning and erudition, especially in matters of language. Claude Lancelot, co-author of the *Grammaire*, provided expertise in Greek, Latin, Italian, and Spanish. (He had in fact written for young learners a very successful series of *Méthode* books advocating a concise, "common sense" approach to language learning that would have found favor with Descartes.) Prior to the advent of historical linguistics, Lancelot thus found himself in a position to observe the similarities of various languages as well as their general relationship to Latin and appeared eminently qualified to collaborate on Arnauld's project of producing guides for the teaching of grammar and logic to the Port-Royal community. The *Grammaire*, while comparative, hierarchizes taxonomically the languages referenced according to their perceived importance. It is from this key aspect that a telling ideology emerges. "Ce sont, dans l'ordre d'importance," writes Roland Donzé in his probing analysis of the work,

> le français, le latin, le grec, l'hébreu; l'italien, l'espagnol, l'allemand; incidemment le wallon, les langues orientales et les langues du Nord. De toutes, le français est la plus favorisée et c'est à son égard surtout qu'Arnauld et Lancelot s'écartent parfois du véritable objet de leur entreprise, accordant à des considérations propres à une langue particulière un développement qui surprend dans le cadre d'une grammaire générale.

He explains further that the authors found justification for prioritizing the French language in their "common sense," practical goal of explaining "clearly and naturally" the principles of proper usage established by Vaugelas rather than submitting usage itself to analysis. This approach, defined especially in Chapter I of the Part II (Analogy), links word or sign to judgment (Donzé 16). The *Grammaire* combines, therefore, the primary philosophical and linguistic precepts of the era not only to the benefit of the national idiom, but also to the detriment of competing languages and paradigms, both ancient and modern. That notion of superiority, ideologically, is of course subsumed by ancient archetypes: the mythical name-giving in Plato's *Cratylus* and Adam as divinely sanctioned name-giver in Genesis. In accordance with the emphases of the time, the *Grammaire* and its companion work the *Logique ou l'art de penser* intellectualize the paradigm, privileging the cognitive process over origins. Indeed, the *Logique* cements the argumentation by linking inextricably language and thought.

Like the *Grammaire*, the *Logique* uses hybridization to gain its ends. Arnauld and Nicole draw on Aristotle, Pascal, and Descartes in their elaboration of the four essential functions of the mind: conceiving, judging, reasoning, and ordering (Clair and Girbal 2, Arnauld and Nicole 37). The opening lines of the "Premier Discours," titled "Où l'on fait voir le dessein de cette nouvelle Logique," all but name their ascendant.

> Il n'y a rien de plus estimable que le bon sens & la justesse de l'esprit dans le discernement du vrai & du faux. Toutes les autres qualités d'esprit ont des usages bornés; mais l'exactitude de la raison est généralement utile dans toutes les parties & dans tous les employs de la vie. (Arnauld and Nicole 15)

Descartes's name does appear frequently in the text. The parameters of cognition—the prescribed goals and the method governing the conduct of one's reason in the pursuit of understanding and judgment—are familiar indeed: "La Logique est l'art de bien conduire sa raison dans la connoissance des choses, tant pour s'en instruire soi-même, que pour en instruire les autres." "[La] methode consiste principalement à commencer par les choses les plus generales & les plus simples, pour passer aux moins generales & plus composées" (Arnauld and Nicole 37, 306). Cartesian independence (the freedom of the subject to inquire and the means to direct the inquiry) combines creatively here with a communal or social orientation, that is to say the education or edification of others. Problems of language are compounded commensurately; not only do we have to deal with "la confusion dans nos pensées," we also must confront "la confusion dans nos discours." The ideal solution, once again, derives from Descartes. "Le meilleur moyen pour éviter la confusion des mots qui se rencontrent dans les langues ordinaires, est de faire une nouvelle langue, & de nouveaux mots qui ne soient attachés qu'aux idées que nous voulons qu'ils représentent" (Arnauld and Nicole 86). A philosophical language would solve the problem. But that is not what the *Logique* proposes. Rather, the authors point implicitly to the dictionary project already underway at the Academy and the ongoing process of structuring and "purifying" the French language begun by Malherbe and Vaugelas and continued by the Port-Royal *Grammaire*. A series of chapter headings in Part I leaves little doubt: " de la nécessité & de l'utilité de définir les noms dont on se sert," (1: 12); "observations importantes touchant la definition des noms" (1: 13); "d'une autre sorte de définition de noms, par lesquels on marque ce qu'ils signifient dans l'usage" (1: 14); "des idées que l'esprit ajoute à celles qui sont précisément signifiées par les mots" (1: 15).

The notion of the superiority of the French language planted by the *Grammaire* thus finds its way into the companion text. It is true, as Clair and Girbal confirm, that Cartesianism benefited from the dissemination of the work:

> N'est-ce pas enfin souligner une évidence que de rappeler le rôle joué par la *Logique de Port-Royal* dans la diffusion du cartésianisme? Publiée douze ans après la mort de Descartes, quelque temps seulement avant la mise à l'Index de la plupart de ses œuvres *donec corrigantur*, elle a contribué à défendre et à véhiculer la pensée cartésienne. (2)

It is also true that the *Grammaire* and the *Logique* did much to formalize the mystique of the French language and build confidence in its ability to serve as intellectual as well as cultural medium in Europe. The Port-Royal texts brought order and reason to *le bon usage* of Vaugelas. Their success and influence are undeniable. Both were edited time and time again. For the *Logique* alone, between 1697 and 1871, Clair and Girbal list forty-nine editions in French, nine editions in English, thirteen editions in Latin, among others (5–10). Jill Vance Buroker goes so far as to say that "the *Port-Royal Logique* was the most influential logic from Aristotle to the end of the nineteenth century," the 1818 English edition having "served as a text in the course of education at the Universities of Cambridge and Oxford" (Buroker xxii).

Moreover, single-handedly, these works institutionalized grammar and led to the veneration of the grammarian. They signal the birth of an era, "une nouvelle période dans l'histoire de la langue," writes Brunot; "en un siècle, l'empire de la langue a passé à des théoriciens professionnels" (4: 60–61).

2.6 Prestige factors: nature's order and the *Dictionnaire*

Henceforth members of the Academy could rely on theory to authenticate their dictates. Two of them, Louis Le Laboureur (*Avantages de la langue Françoise sur la langue latine*, 1669) and François Charpentier (*De l'excellence de la langue Françoise*, 1683), would expand the importance of the syntactical paradigm (subject noun/copula/predicate noun) they found in the Port-Royal texts and which is related to the concept of "clarity" in language. The academicians elaborated an amplified derivative theory that identified the paradigm both as an attribute of the French language and, most importantly, as the basic paradigm of cognition. Roberto Pellerey, who has written an absorbing study of the phenomenon of "direct sentence construction" as "linguistic ideology," explains just how pervasive the elaboration became. Pellerey divides the theory into three levels: 1) Interior composition of the theory of direct order, 2) collocation of the theory in grammar, 3) epistemic function of grammar and social determination (218–20).

The first level defines the order as being "direct," "natural," "logical" because it follows "the order of thought in its progressive, natural, and universal linearity." The grammatical order nominative/verb/oblique is one with the ontological order of "Sub-stance-Action-Object." Hence the Subject is the center of the unification, Subject-Object linked by means of the Copula. The paradigm Subject/Verb/Object thus obtains.

The second level defines such syntactic constructions as cognitively complete verbal expressions of judgment; in series it is they that constitute and structure discursive reasoning.

The third level posits "Rationalism" as the basic philosophy underlying the theory of language as the expression of thought. It also identifies social or cultural determinations. Individual languages differ in phonetic attributes ("douceur," "harmonie" [for which French is known]), syntax, and logicality, due to the indigenous nature of speakers. French follows the most perfect construction which is "direct."

Thus the recognition of the linguistic superiority of the French language contained in the Port-Royal texts was broadened to include the cognitive process, an extension that translated as both cultural and intellectual superiority. The long-awaited publication of the Academy's dictionary would add credence and prestige in 1694. The Académie Française had increased its purview with the addition of the Royal Academy of Inscriptions (1663) and the Royal Academy of Sciences (1666). Charpentier's preface to the *Dictionnaire* voices praise for the institution, praise for the national idiom, indeed, praise for French civilization. The French language has attained a state of perfection, he asserts, owing to:

> la gravité et la variété de ses nombres, la juste cadence de ses périodes, la douceur de sa poësie, la regularité de ses vers, l'harmonie de ses rimes, et sur tout cette construction directe qui sans s'esloigner de l'ordre naturel des pensées ne laissent pas de rencontrer toutes les delicatesses que l'art est capable d'y apporter. (qtd. in Rickard 1992: 213)

As for the dictionary itself, Charpentier explains the compilation process and product. The work has been compiled by moderns for a modern age, an age of scientific exactness that requires words to be defined with the greatest care and clarity, including secondary definitions. Points of grammar are sometimes elaborated in great detail. Synonyms are listed, with the admonition that each word has its own identity. Obsolete terms, technical terms, trendy clichés, and neologisms, are omitted. The overriding concern of the compilers was the recording of "good usage."

2.7 Language, politics, and the idea of a "Republic of Letters"

In the development of the French language, from Montaigne to the publication of the *Dictionnaire*, the historian Gabriel Spillbout proposes 1660 as a watershed year, as had his mentor Ferdinand Brunot before him. His determination derives from different considerations, however. Brunot utilized as convenient marker the change in political dynamics that came with Louis XIV's ascendancy. Spillbout, conversely, points to the first edition of Pierre Corneille's *Œuvres complètes* published that same year. His reasoning is convincing: not only does Corneille revise and clarify his critical thinking about aesthetics and techniques in light of the lessons of intervening years (as documented in his various *Discours* and *Examens*), he also corrects the language to conform to evolved standards: "j'y vois surtout un point de départ, en ce que le Grand Corneille y corrige minutieusement, même ses plus purs chefs-d'œuvre, pour les insérer plus intimement dans le courant de la langue de ses contemporains" (Spillbout 13). Most importantly, Spillbout notes that Corneille's corrections are less numerous and less severe beginning with the play *Pompée* of 1644. The Academy, influenced as it was by Malherbe and Vaugelas, had voiced formal disapproval of the aesthetics and language of Corneille's *Le Cid* in 1636. By 1644, it would seem then, Corneille had responded, and by 1660 he found himself in the mainstream.

The mainstream, as time went on, grew to be identified syntactically with direct or natural word order, lexically with a certain logocentric fixity of meaning, and aesthetically with a decorous, eloquent style that shunned the bizarre and the untoward. These are the purported dynamics of the language of mainstream French culture, the French national idiom as it was packaged for export. They are not to be confused with the language of the majority or with mass culture. Indeed, mass culture, as such, did not exist in the seventeenth century. Regional culture, regional language, dialect, patois: little had changed for a vast peasantry that toiled largely unaware of the splendor of the Court and the Sun King.

In 1685, nevertheless, Pierre Bayle felt quite justified in declaring French to be the leading language of Europe. His *Nouvelles de la République des Lettres* of November of that year contains the following appraisal of the Continent's linguistic status: "la Langue Françoise est désormais le point de communication de tous les peuples de l'Europe, & une Langue que l'on pourrait appeler transcendentelle" (qtd. in Yadav 91). The title of the work is significant. *Lettres*, here, denotes first and foremost, "lettered." The constituents of the Republic are the educated people of the principal geographic regions of Europe, literate in their respective languages. *Transcendentelle* (today *transcendentale*) signified either *supérieure* or *essentielle*, the latter a scholastic valorization. In other words, the assertion is that French had assumed the place of Latin in the early modern era. Little did it matter not only that such a republic did not exist in any meaningful geopolitical sense, nor that the sale of Bayle's journal was prohibited in France at the time (Yadav 91–95). Bayle may have been premature, but forces were gathering that would render his claim prophetic. Such a republic, conceptually, was in the making.

The year 1685 proved to be eventful for another reason. In that year Louis XIV signed the Revocation of the Edict of Nantes and sent more than two hundred thousand Protestants fleeing to other lands: Holland, Prussia, England, the New World. With them they took their industriousness, their wealth, their erudition, their artisanship, and their language. Inadvertently, this political decision, after two decades of suppression, served to disseminate French language and culture more broadly throughout Europe than ever before. Politics also intervened in another way. Even before Louis XIV came to power, the French language had indeed begun to fill the void left by a diminishing Latin presence. François I's plan to enhance and empower the French language through its use in the courts had resulted in the development of an enviable juridical lexicon. (Though Germany had granted its own language similar status earlier than France, the several competing dialects and political divisions militated against uniformity.) As early as the Treaties of Westphalia (1648) that put an end to the Thirty Years War, French was already vying for the role of language of negotiation. (Latin won out, it is true, but only after narrowly defeating stiff competition primarily from the French, but also from the Spanish, the Italians, and the Germans.)

That ambition found fulfillment in the aggressive expansionist policy enacted by Louis XIV. By 1672 the Marquis de Louvois had fashioned for France the mightiest and best commanded army since the Romans (Erlanger 279). The designs the king had been unable to attain through manipulation, extortion, or purchase could be imposed by force. Furthermore, his troops had been armed with a formidable new weapon: the bayonet. So France went to war against the Dutch and the federation known as the United Provinces, the seven northern provinces of the Low Countries. Soon the Empire, Spain, Denmark, and Lorraine had been drawn into the fray. The Peace of Nijmegen in 1678 did not result in the annexation of Holland, but the French-imposed terms did deliver the French-speaking Franche–Comté for Louis XIV and increased France's prestige considerably. The French-speaking populations in Lorraine, Savoy, Switzerland, and nearby Germany took notice. Their own identity and cultural proclivities were thus buttressed. Moreover, the treaty itself was negotiated privately in the wings in French, the various federation and foreign ambassadors having adopted it as common language (Schwab 105).

By the time it came to drafting the treaties that put an end to the War of Spanish Succession, French could no longer be confined to the wings. The 1713–14 texts pertaining to France, England, Holland, Spain, Prussia, Savoy, and Portugal were negotiated and written in that idiom. The treaties themselves would affect the future of Europe for many years to come. England walked away the winner. Newfoundland, the Hudson Bay Territory, and French *Acadie* (Canada) were ceded to the kingdom across the Channel. France also recognized the rights of succession of the Hanovers over the Stuarts. Holland was granted the request to establish fortifications on the northern border of France, as a means of protection against further aggression. France also agreed to destroy its own fortifications along the Rhine. Yet Louis XIV's grandson (Philip V) was confirmed as king of Spain (the reason France had entered the war), and his rights to the French throne were relinquished. Louis also recovered several territories, including Lille and Orange. If the cessions of the treaties (completed by the treaty of Rastadt in 1714) would ultimately impoverish France and place the monarchy itself in jeopardy, the treaties would nevertheless enable Europe to experience an extended period of relative peace during which France would establish itself as the center of the Enlightenment and the French language would become the diplomatic and intellectual language of Europe.

2.8 The *Encyclopédie* and Condillac

Louis XIV died September 1, 1715. The Splendid Century had come to an end. Its progeny would generate a new image and new epithets: *le Siècle des Lumières*, the Age of Reason, the Age of Voltaire, all of them orbiting around *la Ville Lumière*, the City of Light. It was a time of explosive inquiry and identity altering redefinitions. *Les philosophes*, so known throughout Europe, became collectively the gurus of an international rush to knowledge: Montesquieu, Condillac, Maupertuis, Diderot, d'Alembert, Helvétius, d'Holbach, Buffon, Condorcet, Rousseau, and the ubiquitous, chameleonesque Voltaire—who seemed to be able to be all things to all people. Only the specter of John Locke rose as a rival of standing; but his empiricism was quickly appropriated and reformulated to French ends. The resulting *isms* appear quite disparate: hold-over Cartesianism, rationalism, relativism, sensationism, materialism, deism, atheism, among others. Philosophical consistency and solidity of argumentation did not constitute priorities. Social, political, religious, and scientific concerns intermingled, mutated, stirred the endless polemics that kept the movement going. As the century unfolded a new project replaced the *Dictionnaire* as monument to the age: the *Encyclopédie*, the compilation of knowledge to serve as foundation for a new society governed by reason, tolerance, liberty, compassion, a compilation of knowledge, written for the betterment of the entire world—in French.

The *philosophes*, of course, saw language as a primary object of inquiry. Indeed, the eighteenth century pursued language origins and development relentlessly. Theories abounded, from the primacy of sensation expounded in Condillac's *Essai sur l'origine des connaissances humaines* (1746) and expanded by Scotland's Thomas Reid (*Inquiry into the Human Mind*, 1764) and Lord Monboddo (*The Origin and Progress of Language*, 1773) to Rousseau's exploration of the relationship of music to language in his *Essai sur l'origine des langues* (probably written between 1755 and 1767, published posthumously in 1781) and finally to the behaviorist notions expressed by a young Herder in his prize-winning submission (*Abhandlung über den Ursprung der Sprache*) in the 1770–1771 theory of language origins contest sponsored by the Berlin Academy of Sciences and Letters (Wells 7–47).

The *Encyclopédie* itself, which began to appear in 1751 under the direction of Diderot and would eventually fill twenty-eight volumes, addresses various aspects of language in numerous articles. Given the composite character of the work and the inevitable contradictions germane to any speculative dimension of human understanding, researchers have faced a formidable task in endeavoring to sort out and contextualize prevalent concepts relating to language. In the late-1970s, at the height of the structuralist movement, Michèle Duchet and Michèle Jalley accepted the challenge. At the Ecole Normale Supérieure of Fontenay, they fashioned an interdisciplinary seminar that examined both "theory of discourses" (*théorie des discours*) and "signifying systems" (*systèmes signifiants*) of the eighteenth century. Students were exposed to the analyses of eleven prominent scholars, Jean-Claude Chevalier and Julia Kristeva among them. The resulting publication, *Langue et langage de Leibniz à l'Encyclopédie* (1977), is an important contribution to the fields of history, philosophy, anthropology, literature, linguistics, and perhaps others as well. It is essential to remember, Duchet and Pierre Kuentz emphasize in their introduction (13–23),

> Dumarsais ou Beauzée sont des "grammairiens-philosophes," la *Grammaire* et la *Logique* de Port-Royal forment un tout. Science de l'homme, science du langage, étude des langues, genèse de l'entendement, histoire des sociétés, production littéraire tout cela constitue pour les hommes des Lumières une seule et même activité et participe d'un même discours. (16)

César Chesneay, sieur du Marsais, became the *Encyclopédie*'s primary consultant on subjects pertaining to grammar. He had published *Exposition d'une méthode raisonnée pour apprendre la langue latine* (1722) and *Traité des tropes* (1730). These works, even more abstract that those of Port-Royal, tie language to cognition, thereby reinforcing the idea that "grammar" is a dominion of philosophy, indeed, of metaphysics (Brunot 6: 904–06). Dumarsais was succeeded by Nicolas Beauzée, author of *Grammaire générale, ou Exposition raisonnée des élémens necessaires du langage pour servir de fondement à l'étude de toutes les langues* (1767). Together the two not only contributed the majority of language oriented articles, they also influenced the production of grammars and perpetuated the theory of "rationalized language" into the nineteenth century.

Of the fourteen chapters that constitute the Duchet-Jalley seminar, G. Renucci's "Notes sur quelques articles de l'*Encyclopédie*" (293–304) is of primary interest here. Beyond recognizing the Port-Royal writings as source books, it reveals the extent to which contributors drew on Condillac's essay on human understanding, most importantly with regard to the logocentrism with which the French language was credited and that was associated with its superiority. Under the rubric *La toute-puissance du mot* in relation to which he analyses the articles "Signe," "Parole," and "Accent" (among others), Renucci writes the following: "D'une part, on sent et on pense le langage comme un langage parlé. Et d'autre part, on considère le mot comme l'unité fondamentale du langage. Cette contradiction peut s'expliquer par la dignité de la langue écrite, sa prééminence sur la langue parlée du XVIIIe siècle" (300–01). That dignity is to be found, explicitly, in Condillac's *Essai sur l'origine des connaissances humaines* (1746) and a later reformulation of cognitive theory written at the end of his life: *La logique ou les premiers développements de l'art de penser* (1779).

If the Abbé Condillac (1715–1780) did not participate in the Encyclopédie project, he did move freely within the intellectual circles of the time. His essay on human understanding reflects Enlightenment concerns in general, and, in particular, constitutes a response to Locke's *Essay Concerning Human Understanding* (1690). Condillac's thought has attracted the labels "sensationalism," "sensationism," or "sensualism." Perhaps the most accurate designation is found in Michèle Crampe-Casnabet's preface to her edition of Condillac's essay. She refers to an "empirisme sensualiste," which credits Locke as predecessor and which, she is careful to emphasize, is underpinned at every turn by Condillac's theory of language (12–13).

Condillac's subtitle points the way: *Ouvrage où l'on réduit à un seul principe tout ce qui concerne l'entendement humain.* That sole principle, sensation, which would be appropriated by materialists later in the century, leads Condillac back in time to the birth of thought. He finds that cognition and language are born of sensation and need. Accordingly, in the beginning, thought was translated into language in the form of cries and gestures executed not for the sake of communication but for the sole sake of expressing sensation and need. This language, a "language of action," expanded over time and evolved to incorporate artificial signs of an arbitrary character, a development involving two notions dear to the Enlightenment: progress and the drive to perfection. Words thus serve both to designate pre-existing ideas and to form new, more sophisticated or complex ideas, elevating language to a higher order. Language is logic and logic is grammar: an analytical process that divides thought into its constitutive elements—"en un mot la langue est une méthode d'analyse" (Crampe-Casnabet 16).

Conceptually, Condillac's debt both to Port-Royal and to Descartes is obvious. Like Descartes, Condillac establishes the independence of the individual and therefore the primacy of subject coupled with method: "nous ne sortons point de nous-mêmes, et ce n'est jamais que notre propre pensée que nous apercevons" (Condillac 31). Like Descartes as well, Condillac took care to navigate around Catholic dogma—although he would follow a divergent course in doing so. He recognizes an Adamic language (a gift from God), but points out that the Original Sin had made the soul dependent on the body (and therefore the senses). He also recognizes the Babel event that scattered language into multiplicity. Postdiluvian history, however, belongs completely to the descendents of Noah. The Deluge having wiped the slate clean, Condillac imagines two children, isolated, developing naturally both physically and cognitively. He follows them through the "language of action" stage into the later stages of language formation. From there he leads the reader across history through the ancient world and into the modern era.

Ancient languages exhibit a "natural order" derived from the early stages of language development. Their tonal systems and declensions appear as adjuncts to an indirect, undulating syntax that privileges rhythm, sound, and variety—all attributes of early civilizations that value metaphor, dance, song, and epic poetry over expository discourse. As civilization progresses, as it approaches the scientific age, language moves from phonocentrism to logocentrism; thus the order natural to prior stages gives way to the new, evolved "natural order": direct word order, precision, clarity, fixity of meaning. Unaware of or oblivious to the incongruence of Condillac's theory of simultaneity of verbalization and thought that placed him at odds with rationalists such as Beauzée (Pellerey 242–53),[7] adherents in important circles savored the evolved attributes hypothesis—which they enthusiastically ascribed to the superiority of French culture. As recognition Condillac was honored with seats both at the French Academy and at the Academy of Sciences and Letters of Berlin.

2.9 Another opinion: Jean-Jacques Rousseau

Rousseau, to the contrary, found little to savor in Condillac's theories. One wonders how that could have been otherwise, given Condillac's position on music and logocentrism. Rousseau was after all a composer and music theorist who wrote articles on the subject for the *Encyclopédie* and published widely on related matters. Rousseau had a good deal to say about language, particularly as it relates to music. His views may be found scattered throughout his works, including the two *Discours*, *Emile*, *La nouvelle Héloïse*, *Les confessions*, the *Dictionnaire de musique*, and of course the *Essai sur l'origine des langues*. The genesis of the *Essai* is clouded. It is in part the product of *Encyclopédie* polemics and the exceptions Rameau took to Rousseau's music theory. It is a complex work, as Rousseau's works tend to be; its inherent lack of coherence has spawned widely divergent interpretations penned by such well-known writers as Jean Starobinski, Jacques Derrida, and Aram Vartanian.[8]

---

[7] It is in Chapitre 9 of the Seconde Partie (Condillac 219–35) that Condillac discusses this evolution. In effect, if there is no pre-verbal, then verbalization itself equates with both cognitive paradigm and expression, no matter the stage of development or the language in question. Notions of superiority based on syntax thus dissipate in the face of a linguistic egalitarianism not conducive to the promotion of cultural or national interests—hence the adverse reaction on behalf of French grammarians. Moreover, Condillac's theory of the "original natural order" (privileging "inverted word order") would be used later by German nationalists in their revalorization of the German language.

[8] Downing A. Thomas (85) attributes this divergence to the neglect of the chapters devoted specifically to music in their respective readings of Rousseau's *Essai*: Starobinski's edition of the *Essai* (Paris: Gallimard, 1990); and Derrida's *De la grammatologie*. Thomas credits Aram Vartanian with recognizing that Derrida, in a usual tactic, upgrades what he believes to be a "marginal, or at least accessory, aspect of Rousseauism," but maintains that the theme of "the origin and present state of music and language [...] permeates a healthy number of Rousseau's 'major' works." Thomas is referring to Vartanian's 1989 "Derrida, Rousseau, and the Difference."

Rousseau and Condillac do share some common ground. Like Condillac, Rousseau posits the initial (pre-linguistic) stage of language development as consisting of cries and gestures as an expression of sensation and need. It is in chapter two of Rousseau's *Essai* that the two part ways. The chapter heading reads: "Que la première invention de la parole ne vint pas des besoins mais des passions." Whereas Condillac theorizes a social continuum, Rousseau postulates both division and a different stimulus leading to the development of speech:

> Il est donc à croire que les besoins dictèrent les premiers gestes et que les passions arrachèrent les premiéres voix. En suivant avec ces distinctions la trace des faits, peut-être faudroit-il raisonner sur l'origine des langues tout autrement qu'on n'a fait jusqu'ici. Le genie des langues orientales, les plus anciennes qui nous soient connües, dément absolument la marche didactique qu'on imagine dans leur composition. Ces langues n'ont rien de méthodique et de raisonné; elles sont vives et figurées. On nous fait du langage des premiers hommes des langues de Géométres, et nous voyons que ce furent des langues de Poëtes. [...] On pretend que les hommes inventérent la parole pour exprimer leurs besoins; cette opinion me paroit insoutenable.

Of course Rousseau has brushed aside Condillac's emphasis on metaphor, song, and dance in ancient societies. But the essential difference here is that Rousseau views the cries and gestures stage as being a pre-social stage, a state of isolation, a state of nature. Rousseau the anthropologist/moralist states the theory emphatically:

> l'origine des langues n'est point düe aux premiers besoins des hommes; il seroit absurde que de la cause qui les écarte vint le moyen qui les unit. D'où peut donc venir cette origine? Des besoins moraux, des passions. [...] Ce n'est ni la faim ni la soif, mais l'amour la haine la pitié la colére qui leur ont arraché les premiéres voix. (Rousseau 5: 380, both quotations)

Given this chronology, however inconsistently Rousseau may have presented his theory, two aspects stand out: Rousseau's phonocentrism and language as loss. The second half of Rousseau's *Essai* deals with the originary elements of music: melody/song (the "speaking of melodies"). Downing Thomas underscores the importance of music as it relates to his social theory: "For Rousseau, then, music plays a determining role in the events which lead humans from solitude to society and culture. [. . .] The emergence of desire, the move away from the unmediated pleasure of self-sufficient solitude, and the 'speaking' of melodies are all inextricably linked." Rousseau suggests "that the first melodic speech set up an original social contract" and "claims that there can be no society or culture without music" (121). That original social contract has been broken, however. Originally (according to Rousseau), laws were sung. Thus, in the scheme of things, the acquisition of speech coincides with the fall from the state of nature, on the one hand, and, on the other hand, written codification signals social degeneration and rupture.

2.10 Cosmopolitanism: emulation and exportation

Rousseau's theories belonged to the future; they would impact the French Revolution and the Romantic movement that would follow in the 1820s and 1830s. Condillac's ideas, conversely, were widely disseminated and appreciated in his own day. Outside France, pre-Revolution Europe continued to value the legacy of the Splendid Century. The French classical frame, identified especially with the writings of Corneille, Racine, and Molière, was openly emulated in Germany and Spain, the latter forsaking centuries of exuberance to form the Escuela de Buen Gusto. Elsewhere such works were read as an integral part of a proper education, essential reading for those who wished to take their place in an increasingly cosmopolitan world. They were read in French, of course, lessons in the language having become a component of the curriculum offered gentry and commoners of status. Indeed, French translations soon became the norm for accessing foreign literatures. The large French-reading audience made for a lucrative enterprise. From Young's *Nuits* to Gessner's *Poésies*, French translations were shipped in all directions. Beyond their commercial success, these translations reinforced French cultural and aesthetic values. They are known to us today as the *Belles Infidèles*, more appropriations than translations, for they Gallicize source texts by imposing French standards in both form and content. Alexandrine verse and a highly decorous sense of the proprieties replace indigenous prosody and social constructs. Romy Heylen's 1993 study of eighteenth-century French translations of Shakespeare (*Translation, Poetics, and the Stage*), for example, documents the flagrant liberties taken by Letourneur, Ducis, and Voltaire, including extensive elaborations.

The French language thus served as cultural, intellectual, commercial, and diplomatic intermediary. For emissaries it was the required tool. Marc Fumaroli of the French Academy has provided a collection of texts in French (twenty-six in all) culled from the writings of prominent figures of the time. The names read like a Who's Who: the Viscount Bolingbroke and Lord Chesterfield of England, Prince Eugene of Savoy, Frederick the Great and Frederick Melchior Grimm of Prussia/Germany, Catherine the Great of Russia, Gustavus III of Sweden, Benjamin Franklin and Gouverneur Morris of the United States, Stanislas II of Poland, to mention only ten of them. Fumaroli's title, *Quand l'Europe parlait français* (2001), reflects the pervasiveness of the phenomenon. He could have added countless examples drawn from other countries.

The degree to which France had successfully exported its language and its culture was nowhere more evident than in nearby Prussia. If Germany was to become France's most redoubtable adversary in the following century, Frederick the Great's Prussia of the eighteenth century sought identity and fortune vicariously, by following the French model. The emulation dates from the early years of the century. Having already founded an Academy of Sculpture and Architecture, in 1700 Frederick I (Elector of Brandenburg) called upon Wilhelm Gottfried Leibnitz to establish a Society of Sciences. The resulting institution resembled its French counterpart down to the four "classes" into which it was divided (Physics and Medicine, Mathematics, Philology, History of Germany) and the goal of perfecting the German language. The latter goal soon evolved into the project of producing a dictionary of the German language (Formey 7–38). The monarch's death in 1713 brought Frederick Wilhelm to power. The Society would languish under his auspices, his priorities lying with militarism and economics.

The succession of Frederick II in 1740 changed emphases drastically. The contentious relationship with his anti-French, insular father (Frederick Wilhelm) had fostered resolve: he was determined that his Prussia would attain the social refinement and the progress in the sciences that set France apart from other European countries. Frederick had been reared in the French manner, having been tutored by French Huguenots. He had come to adore French culture and had learned to speak and write the language fluently and well (which could not be said for his "native" German). A Francophile of the first order, at an early age he thought of himself as "philosophe," and even took to signing his name in that fashion. Over the years he would seek out French intellectual contacts at the highest levels and would maintain correspondence with Diderot, d'Alembert, Voltaire, and others. As for the arts, Frederick wrote poetry in French (in addition to being an avid flutist). On a daily basis he discussed current topics of interest in French and he sent orders to his officers in French.

These proclivities did not exist in a vacuum. They were nurtured in part by a demographic ambiance inherited from the seventeenth century. The Berlin region had become a haven for French Huguenots fleeing Louis XIV's purge (1685). They had thrived there, had formed a vibrant colony that left an indelible mark on society at large. As artisans they prospered, as intellectuals they excelled, as linguists they disseminated their language throughout the land. French language publications of all sorts soon took their place alongside their German counterparts: *Le Journal de Berlin*, *Le Spectateur en Allemagne*, *La Gazette de Berlin*. For all practical purposes, the region had become bilingual, and in matters of culture it was to French tradition that esthetes turned.

Thus, when Frederick sought to reform and revitalize the Society of Sciences founded forty years before, it was quite natural that he should look to France once again. The resulting Académie des Sciences et Belles-Lettres de Berlin would not only look French, it would "sound" French as well. In addition to the borrowed structure, in addition to the members representing the French Huguenot community, there would be a Frenchman to preside, Pierre Louis Moreau de Maupertuis, the scientist who had introduced Newtonianism in France. What is more, he would preside in French, the official language of the Académie. Before long he would welcome as member the author of the *Essai sur l'origine des connaissances humaines*, Etienne Bonnot de Condillac.

The French language, supporters reasoned, could alone breach the language gap and serve as "universal" vehicle for the dissemination of knowledge in Europe and beyond. After all, even the Academy at Saint-Petersburg had taken to publishing its reports in French. Their position was bolstered by the willingness of Voltaire, "l'homme universel," to come to Berlin to share his wisdom, his notoriety, his social agenda, and his continued enthusiasm for the aesthetics of the Splendid Century. He came at great expense to Frederick, both monetary and political. From 1750 to 1753 he postured and riled, succeeded in alienating Francophiles and Germanophiles alike, coveted Maupertuis's position, and finally broke with Frederick himself.

The seeds of the Germanic revolt had been sewn, although it would take many years for them to mature. The French connection continued to dominate, thanks to Frederick's direction. Yet dissent brewed as the decades passed. Maupertuis died, and d'Alembert, who was to be his replacement, refused to relocate to Berlin. Anti-French factions became vociferous. Frederick felt threatened. He took to the fray himself, publishing in 1780 a scathing rebuke of German language and culture, written in French: *De la littérature allemande; des défauts qu'on peut lui reprocher; quelles en sont les causes; et par quels moyens on peut les corriger*. Adversaries recognized that Frederick had fallen out of touch: the recriminations derived from the Germany of Frederick's youth and from the prestige of the "Siècle de Louis XIV," which, according to Voltaire himself, had faded into mediocrity. Opposition fomented, leading to the adoption of the tripartite topic of the Academy's essay contest for 1782–84:

> *Qu'est-ce qui a fait de la langue Françoise la langue universelle de l'Europe?*
> *En quoi mérite-t-elle cette prerogative?*
> *Peut-on présumer qu'elle la conserve?*

Two winners were crowned, both of them supporters of the continued dominance of the French language, Johann Christoph Schwab and Antoine de Rivarol. The Frenchman alone would receive historical accolades, however, an injustice that has taken more than two centuries to rectify (Storost, Henry [2003, 2005]). In research, thoroughness, and acumen, Schwab's work surpassed his rival's by far. He even had the prescience to envision the eventual ascension of the English language as a plausible consequence of the socio-economic impact of the former colonies in America (Schwab 131). Nevertheless, Rivarol's work, known to posterity as *Discours sur l'universalité de la langue française*, would attain the rank of sacred writ in France. His mantra, *CE QUI N'EST PAS CLAIR N'EST PAS FRANÇAIS* (Rivarol 32), was destined to be chanted by generations of school children and would serve as precept for a Flaubert bent on reining in his congenital taste for metaphor. Little did it matter that Rivarol's text exploits metaphor, allegory, and fallacy. His irresistible style and play on emotions, allegiances, and inveterate biases are the stuff of seduction, his audience a willing participant to the point that even framers of the Revolution would be compelled to applaud the triumphs of this *monarchiste émigré*—for the sake of Nation (Henry [2005] 26–31, 38–43).

Prussia was part of a vast French-speaking network. Fumaroli emphasizes its "in-house" character. Family ties of aristocrats and royalty dispersed throughout Europe fostered its use as common language; those attached to or supported by their houses (jurists, writers, associates of all descriptions) were compelled to follow suit. Moreover, diplomats and commercial negotiators—official and clandestine alike—were all subject to the "universality of the French language." Such was the République des Lettres, such was the "grand jeu politico-diplomatique dont tous parlaient la langue: le français" (Fumaroli 235). Such was the Court of Catherine II of Russia. Upon coming to power in 1762, the Czarina (herself a German princess and an admirer of Frederick II), charted a course similar to Prussia's. She courted the favor of Voltaire, maintained a regular correspondence with him (and with other *philosophes*), sought his counsel on political and social matters, and supported his humanitarian causes as well as the work of the Encyclopédistes. Such too was the Court of Gustavus III of Sweden who ruled from 1771 to 1792. Sweden had long been under the cultural and political influence of France. Christina had set ample precedent. Gustavus's mother, Louisa Ulrique whom he succeeded, was sister to Frederick II and shared her brother's affinity for things French. She reared her son in the same fashion. Gutavus did not disappoint. As Crown-Prince he could not wait to sojourn in Paris where he was overwhelmed by the hospitality of Louis XV and his contacts with various *philosophes*. Inspired by their thinking, he altered Sweden's fortunes by suspending the aristocratic assembly and subjecting it to constitutional law. In effect, he saw himself as an "enlightened despot" in the French ideological mold and paid special tribute to Voltaire. He kept abreast of events in the French capital by reading the widely disseminated *Annales politiques, civiles et littéraires* and *Courrier de l'Europe*, both of which were published in London. In 1784 Gustavus would visit Paris again. The warm welcome from Louis XVI and Marie-Antoinette, Versailles, the festival in his honor, and a performance of Piccinni's *Dido* left him convinced that he had been to the cultural center of the world. Back in Stockholm he began a series of projects designed to bring the Swedish capital in line with Paris, among them a national academy based on the French model and a theater technically fitted to stage the sort of productions he had attended.[9]

---

[9] Fumaroli 346–51. Leigh Oakes, in *Language and National Identity: Comparing France and Sweden*, marvels at the influence France exerted on Sweden over the centuries:

2.11 Voltaire's Europe, Voltaire's language

Voltaire's prominence in the Republic of Letters extended into the realm of language itself. Indeed, his notoriety as spokesman for French civilization in general and the virtues of the French language in particular moved Brunot to devote an entire section of volume VI of his history of the language to "la grammaire voltairienne" (6: 863–98). The subdivisions convey emphases: "la langue fixée," "les commentaires d'auteurs classiques," "la tradition grammaticale." The eighteenth century rewrote history: grammarians and the French Academy were now cast in a supporting role. A group of new stars assumed the lead: the great authors of the "classical period." In Voltaire's *Le siècle de Louis XIV* only Vaugelas retained an elevated position—not owing to his contributions as grammarian, but rather his translation of the histories of Quintus Curtius. Heading the bill was Blaise Pascal and his 1656 *Lettres provinciales*, followed by the writers that would constitute the core of the French humanities curriculum into the twentieth century: Racine, Boileau, La Rochefoucauld, et al. Thus, as Brunot infers, the official history of the French language became inseparable from the history of French letters, a standing that would be difficult to assail, even in light of the discoveries of Sir William Jones and the achievements of German philologists.

Of course the dynamics of eighteenth-century France differed significantly from those of the Splendid Century, which had in many ways attained mythical status. The Court no longer enjoyed the prestige of its predecessor, nor was it seen as paragon in matters of style. Paris itself had become the trendsetter—innovative, ostentatious, incorrigible. Purists looked to the past, nostalgically. Voltaire, concerned about the state of the French language, urged the Academy to undertake the compilation of a new dictionary bolstered by examples drawn from "approved authors." Curiously, on the surface he appeared to support uniformity of spelling. He encouraged for

---

"The construction of linguistic and national consciousness in Sweden" the author writes, "mirrored that in France for many centuries: François I's Edict of Villers-Cotterêts of 1539 was followed, albeit over a century later, by guidelines in 1661 reinforcing the use of Swedish in diplomatic correspondence; the Swedish Academy set up in 1786 modelled itself on the French equivalent established in 1635; and the effect of nineteenth-century Romanticism in Sweden resulted in similar efforts to consolidate national identity as those observed under the Third Republic in France. It is not until World War II that a clear divergence between the two countries can be observed" (230).

example the orthographic change from "*oi*" to "*ai*" (*françois* > *français*), among others. Yet his own manuscripts reflect an indifference to spelling shared by many writers of the period, including Montesquieu. Attempts at reform, supported enthusiastically by scientists, encountered resistance. The problem lay with finding a uniform system. Progress did ensue, nevertheless. Simplifications led the way, *sç* (*sçavant, sçavoir*) yields to *s* (*savant, savoir*); *ct* (*défunct, conflict*) becomes *t* (*défunt, conflit*); intervening *s* (*maistre, honneste*) disappears as well (*maître, honnête*), in favor of a diacritic. In addition to the aforementioned *oi* > *ai*, traditional *e* disappears completely from the following clusters: *creu* > *cru, insceu* > *insu*. Similarly, *i* replaces the ornamental *y*: *cecy* > *ceci, gay* > *gai*; and *z* disappears as a plural marker in words ending in *é*: *véritez* > *vérités*. The fate of plurals in *ent* and *ant* remained unresolved, most grammarians (including the Academy) opting for suppression (*enfans, parens*). (Reinstatement would not occur until the following century.) Double consonants, under attack from some quarters, tended to remain intact (*affirmatif, commode*) and would be increasingly recognized as standard as time went on. The practice of using *i* and *u* to represent *j* and *v* disappeared progressively. Diacritics underwent major reform. Until the eighteenth century accents had been haphazard at best. Whereas modifications would continue into the nineteenth century, typographical usage became largely as we know it today. Orthography thus made important strides, however grudgingly, and foundations were laid for standardization in the decades following the Revolution. Interestingly, in France, resistance continues to be the norm. Further efforts to simplify or "phoneticize" orthography (as late as the final decades of the twentieth century) have all met with little success.

Brunot includes no rubric for punctuation. Understandably so. It is fair to say that even today standardization is lacking. Whereas norms do exist, there is no universal style sheet; editors and publications impose their particular desiderata. Teachers abroad, not trained within the French frame, are left to puzzle out the system. As for pronunciation, a basic change in attitude had occurred since the sixteenth century. Brunot describes it succinctly:

> Au XVIIIe siècle le renversement qui avait commencé au XVIe siècle est complet. Il n'y a plus à la base une langue parlée, que l'écriture reproduit, en essayant de suivre de près ou de loin les variations. [...] Ce qui est à la base, c'est une langue écrite, fixée par les textes des écrivains, les observations des lexicologues, et que reproduit bien ou mal la parole. (6: 973)

The written language had thus become dominant, "fixing" basic forms and halting major shifts. The sound system was affected as a consequence. Henceforth only minor adjustments would find their way into the spoken language. Closed vowels, for instance, could open, causing eventual orthographic modification as in the case of *é* > *è*. The sole exception was the change ([wɛ] > [wɑ]) in instances where *oi* was not pronounced [ɛ]: roi ([ʀwɛ > ʀwɑ], loi [lwɛ > lwɑ]. It goes without saying that such changes occurred inconsistently; outdated pronunciations persisted regionally and colloquially even in higher social circles and at Court, the retention of the nasal vowel [ɔ̃] in *homme*, for example. (Louis XVIII, historians are fond of repeating, had to be reminded to refer to himself as ʀwɑ, not ʀwɛ, de France).

Despite polemics sparked by theorists, the syntax of the written language prevailed as well. Norms derived from seventeenth-century canonical works were adopted by aspiring writers, publishers, and grammarians alike. A purified literary language evolved over time. Indeed, stylistically, as the century approached its end, imitation became servile. "Le style noble" attracted the would-be Racines, Pascals, and Voltaires of the latter day who exaggerated "classical" sobriety and turned it into wooden snobbery. In place of the creative use of vocabulary, for instance, terms adjudged to fall outside the canonical lexicon could be introduced only if their placement in the utterance resulted in their ennoblement. Thus a common word such as *métier* had to be used figuratively in tandem with an ennobling factor that would rid it of its quotidian dimension, *le vil métier du tyran*, for example.

That is not to say vocabulary remained static in the eighteenth century. To the contrary, the constraints of the seventeenth century soon gave way to the lexical exigencies imposed by the social, political, and intellectual dynamics of the Enlightenment. Change became increasingly the norm as the century progressed. Advances in the sciences, agriculture, commerce, and industry were accompanied by shifting demographics, increased social concerns, philosophical innovation, institutional expansion, and broadened political horizons—including democracy in the New World. A language crisis ensued. Neologisms had to be summoned by the score to fill the many voids and to provide increasingly specialized lexicons. These new words were drawn from traditional quarters such as Latin and Greek as well as from modern foreign languages and localized trade talk. English enjoyed special favor. Anglicisms slipped into the language in significant numbers: *budget, club, congrès, jury, jockey, redingote, bifteck, pudding, punch, boxe.* Germany's prominence in mineralogy and geology led to the adoption of words such as *quartz, gneiss, feldspath, cobalt,* and a wealth of mining terms. Italy continued to be a source for music and the arts: *arpège, cantate, cantatrice, contralto, piano, aquarelle, pittoresque* (Wartburg 199–200).

As needed as the neologism was, necessity soon turned to vogue. The "précieux" movement that again swept over high society coveted euphemism and periphrasis. An elitist social jargon developed akin to the "style noble," an "aristocratic" code that identified the speaker as upper echelon. At the same time, popular expressions viewed as being of unfortunate taste (vulgarisms) "invaded," democratically, other registers. Reformers protested, but the swell swept on unabated. Predictably, then, language was to become a focus of the Revolution—albeit in several unpredictable ways.

3

Revolution, Restoration, Language for Profit

THE REVOLUTION OF 1789 changed France forever. The decade of upheaval restructured institutions, blurred the social strata, and initiated a reconfiguration of the myth of Nation that would not culminate until the *débâcle* of the Franco-Prussian War and the Commune had once again underscored the pressing need for consolidation. The period known as the Restoration, following the exit(s) of Napoleon and encompassing the reigns of Louis XVIII (1814–1824) and Charles X (1824–1830), marked the return of the House of Bourbon to the throne. That return, however, did not entail putting France back together as the country had been. The Ancien Régime was no more. The Revolution had touched every corner of France. The peasantry knew how the king and queen had met their demise. Some of them had participated in events and had brought back first-hand descriptions. Regional Jacobin Clubs had spread the word beyond urban areas and into their very midst. Later Napoleon would recruit them and take them on a devastating tour of Europe (as far as Moscow) and North Africa (all the way to the Pyramids). Most importantly, the tithing system that had benefited Church and gentry alike fell prey to the restructuring (Barral 6). Likewise, a sense of empowerment that would not soon subside had filled commoners in the many cities. Those who joined in the process or who looked on saw how thin and vulnerable the "upper crust" truly was. New possibilities swirled in their heads as they witnessed the crumbling of social bastions and economic impediments centuries old. New values seemed within reach: lineage was finally yielding to enterprise and self-worth. Many looked to move up the ladder, to elevate their socio-economic status amidst the restructuring. Other factions, carried away by enthusiasm turned frenzy, sought to dismantle the ladder completely.

3.1 Lexis and the *bonnet rouge*

The institution of the French language did not escape the tumult. The lofty status it had acquired under the Ancien Régime hardly corresponded to the newly defined construct of Nation as a manifestation of the people. The pressures brought to bear on it differed little from those of other institutions: pressures to liberate and democratize language, to abolish elitism and hierarchy, to grant equality to all words, expressions, and dialects in a classless society. Victor Hugo, in retrospect (he was born in 1802), would romanticize the phenomenon. He would link the metaphors of Ocean/People and Sea/Language and in so doing would assail the very attributes for which the French language had been admired for so long:

> La langue française n'est pas *fixée* et ne se fixera point. Une langue ne se fixe pas. [. . .] Les langues sont comme la mer, elles oscillent sans cesse. [. . .] Il en est des idiomes humains comme de tout. Chaque siècle y apporte et en emporte quelque chose. Qu'y faire? Cela est fatal. C'est donc en vain que l'on voudrait pétrifier la mobile physionomie de notre idiome sous une forme donnée. (*Préface de Cromwell* 94)

Later still, in his poem "Réponse à un acte d'accusation," Hugo would claim to have broken the shackles that had been placed on the French language by the Academy, the State, and a pretentious aristocratic society. "La langue était l'Etat avant quatre-vingt-neuf/Les mots, bien ou mal nés, vivaient parqués en castes," he would write. Whereas words of "noble" lineage "boarded carriages at Versailles," the others, "sans perruque," went about in rags. Hugo boasted that he had changed all that:

> Je fis souffler un vent révolutionnaire.
> Je mis un bonnet rouge au vieux dictionnaire.
> [. . .] Et déclarai les mots égaux, libres, majeurs;
> [. . .] et je criai dans la foudre et le vent:
> *Guerre à la rhétorique et paix à la syntaxe!*
> *Et tout quatre-vingt-treize éclata.*

Of course Hugo's frame of reference was primarily French poetry, the alexandrine verse that had been the mainstay of "classical" aesthetics in France for nearly two centuries. This new, egalitarian footing provided the theoretical basis for all sorts of lexical "audacities" which Hugo exploited systematically and which allowed him to rhyme such unlikely couplings as *bibliothèque* and *pastèque* (*Ruy Blas* 1838). Needless to say, in the heat of the Revolution and in its aftermath, it was not poetry that occupied minds and spirits. Indeed, street language had moved into higher quarters. When the dust began to settle, concern arose regarding the "fallen status" of the French language. In response and in order to provide direction for those who sought to improve their lot in society, numerous self-help dictionaries were published in the years following the conflict. The title of one of them reveals the magnitude and contemptibility "popularisms" had come to acquire by 1808: *Dictionnaire du bas-langage ou des manières de parler usitées parmi le peuple; ouvrage dans lequel on a réuni les expressions proverbiales, figurées et triviales; les sobriquets, termes ironiques et facétieux; les barbarismes, solécismes; et généralement les locutions basses et vicieuses que l'on doit rejeter de la bonne conversation.* The disdainful tone carries over into a vituperative preface:

> Le plus bel apanage d'une langue est sans contredit l'élégance et la pureté; et où doit-on le plus s'efforcer de faire briller ces précieux avantages, si ce n'est dans l'intimité et l'abandon de la conversation? L'ouvrage que l'on publie, est loin, assurément, d'offrir un recueil de ces pensées nobles et pures qui élèvent l'âme et l'imagination, de donner un choix de ces mots dont le son doux et harmonieux flatte si agréablement l'oreille; la langue, dépouillée de tout ornement, ne s'y laisse apercevoir que sous des formes burlesques ou triviales. Des peintures hardies, mais grossières, des termes ignobles ou barbares, y remplacent continuellement des nuances fines et délicates, ces métaphores ingénieuses qui concordent avec la politesse et l'urbanité françaises.

A couple of entries suffice to indicate the specific character of the language targeted:

> **CHIER**. *Il a chié dans ma malle jusqu'au cadenas.* Se dit d'une personne dont on a sujet de se plaindre, et à laquelle on garde rancune. On dit bassement d'une personne grossière et mal élevée, qui est sujette à lâcher des vents, qu'*elle ne fait que chier. Bientôt, s'il n'y prend garde, on lui chiera sur le nez.* Locution grossière et exagérée qui signifie qu'un homme est d'une foiblesse impardonnable; qu'il laisse trop abuser de sa patience et de son autorité. On dit bassement d'une personne pour laquelle on a le plus grand mépris, que l'*on chie sur elle. Chier sur sa besogne.* Dédaigner l'ouvrage dont on est chargé.

CLAVIOT. Terme bas et populaire qui équivaut à expectoration, crachat; flegme qui s'arrête dans la gorge. *Un gros claviot*. Pour dire un crachat très épais.

3.1.1 The counter-revolution: a war of words and values

Examples of another sort emanate from the political process itself. The term *propagande*, according to the *Petit Robert* dictionary, derives from the Latin expression *congregatio de propaganda fide* documented in 1689 and meaning to "propagate the faith" ("propager la foi"). It finds its way into the French language in 1790 and appears amidst the Convention (1792) where its semantic value has been appropriated to denote an "action exercée sur l'opinion pour l'amener à voir certaines idées politiques et sociales, à soutenir une politique, un gouvernement, un représentant." This sort of politicization common to Revolutionary rhetoric did not go unchallenged as events ran their course. A linguistic counter-revolution, captured in Hugo's lines "Guerre à la rhétorique et paix à la syntaxe! / Et tout quatre-vingt-treize éclata [...]," surged to remedy perceived abuses. Jean François de La Harpe (1739–1803) of the Academy, a dramatist and esthete in the old style, rose to the challenge. In his *Du fanatisme dans la langue révolutionnaire* (completed in1799), he focused on the shift in semantics emanating from eighteenth-century rationalism and attaining its zenith at the height of the Revolution. The subtitle is more revealing still: *De la persécution suscitée par les barbares du dix-huitième siècle, contre la religion chrétienne et ses ministres; suivi d'un appendice sur le calendrier républicain*. The epigraph in Latin and French comes from Psalms xxxiii: "*Firmaverunt sibi sermonem nequam. Ils se sont affermis dans l'habitude d'un langage pervers.*"

La Harpe thus viewed both the Revolution and its language as perversions. He had little sympathy for the recontextualization history had foisted upon people and institutions. His claims of ideological manipulations have been borne out by countless studies,[1] of course, but it is also apparent that his own reactionary perspective springs from the "*propaganda fide*" ideology against which so much Revolutionary rhetoric was directed. The "linguistic"

---

[1] Most recently Caroline Weber's *Terror and its Discontents: Suspect Words in Revolutionary France*, 2003. See her extensive bibliography and ample index. A quotation from the chapter titled "Epilogue: The Revolution Eats its Children" sums up her thesis: "Precisely because moral and political categories are as malleable as the words that constitute them, today's 'good' citizen may very well be tomorrow's bad apple, and vice versa" (232).

value of his work resides, then, in counterpoint or rather "différend": two essentially different and incompatible rhetorics/ideologies (not languages)—the Ancien Régime and the Revolution at antipodes. The problem of how to bridge the chasm would befall both Napoleon and the Bourbons. It is the breadth of the chasm that La Harpe's work documents.

The base word of the title, *fanatique/fanatisme* (denoting divine or religious inspiration according to its sixteenth-century origins), serves as crux; it is presented as a newly secularized "perversion" that turns the vocable against itself. La Harpe writes:

> J'ai de ce qu'était le fanatisme dans la langue du bon sens, ce qu'il a été jusqu'ici dans la pensée et dans la bouche de tous les hommes raisonnables. Il fallait bien que dans la langue inverse, appelée *révolutionnaire*, il fût autre chose. [...] Le fanatisme est croyance à une religion quelconque [...] Voilà le fanatisme. Quiconque en est atteint est un ennemi public, et doit être exterminé (La Harpe 9–10).

"Fanaticism" redefined thus embraces intolerance, oppression, tyranny. La Harpe cites appropriation upon appropriation. He casts the term *liberté* itself within the negative semantic frame of temptation and misguidance—all that serves to lead the flock astray. It is true that "Dieu a fait l'homme libre," he says, but what is liberty? It is "la liberté de préférer le mensonge à la vérité et le mal au bien, selon sa vanité et ses passions" (2). Perhaps the greatest semantic (and institutional) "injustice," La Harpe suggests, took the form of a document and a policy: *la Constitution Civile du Clergé*. The priests who refused to submit were not only justified, it is obvious to him, they were the true "heroes," those who chose to obey a higher authority (13–14). From there La Harpe lists some eighty words that the Revolution had invented or redefined politically and/or ideologically. Some of the more salient ones are: *abus, bienfaisance, carmagnole, exécrable, fidélité, montagne, moral, Patrie, patriotique, peuple, propriété, raison, saint(e), sans-culottes, serment, suprême, sûreté, temple, tort*, and so on.

Language itself, then—the French language—found itself ideologically embroiled. Outside France even the most ardent supporters of French language and culture found reason for concern. Rivarol himself would spend the rest of his days in exile. He wandered from Belgium to Holland to England and finally to Germany where he would publish the definitive edition of his *De l'universalité de la langue française* in 1797, four years before his death in

Berlin in April of 1801. Schwab, the co-winner of the "grand concours," all but recanted in1796 the panegyrics he had written in favor of French civilization a decade before. In that year he wrote to Denis Robelot a letter that the former canon of Dijon incorporated into his 1803 translation of Schwab's *Dissertation sur les causes de l'universalité de la langue Françoise.* Schwab minced no words. "En relisant mon ouvrage, que j'ai composé il y a plus de dix ans," he confided,

> Je me suis souvent demandé si je n'y ai pas trop dit de bien d'une nation devenue depuis, par les crimes dont elle s'est rendue coupable, et par les horreurs qu'elle a commises, l'opprobre de l'humanité. (Schwab 63)

Moreover, not unlike La Harpe but for other reasons, he admitted having praised a culture that had not existed for some time, a culture that had slipped into decline and whose mores and language had been depreciated to the point of corruption, compromising the very logocentric stability that had been touted as its primary asset:

> Je remarque d'abord, que j'ai pris les François tels qu'ils étoient, et non pas tels qu'ils seroient un jour. J'ai même dit expressément que je les considérois tels qu'ils avoient été dans les plus beaux temps de la monarchie Françoise, en ajoutant que je ne disconvenois pas que, "chez une nation où trop de raffinement dégénère en corruption, la politesse se réduit enfin à de simples formules et à de pures cérémonies, qu'elle devient même le vernis et le véhicule de la dissimulation et de la fraude. (Schwab 63)

Similarly, writing before the suspended Academy had been reconstituted under the umbrella of the Institut (1795), Robelot bemoaned in an explanatory note the excruciatingly bad taste that had come to dominate his compatriots' penchant for neologisms. "Depuis que l'Académie françoise n'existe plus," he laments, "nous avons, en cinq à six années, fait une riche conquête de mots nouveaux, qui justifieroit les regrets qu'on pourroit donner à la suppression de ce tribunal littéraire." He then represents linguistic and political "misdeeds" as products of the same misguided zeal. The example he cites is so well chosen that it needs no commentary:

> Plût à Dieu que quelques-unes de ces expressions s'effaçassent à jamais de la mémoire des hommes, à qui elles ne rappellent que des forfeits! [...] Personne, je pense, ne répétera après Anacharsis Cloots: "*Gallophile,* de tout temps, mon cœur est sans fard, et mon âme est *sans-culotte.*" (Schwab 146)

3.1.2 French: the "common" language of the New Order

Of course Robelot had fled to Germany as a consequence of the Civil Constitution of the Clergy. Both he and Schwab were Ancien Régime partisans who, as outsiders removed from the daily events, currents, and crosscurrents of the Revolution, could not have known that their concern for the French language was shared by many of the framers of the new order. Indeed, in the very midst of the Convention—as architects of the early Revolution grappled with their responsibilities to the State and humanity—a piece of disturbing news caused them to focus on the French language. What they learned, to their dismay, would shape French language policy for more than a century.

In 1792 François Lanthenas (translator of Thomas Paine's *The Rights of Man*) presented a multidimensional report before the Convention's Public Education Committee. In it he outlined a plan for reorganizing the nation's primary schools. That plan included modest yet practical measures designed to make the French language "en peu de temps la langue familière de toutes les parties de la République." His goal in doing so was both patriotic and political. "Il faut que les intérêts de la République soient maintenus et connus de tous ses membres," he wrote.

> D'ailleurs, le moyen de répandre les principes de notre liberté et d'aug-
> menter l'ascendant de notre industrie, c'est de mettre à même les Français
> de nos frontières de parler avec une égale facilité la langue qui les voisine et
> celle qui doit désormais les unir davantage avec leurs frères.

Since the Committee had already discussed the status of the French language in Corsica and Brittany, Lanthenas focused on the German-speaking departments of France. He proposed an initial phase of bilingual education (to be implemented according to available resources) that privileged reading and writing in French but allowed instruction in other subjects to be rendered in both languages. That formula was to be generalized throughout the country and would address other language communities as well. At this stage dialects do not come under negative scrutiny. The proposal thus conveys a federalist vision of a new France that would allow linguistic diversity while promoting the national idiom.

That vision would soon be challenged by Bertrand Barère (de Vieuzac) in his capacity as spokesman for the Committee of Public Safety.

The shift from the Education Committee to the redoubtable committee that would oversee much of the violence to come signals a decisive change in perspective. First, in his report of 8 Pluviose of the year II (1794), Barère characterized languages other than the official idiom of public instruction as tools of tyranny, ignorance, and fanaticism. Second, he portrayed the French language in the following way: "la plus belle langue de l'Europe, celle qui la première a consacré franchement les droits de l'homme et du citoyen, celle qui est chargée de transmettre au monde les plus sublimes pensées de la liberté et les plus grandes spéculations de la politique" (Barère 291). The French language so described combines a pretension of aesthetic superiority and a mission as conveyor of a politicized, secular proselytism that makes Liberty the new messiah. Third, the French language under the Ancien Régime had been the prerogative of the privileged classes and therefore had fragmented the country linguistically, culturally, and politically: "on eût dit qu'il y avait plusieurs nations dans une seule" (Barère 292). Hence, language diversity, including the federalist bilingual solution, placed the Republic itself at risk: "Le fédéralisme," Barère wrote, "et la superstition parlent bas-breton; l'émigration et la haine de la République parlent allemand; la contre-révolution parle italien, et le fanatisme parle basque. Cassons ces instruments de dommage et d'erreur" (295). Dialects or "patois" are treated less severely because they are perceived as being more unfortunate than menacing. Barère assumed that they did not hinder communication, as the following lines reveal: "Ce n'est pas qu'il n'existe d'autres idiomes plus ou moins grossiers dans d'autres départements; mais ils ne sont pas exclusifs, mais ils n'ont pas empêché de connaître la langue nationale. Si elle n'est pas également parlée partout, elle est du moins facilement entendue" (295).

Barère's proposal differed significantly from the one Lanthenas had outlined two years before; it conveyed his sense of urgency. Within ten days of the enactment of the decree, at the Republic's expense, teachers were to be selected "by the people" in all the affected communes to begin instructing all citizens, young and old alike, in the French language, the Rights of Man, and the laws of the Republic—especially laws relating to agriculture (Barère 298).

3.1.3 Grégoire's call for annihilation of *les patois*

The assembly adopted Barère's measures, but not before questioning the limited spectrum to which they applied. Some wished to refer the matter back to the Education Committee in order to broach implementation on a broader level. Specifically, abbé Henri-Baptiste Grégoire pointed to the patois problem and the multitude of people in the provinces who, as a consequence, were unable to communicate in French. Barère responded that his solution, because limited, could be expedited more quickly and that, moreover, it targeted potential insurgencies such as the Vendée uprisings.

Grégoire would have to await another day. His opportunity came some months later in the Education Committee's session of 16 Prairial of the same year (1794). There he presented another report on the languages of the Nation. Grégoire, with the assistance of various regional Jacobin Clubs, had conducted a language survey designed to determine with greater accuracy the veritable extent to which the French language was known and utilized throughout the country. The report carried the title *Rapport sur la nécessité et les moyens d'anéantir les patois, et d'universaliser l'usage de la langue française.* Grégoire prefaced his findings with encomia:

> La langue française a conquis l'estime de l'Europe, et depuis un siècle elle
> y est classique. [...] Il y a dix ans qu'au fond de l'Allemagne (à Berlin) on
> discuta savamment cette question qui, suivant l'expression d'un écrivain,
> eût flatté l'orgueil de Rome empressée à la consacrer dans son histoire
> comme une de ses belles époques. On connaît les tentatives de la politique
> de Rome pour universaliser sa langue: elle défendait d'en employer d'autre
> pour haranguer les ambassadeurs étrangers, pour négocier avec eux; et
> malgré ses efforts, elle n'obtint qu'imparfaitement ce qu'un assentiment
> libre accorde à la langue française. (1–2)

Grégoire began by touting the storied history and linguistic efficacy of the French language and by evoking the challenges it faced in the making of a new France. The thinly veiled reference to Berlin and Rivarol situates its prominence within the Republic of Letters, a status acquired by dint of cultural and linguistic superiority. The explicit reference to the Roman Republic, conversely, posits the newly formed French Republic as political successor to its esteemed antecedent and, implicitly, torchbearer of Western Civilization. The attributes of the French language, in a very practical sense, had already served that purpose well, Grégoire emphasized. The French language had succeeded where Latin had failed: "Dans sa marche claire et méthodique la pensée se déroule facilement; c'est ce qui lui donne un caractère de raison, de probité que les fourbes eux-mêmes trouvent plus propre à les garantir des ruses diplomatiques" (2). Thus within the context of the Revolution bent on eliminating the intrigues and deceit of the Monarchy, the clarity of the French language itself (especially syntax) emerges as guarantor of liberty. If it had been "prostituted" to other ends in the past by misguided factions and had lost a measure of its efficacy, it remained nevertheless the surest vehicle of communication for the people who, by using any other language, lent themselves all the more readily to victimization. In order for it to fulfill its function, in addition to undergoing certain modifications, it needed to be the universal language of the land. Therein lay the problem, Grégoire lamented. Feudalism had left France linguistically divided. France had been newly partitioned into administrative departments in the interest of centralization and consolidating the Revolution, yet this vestige of feudalism persisted as a threat to the Nation:

> Nous n'avons plus de provinces, et nous avons encore environ trente patois qui en rappellent les noms [...] On peut assurer sans exagération qu'au moins six millions de Français, sur-tout dans les campagnes, ignorent la langue nationale; qu'un nombre égal est à-peu-près incapable de soutenir une conversation suivie; qu'en dernier résultat, le nombre de ceux qui la parlent purement n'excède pas trois millions; et probablement le nombre de ceux qui l'écrivent correctement est encore moindre.
> (Grégoire 3, 5)

It is impossible to validate the accuracy of Grégoire's statistics. They were certainly viewed as credible and worthy of action by the Convention, however. Members readily bought into his project of standardizing ("uniformer"/"révolutionner") the national idiom and of bringing to the "République une et indivisible, l'usage unique et invariable de la langue de la liberté" (Grégoire 6). Exactly why the Convention took such an uncompromising stand against regional languages and patois at this juncture is another matter. Barère's interests are easily documented. Haling from Tarbes and having studied law in Toulouse amidst the many Occitan speakers, he sensed the dangers federalism posed to national unity. Indeed, it was he who initiated the creation of a special department (Hautes-Pyrénées) for the Bigorre region rather than let it be attached to Béarn (present Bas-Pyrénées) because he recognized that "les deux nations sont trop séparées par les mœurs et une sorte d'antipathie qui rendront à jamais toute liaison impossible" (Barère 1).

The use of the term "nation" to describe the two regions underscores Barère's apprehension.

3.1.4 One language for all: egalitarianism and empowerment

David A. Bell, in the chapter "National Language and the Revolutionary Crucible" of his admirably researched *The Cult of Nation in France* (2001), offers further explanation. Initially, he notes, revolutionaries were anxious to extend the Revolution into the provinces. As a consequence, translations of essential government texts into the country's various idioms was policy until 1792. Progressively however, Bell clarifies, language policy came to reflect the concern that even though local clergy had acquiesced to the Civil Constitution of the Clergy (which Grégoire was the first to sign), their empowerment as moral and spiritual guides to the peasantry and as speakers of local vernaculars jeopardized the central religious authority and therefore the well-being of the Nation. The means to combat the threat thus took the form of a program of national language empowerment, in other words the decree stemming from Grégoire's report. The measure, Bell contends, borrowed a page from Protestantism:

> Had Protestantism succeeded in France, it is virtually certain that the French language would have spread far more rapidly than it did. The Protestant churches that mushroomed in the mid-sixteenth century used the French of the court and the high nobility almost exclusively, even in the south of the country. [. . .] In short, when Grégoire proposed to abolish patois and universalize the use of French in France, he was effectively introducing a Protestant solution to the problem of linguistic diversity. (193)

The point is well taken. Moreover, Grégoire (like Lanthenas) was first and foremost an egalitarian whose "universalism" included equality for the "races." He had published in 1788 *Essai sur la régéneration physique, morale et politique des Juifs* and his activism would be in large part responsible for the Revolution's decrees abolishing the slave trade.

In this sense his name deserves to be cited as a true humanitarian of the Revolution, alongside abbé de L'Epée and abbé Sicard, for example— subjects of the following chapter—whose concern for the impaired led to the founding of the national school for the deaf and the development of *la langue des signes française*. Indeed, the French government's recognition of his stance on human rights would earn him a place in the Pantheon in 1989, generating a flood of attention and in its wake numerous studies and biographies.[2]

In Grégoire's view the concept of one language for all would certainly eliminate the inequities associated with regional speech. He came from the Meurthe-Moselle area of Lorraine, after all, where he would have been sensitized to local dialectical and ethnic diversities. Furthermore, as his report attests and given the region's Franco-German dichotomy, he was aware of the 1782–1784 contest sponsored by the Berlin Academy of Sciences and Letters that produced the essays by Rivarol and Schwab predicting that French was to remain the universal language of Europe for the foreseeable future. Those predictions notwithstanding, there is incontrovertible evidence that he shared the opinion of Voltaire, Frederick the Great, and later Schwab according to which the French language was in decline and therefore in jeopardy. A key word may be found in his 1788 title: "regeneration." For Grégoire's proposal included five provisions designed to "regenerate" the French language and to elevate it to a greater state of perfection. The provisions, it is obvious, offered nothing that had not been suggested by past reformers: 1) orthographic reform, 2) semantic reform fixing denotation and usage, 3) the production of a new dictionary and grammar to those ends, 4) the paring of frivolous synonyms from the language, and 5) enrichment of the language through the addition of augmentatives, diminutives, and privatives (Grégoire 28).

3.1.5 Revolutionizing the heritage

Ironically then, the Convention, faced with instituting the new order, took a conservative and largely preservative stance with regard to the French language. Brigitte Schlieben-Lange, in *Idéologie, révolution et uniformité de la langue*, summarizes succinctly the polarities involved:

> La politique linguistique "jacobine" s'est trouvée confrontée à un dilemme devant la variation sociale. Elle se sent d'une part redevable aux couches populaires, sujets de la Révolution à Paris; il faut en outre faire régner l'égalité en matière de langue. Tout sujet du souverain doit avoir le droit de s'exprimer librement et dans la variété du français qu'il connaît. L'ennemi

---

[2] The diversity of these works underscores the complexity of the man and his thought. See especially Certeau et al. (1975), as well as Plongeron (1989 and 2001), Popkin (2000), Boulad-Ayoub (2005), and Sepinwall (2005).

de l'égalité linguistique est avant tout l'aristocratie qui a développé le jeu capricieux et artificiel de la diversité des styles.

[...] Mais d'autre part, les variétés populaires sont, à y regarder de plus près, tout aussi capricieuses et sujettes à l'anomalie que les variétés plus "polissées". Il faudra donc une langue nouvelle, analogue destinée à une universalisation touchant toutes les classes sociales. (Schlieben-Lange 172)

Grégoire's report produced a decree charging the Committee with drafting legislation for the production of a new grammar and the compilation of a new dictionary as well as plans for instilling a "regenerated" and "universalized" form of the French language throughout the realm—in city and province alike—based on the Enlightenment principles of "analogie" as opposed to the "caprices de l'usage" (Schlieben-Lange 218). Of course the Convention soon gave way to more radical factions and other agendas, leaving those projects unaccomplished. The significance of Grégoire's report cannot be overestimated, nevertheless. In the interim the Convention had rejected Citizen Jean Delormel's call for development of an artificial universal language based on logical classifications and, more significantly, had also adopted for schools (30 Brumaire year III) Charles-François Lhomond's *Elémens de la grammaire françoise* (1780)—a short, analytical grammar employing as models examples of "le bon usage" as it had evolved in the writings of the most esteemed, "linguistically enlightened" authors of the Ancien Régime and designed to be used alongside his Latin grammar.[3] "Nationalizing" the French language was therefore a means of appropriating the writings themselves, of "revolutionizing" them, so to speak, and of converting the cultural heritage of

---

[3] In her article "Universal Languages during the French Revolution" (1999) and in her book (*A Revolution in Language* published two years later) Sophia Rosenfeld contextualizes Delormel's proposal and points to the lobbying strategies of proponents of a universal sign language based on the abbé de L'Epée's "natural" language developed for the hearing impaired and modified by abbé Sicard (see Chapter Four). She concludes that the language policy ultimately adopted by the Jacobins reflects the "revolutionary efforts to standardize and propagate a single national tongue [that] depended on the idea that the French language could be remade in the image of the original universal language: the instinctive language of the first human societies. In other words [...] a single language for the world" (Rosenfeld 1999: 121). As enticing as this notion may be, however, the realities brought to light in the Convention's various reports on the domestic status of the French language proved to be sobering indeed. Framers were thus compelled to set aside such idealism and to target more practical and realizable goals.

privilege from liability to national attribute. Henceforth Corneille, Racine, Molière, Voltaire, and all others deemed worthy could justly take their place in the pantheon of a "regenerated" legacy to be taught in the *écoles centrales* (created in 1795).

Likewise, the French Academy, "regenerated" as the five divisions of the Institut de France (1795), could continue to bring prestige to the nation in the sciences and in letters alike.[4] As a consequence, in 1798, one hundred four years after its initial publication, the fifth edition of the *Dictionnaire de l'Académie Française* was allowed to be released to the public. The preface, like the original penned by Charpentier, extols the idiom itself, the "Nation"/ "Civilization" that perfected it, and the institution that produced the work. There, however, the similarity comes to an abrupt halt. Composed by Jean Garat (the then Minister of the Interior), the "Discours préliminaire" reflects the lengths to which politicians were willing to go in their efforts to rewrite cultural history and to draw the Academy and its dictionary into the ideology of the Revolution. Garat's contrived apologetics would be amusing were they not so pathetic. "Entre les trois académies," he wrote of the former units,

> l'Académie Françoise, cependant, est celle qui a le plus contribué au change-ment de l'esprit monarchique en esprit républicain: en caressant les Rois, c'est elle qui a le plus ébranlé le trône: ce n'étoit pas le but qu'on lui avoit marqué, ni celui qu'elle avoit a remplir; et cette influence a été l'effet néces-saire, quoique très-imprévu, de plusieurs circonstances de son institution.
>
> Par un statut, ou par un usage, l'Académie Françoise étoit composée d'Hommes-de-Lettres, et de ce qu'on appeloit grands Seigneurs. Ses Mem-bres, égaux comme Académiciens, se regardèrent bientôt comme hommes: les futiles illustrations de naissance, de la faveur, des décorations, s'évanouirent dans cette égalité académique; l'illustration réelle du talent sortit avec plus d'éclat et de solennité. Cette espèce de démocratie littéraire étoit donc déjà, en petit, un exemple de la grande démocratie politique. (Garat i–ii)

So rather than an elitist institution subverted by wealth and privilege, Garat insisted, the Academy had been in microcosm a "republic of letters" whose sense of Nation had nurtured the democratic spirit of the Revolution. As

---

[4] The five divisions of the Institute as restructured in 1795 were L'Académie Française, L'Académie des Inscriptions et Belles-Lettres, L'Académie des Sciences, L'Académie des Beaux-Arts, and L'Académie des Sciences Morales et Politiques. Their fascinating history may be read in the Institute's own *Histoire des cinq académies*.

for any complicity in the malfeasances of the monarchy, Garat denied it categorically and cited the Academy's independence, integrity, and patriotic discourse:

> Tous ceux qui, dans tous les états et dans tous les genres, avoient servi avec éclat, avoient illustrée et éclairé la Nation, reçurent ses hommages dans les séances publiques de l'Académie Françoise; ce qui n'eut d'abord l'air que d'un concours d'éloquence, devint un établissement vraiment politique et national: dans ces discours, dont plusieurs offriront éternellement des modèles à l'éloquence du patriotisme, tout prit le ton simple et auguste de la Langue républicaine; là le nom de *Roi* étoit rarement prononcé; le nom odieux de *sujet*, ne l'étoit jamais. Placés par les objets au milieu des grands intérêts de la Nation, les Orateurs ne voyoient qu'elle, ne parloient qu'à elle; et comme si, par un don de prophétie accordé aux sublimes inspirations des talens, ils voyoient déjà la République, en adressant la parole aux François, déjà ils les appeloient *Citoyens*. (Garat ii–iii)

Curiously, the fifth edition had been in the making for some time, but the Directory chose to modify it only by adding a supplement containing certain neologisms issue of the Revolution—*Carmagnole*, *tyrannicide*, and *lanterner* (the latter meaning "faire subir le supplice de la lanterne"), for example. The *Dictionnaire*, the language it codified, and the culture it represented—shared by Revolutionary and Royalist alike—thus remained indispensable to French national identity despite the radical shifts in ideology. It is not surprising, then, that standardization and universalization of the French language, in the name of national unity, would become a permanent plank in the platforms of the various forms of governments to follow—empire, monarchy, or republic. Indeed, it is clear that France's initial refusal to sign the Charter of Regional or Minority Languages (adopted by the European Council in 1992 and ratified in 1997) and subsequent refusal to ratify it represent a continuation of a language policy two centuries old that finds its latest justification in article 2 of the present French Constitution: "La langue de la République est le français."

3.1.6 Mercier's *Néologie*: usage and *les bons auteurs*

Three years later, in 1801, Louis Sébastien Mercier, drama theorist and playwright, author of a series of books contrasting Parisian society before and after the Revolution, and a member of the Institute, published a work designed both to constrain and to consolidate the lexical innovations accumulated over the preceding decades. His objectives drew on Grégoire's call for further enrichment of the language, on the one hand, and La Harpe's acrimonious admonitions on the other. In producing his *Néologie ou vocabulaire de mots nouveaux, à renouveler, ou pris dans des acceptions nouvelles*, he contrasted his dictionary with the latest edition produced by the Institute itself and voiced a criticism that would be frequently repeated in years to come. He viewed the Academy's dictionary as being out of date and out of touch with the language. "L'Académie ne crée pas les mots," he wrote; "son emploi est d'enregistrer ceux que l'usage autorise. Un mot est donc français avant qu'il soit inséré dans son Dictionnaire" (1:52). Mercier thought of language as a living entity constantly "regenerating" and rejuvenating itself. "Il est d'une langue comme d'un fleuve que rien n'arrête," he insisted:

> Qui s'accroît dans son cours, et qui devient plus large et plus majestueux, à mesure qu'il s'éloigne de sa source. Mais plus un despotisme est ridicule, plus il affecte de la gravité et de la sagesse. Et qui ne rirait d'un tribunal qui vous dit: *je vais fixer la langue.* Arrête, imprudent! Tu vas la clouer, la crucifier. (1: vii–viii)

New words, Mercier reasoned, are at the heart of the process, and those that truly warrant it should be recognized by lexicographers. Yet such recognition, he was careful to specify in his introduction, must necessarily be selective. He refused the "bonnet rouge" image later poeticized by Hugo: he had systematically excluded terms emanating from the Revolution as well as from the sciences and the arts (judging the latter two categories as being too specialized), offering the following justification:

> Quand j'intitule cet ouvrage *Néologie*, qu'on ne l'appelle donc pas *Dictionnaire Néologique! Néologie* se prend toujours en bonne part, et *Néologisme* en mauvaise; il y a entre ces deux mots, la même différence qu'entre religion et fanatisme, philosophie et philosophisme. (1: vi–vii)

If one senses La Harpe in the wings, this diatribe targets other compilations Mercier believed too liberal in their listings, especially J. Cousin's recently published three-volume *Dictionnaire néologique des hommes et des choses* (1800). He stakes claim to a more stringent method based on both linguistic and aesthetic criteria:

> Tous les mots que j'ai ressuscités, appartiennent au génie de la langue
> française, ou par étymologie, ou par analogie; ces mots viennent de
> *boutures*, et sont sortis de l'arbre ou de la forêt, pour former autour d'elle
> des tiges nouvelles, mais ressemblantes. (1: vii)

The combination of biological metaphor and lexical parentage derives from Mercier's literary penchant and suggests his sources and his priorities. "Tous les grands écrivains ont été Néologues," he writes a few pages later, "et je puis dire qu'il n'y a point d'écrivain qui ne soit tombé plus ou moins dans la Néologie" (1: xiii). Thus, in seeking words meriting inclusion his dictionary, Mercier turned to the concept of *usage* as determined by "les bons auteurs." He consulted an impressive number and variety of works in making his compilations and cited in his entries more than one hundred authors—from the sixteenth to the eighteenth centuries. The list of writers from whom he drew the largest number of entries reveals Mercier's preferences. Heading the list is Voltaire (134 entries), followed by Rétif de la Bretonne (87 entries), Montaigne (83 entries), Rousseau (47 entries), Mirabeau (23 entries), Linguet (21 entries), La Harpe (20 entries), Diderot (16 entries).[5] The diverse proclivities of these writers bear witness to the breadth of Mercier's lexical/ideological spectrum and also attests to Mercier's sense of canonicity. Today only the name of Simon Linguet, founder of the *Journal de Politique et de Littérature* (1774), author of *Mémoires sur la Bastille* (1783), and victim of the Revolution, remains relatively obscure. Mercier's recognition of Montaigne prefigures the essayist's return to the canon with the rise of Romanticism. It is also of special note that Mercier assigned an entry to the word *Romantique*, the source for which he cites as the following Rousseau passage: "Les rives du lac de Bienne sont plus sauvages et plus *Romantiques* que celles du lac Genève, parce que les rochers et les bois y bordent l'eau de plus près; mais

---

[5] Endeavoring to influence or even predict usage is an uncertain business at best. Whereas out of the hundreds of entries many have found their way into the language of today, others seem so unlikely that they bring a smile. Mercier's gleanings from Rousseau's works are a case in point. On the positive side there are a number of recognized words such as *alanguissement, ascendance, brûlerie, borgne, dévoreur, doctoresse, entregent, exubérance, flageoler, grognon, haineux, investigation, penser* (as a substantive), *punisseur, regrettable, trouvable, tortillage* (some of them are now listed as "rare," it is true). On the negative side one finds *anti-despote, bavardises, cajolable, dépersuader, dictamen, imboire, lourdise, platise, ségrégatiement,* among others.

elles n'en sont moins riantes." Mercier then reveals his own leanings by glossing the term in the first person without attribution:

> Romantique. La Suisse abonde en points de vue Romantiques: je les ai bien savourés. Une forêt Romantique (celle de Fontainebleau); un vieux château Romantique (celui de Marcoussis). Je salue tout ce qui est Romantique avec une sorte d'enthousiasme. On sent le Romantique, on ne le définit point; le Romanesque, dans les arts, est faux et bizarre auprès de lui. (2: 250)

In matters of literature Mercier was ahead of his time. As it turns out, so was he in matters of language. Reactionary voices dominated policy. The Reform Act of the following year (1802) turned back the clock and re-introduced precepts supporting the holistic approach of the philosophical grammar promoted by the Idéologues Destutt de Tracy and D. Thiébault whose *Grammaire philosophique ou la métaphysique, la logique et la grammaire réunies en un seul corps de doctrine* appeared that same year. Fortunately, pedagogues recognized the impracticality of the approach and responded by adapting the Lhomond grammar to the revised exigencies of the imperial lycées. Over the next decade they were able to present grammatical analysis and logical analysis as parallel domains, thereby retaining the integrity of the "les bons auteurs" and preparing the way for the 1823 Noël and Chapsal approach that would utilize separate manuals (Delesalle-Chevalier 103–09).

3.1.7 Language as social marker

As the First Empire emerged, ran its course and gave way to Restoration, the demand for books on the French language surged to unparalleled heights. Dictionaries and grammars of varying descriptions rolled off presses at an exponential rate. Jacques-Philippe Saint-Gérand notes the appearance of some one hundred twenty-five new or re-edited dictionaries and two hundred ninety-one such grammars between 1800 and 1823.[6] Dictionaries of

---

[6] Saint-Gérand and the University of Toronto deserve special praise for making available online numerous reference tools that facilitate the needs of nineteenth-century French language students and scholars alike. The two referenced here (and many more) may be found at http://www.chass.utoronto.ca/epc/langueXIX. The second is a reproduction of André Chervel's *Les grammaires françaises 1800–1914. Répertoire chronologique* (1982).

synonyms, rhymes, homonyms and homographs, proverbs and idiomatic expressions, orthography, etymologies, onomatopoeias, philological amusements, dialects, epithets, metaphors, oratory, and compound words all found a place in an expanding market that accommodated both multi-volume sets and numerous "dictionnaires portatifs." Of particular significance are the self-help or corrective books similar to the *Dictionnaire du bas-langage* cited above and whose function was to counteract language abuses and "popularisms" issue of the Revolution. During this time frame (1800–1823) no fewer than twenty-five of them were made available to a public avid to put their lessons to use. Some of them referenced provincialisms to avoid and were marketed to regional populations in Gascony, Lyon, Périgord, the Basses-Pyrénées, the Vendée, and "the southern departments" ("les départements méridionaux"). Others focused either on unsavory vocabulary and expressions ("phrases vicieuses," "barbarismes"); others still on "cacographie" or "cacologie," or simply "mauvais langage." Whereas either curiosity or scholarly interest may have been responsible in part for their popularity, the language phenomenon had acquired new dimensions in post-Revolutionary France. Lineage had lost its cachet and language was replacing it as marker. If it had not yet reached its peak, the ability to speak and write correctly was becoming increasingly the ticket to upward social and economic mobility. Michel Glatigny, in his essential *Les marques d'usage dans les dictionnaires français monolingues du XIXe siècle*, quotes Crevel of Balzac's *La cousine Bette* to underscore the point. "C'est de la Gnognotte," Crevel says; he then adds: "Qu'ai-je dit là... Mon Dieu! Je suis capable de lâcher cela quelque jour aux Tuileries... Non, si Valérie ne fait pas mon éducation, je ne puis rien être." Obviously aware of the humor of Crevel's remark, Glatigny glosses the utterance in deadpan fashion: "Ce n'est pas qu''aux Tuileries' (palais du Roi) qu'une expression inadaptée déconsidère. En effet le langage prend de plus en plus d'importance dans les relations sociales où la naissance a une moindre importance que jadis" (Glatigny 23).

3.2 Restoration and epistemology: Girault-Duvivier's *Grammaire des grammaires*

For those who were disenchanted with the infrequently re-edited *Dictionnaire de l'Académie* (the sixth edition would not appear until 1835), other options materialized to meet their needs. P.C.V. Boiste's all-purpose *Dictionnaire universelle de la langue française*, for example, would support fourteen editions between 1857 and its initial publication in 1800. As for frontline grammars dating from this time frame, Charles-Pierre Girault-Duvivier's *Grammaire des grammaires, ou Analyse raisonnée des meilleurs traités sur la langue Françoise* (1811) would be re-edited systematically until 1886. Girault-Duvivier's grammar warrants scrutiny for a number of reasons. First and foremost it was viewed by many as the ultimate authority in matters of language for seventy-five years. If Racine turned to Vaugelas for counsel, Flaubert relied on Girault-Duvivier. Jesse Levitt begins the introduction of his 1968 study devoted to the various editions of the grammar by quoting the widely recognized master of French prose. Flaubert wrote to the Goncourt brothers in 1862: "Je m'occupe présentement à enlever les *et* trop fréquents et quelques fautes de français. Je couche avec la *Grammaire des Grammaires* et le dictionnaire de l'Académie surcharge mon tapis vert."[7] The Academy's dictionary cited as companion reference suggests the tenor of Girault-Duvivier's work: reactionary, with regard to the liberties that had surfaced during the Revolution, indeed "restorative," as it pertains to the return to order (both political and linguistic) prioritized by Empire and Restoration alike. Furthermore, it would serve even rebellious Romantics well, especially Hugo whose lexical iconoclasm did not extend into the realm of grammaticality. "Hugo savait parfaitement sa grammaire," Charles Bruneau observes, "non pas seulement Lhomond, mais la *Grammaire des Grammaires*, de Girault-Duvivier. [. . .] Il est de tous les poètes du XIXe siècle, le plus grammatical" (Brunot 13.1: 31, 35).[8] As for French Romantics as a group, Gustave Lanson makes a similar observation regarding their respect for syntax:

> Ils déposèrent leurs sensations dans les mêmes phrases, qui avaient con-
> tenu les idées classiques: ils dressèrent exactement comme leurs devanciers
> l'appareil des conjonctions et des relatifs, des propositions subordonnées et
> coordonnées; ils composèrent selon les règles les groupes des sujets des
> verbes et des régimes. (Lanson 944)

---

[7] In Levitt 18. Levitt's work is the primary source of the background information concerning the preparation and early editions of the *Grammaire des grammaires*.

[8] References to the various volumes of Brunot's *Histoire de la langue française* bear the name of the general editor unless, as in this instance, it is a matter of quoting one of the several contributors. Charles Bruneau produced volume 13 titled *L'époque réaliste*. Part I, cited here, chronicles the period "fin de romantisme et Parnasse."

Girault-Duvivier destined his grammar for use in the Imperial schools and for home-schooled girls, who were not provided the same access to public education as were boys. Brunot characterizes succinctly and poignantly what that meant for language manuals and instruction following the fall of Robespierre:

> Il y eut, après Thermidor, un purisme de réaction, où se mélangent, en proportions variables, la haine des nouveautés grammaticales et celle des nouveautés politiques. [...] dans l'enseignement secondaire [de l'Empire], les enfants étaient formés à la grammaire des règles et à la grammaire traditionnelle comme à un dogme que nul n'avait le droit de contester et qui était présenté comme s'il eût été celui du passé, celui des grandes œuvres et des grandes époques. (10.2: 585, 684)

Political reaction, prescriptive/normative grammar, reintroduction of the old order à la Rivarol, *La Grammaire des grammaires* quickly gained prominence within this retrogressive environment. It soon garnered State sanction as well. The second edition was saluted by the Academy in 1814 and was selected to be awarded as a premium to prize-winning students. In 1817 the Institute once again praised the work, commended the improvements brought to the third edition, and ordered that it be granted a permanent place in its library.

Girault-Duvivier himself oversaw the publication of successive editions until his death in 1832. His modifications tell an interesting tale (despite the publisher's claim that each edition was definitive). Flattering references to Napoleon and the Empire disappeared from the text as one regime gave way to the next. As Du Bellay before him, Girault-Duvivier took care to court the favor of the powers that be. He dedicated the work to the king (Louis XVIII until 1824) and, on the title page, quoted the Academy's dictionary in epigraph: "Les difficultés grammaticales arrêtent quelquefois les plus grands esprits, et ne sont pas indignes de leur application."

In his preface (cited in the 1822 edition), Girault-Duvivier defined the binary character of the work; it was to serve both as "universal grammar" and as "grammaire particulière." As such it was to be the purveyor of "universal truth," on the one hand, and—consequently—on the other hand, an ideo-linguistic guide for its finite articulation in the French language. Finite, in this context, denotes the state of the French language as it is found in the works of "Bossuet, Fénelon, Pascal, Boileau, Racine, Voltaire, les deux Rousseau, Buffon, Delille, etc." (1: iv [1822]). Thus the French language had reached its pinnacle (epistemological and linguistic) in pre-Revolutionary, eighteenth-century France. The challenge was to restore and preserve it: "il ne faut plus que la fixer, au moins pour nous, au point auquel ces grands écrivains l'ont élevée" (1: iv–v [1822]).

Fixity is implicit in the motto of the work that forms the conclusion of the preface: "Il n'y a de Grammairiens par excellence que les grands écrivains" (1: vii [1822]).[9] If canonicity is conferred on the authors cited, it is also obvious that quotations drawn from their works as examples of correct usage also need to carry ideological messages beyond the scope of grammar. Girault-Duvivier made no attempt to hide the socio-philosophical emphases of his "grammatology":

> Bien convaincu que la religion et la morale sont les bases les plus essentielles de l'éducation; que les règles les plus abstraites sont mieux entendues lorsqu'elles sont développées par des exemples; et qu'à leur tour les exemples se gravent mieux dans la mémoire, lorsqu'ils présentent une pensée saillante, un trait d'esprit ou de sentiment, un axiome de morale ou une sentence de religion, je me suis attaché à choisir de préférence ceux qui offrent cet avantage. (1. vi [1822])

He could well have added politics to the rubrics of religion and morality. An abbreviated survey of such pronouncements found at random in the two volumes (1822) further clarifies his perspective and intent.

> Le peuple, pour ses rois toujours plein d'injustices,
> Hardi dans ses discours, aveugles en ses caprices.
> (Voltaire 1: 149)

> Qui se lasse d'un roi, peut se lasser d'un père
> (P. Corneille 1: 369)

> Le premier qui fut roi, fut un père adoré.
> (l'abbé Aubert 1: 369)

> La valeur, quels que soient ses droits et ses maximes,
> Fait plus d'usurpateurs que de rois légitimes.
> (Crébillon 1: 446)

---

[9] Sources, of course, included grammarians themselves, primarily "Vaugelas, Arnauld, Lancelot, d'Olivet, Dumarsais, Beauzée, Girard, plusieurs Grammairiens modernes, l'Académie Françoise" (1: vi [1822]).

Les prières ferventes apaisent Dieu, et lui
Arrachent la foudre des mains.
>   (L'Académie 1: 101)

L'univers m'embarrasse, et je ne puis songer
Que cette horloge existe, et n'ait point d'horloger.
>   (Voltaire 1: 566)

Entre le pauvre et vous, vous prendrez Dieu pour juge,
Vous souvenant, mon fils, que, caché sous ce lin,
Comme eux vous fûtes pauvre, et, comme eux, orphelin.
>   (Racine 2: 1047)

Homme, qui que tu sois, si l'orgueil te tente, souviens-toi que
Ton existence a été un jeu de la nature, que ta vie est un jeu de
La fortune, et que tu vas bientôt être le jouet de la mort.
>   (Marmontel 1: 226)

Le riche et l'indigent, l'imprudent et le sage
Sujets à même loi, subissent même sort.
>   (J.B. Rousseau 1: 264)

Ainsi qu'en sots auteurs,
Notre siècle est fertile en sots admirateurs.
>   (Boileau 1: 292)

La vie des flatteurs, c'est qu'ils applaudissent
Au mal de même qu'au bien.
>   (Vaugelas 2: 20 [Remarques détachées])

Such imbedded aphorisms are readily recognizable as belonging to the "bourgeois" code of values that became increasingly entrenched as the Restoration matured. Their appeal to an expanding middle class certainly enhanced marketability. It was not the sole device of the sort. The two volumes of the1822 edition devote1086 pages to the presentation and analysis of the French language. These are followed by an ample section of one hundred seventy-four pages that constitute a self-help handbook of the type that had become so popular. It bears a familiar title: "Remarques detachées sur un grand nombre de mots, et sur l'emploi vicieux de certaines locutions." The preface leaves little doubt about the segment of society targeted. The "locutions vicieuses" are characterized as a "contagion" and identified as belonging exclusively to "la classe du peuple" (1: viii [1822]). So the tomes could be marketed as a politically correct, all-purpose grammar suited to the needs of those who sought to distance themselves from the lower echelons of society.

By 1838 the ninth edition had swelled the self-help section to two hundred twenty pages and was advertised thus: "La neuvième édition, revue avec soin, enrichie de plus de 250 corrections, augmentée de deux cent soixante nouvelles remarques détachées." The dedication to the king had disappeared, but otherwise the work remained essentially the same. The preface had not been recast, despite Girault-Duvivier's death six years before. The binary aspect of metaphysical (universal) grammar and "grammaire particulière" persisted intact. The first volume numbered nearly a hundred pages more than the 1822 version, but retained original rubrics. Chapters V and VII of the second volume had been altered somewhat: chapter V (verbs, tense sequences, modes) had been expanded and restructured; chapter VII (adverbs) had an increased number of divisions. While philologists across the Rhine were busy puzzling out the evolution of Indo-European languages in the distant wake of Sir William Jones's discovery fifty years before, this grammar continued to rely on the dictates of Port-Royal. Indeed, scientifically determined historicity is disregarded in favor of received notions generations old, the origin of gender and its expansion to include grammatical gender, for example:

> Genre—Théorie de la sexualité du langage
>
> Les hommes ayant remarqué dans l'espèce humaine une différence sensible,
> qui est celle des deux sexes, ont jugé à propos d'admettre deux Genres dans
> les Noms Substantifs, le masculin et le féminin: le masculin appartient aux
> hommes et aux animaux mâles, et le féminin aux femmes et aux animaux
> femelles. (1: 94 [1838])

The gamut of genders in French, the author postulates without elaboration, was determined by process of "imitation." Too, as the precepts of Auguste Comte's "philosophie positive" were being debated and embraced by forward thinkers, reasoning continued to be defined as a syllogistic process:

> *Raisonner*, c'est se servir de deux jugements pour en former un troisième;
> comme lorsqu'après avoir jugé que toute vertu est *louable*, et que la
> patience est une *vertu*, je conclus que la *patience* est *louable*. (1: 91 [1838])

So much had changed by 1853. The Second Republic had come and gone; the advent of the Second Empire had sent Hugo fleeing into exile.

Steamships crossed vast seas almost effortlessly; locomotives puffed into Paris carrying goods and passengers from afar; and the *Grammaire des grammaires* went into its fifteenth edition. By that time its association with the Academy had been formalized to the point that on the title page it could claim to have been "entièrement revue et corrigée d'après le nouveau dictionnaire de l'Académie." Of course the so-called "new" version was already eighteen years old, (the sixth edition dates from 1835; the seventh edition would not appear until 1878). Since 1842 the grammar's publication had been overseen by Pierre-Auguste Lemaire. In his "Avant-Propos," written for the eleventh edition (1842) and republished in 1853, he noted that the Academy's decision to recognize Voltaire's "orthographic revolution" had been honored in the pages to follow. He cited the Academy as final authority, meekly asserting independence: "Nous savons bien que l'Académie elle-même n'est pas infaillible: une ou deux fois peut-être nous avons cru devoir nous séparer d'elle et combattre son opinion" (1: iii [1853]). That pronouncement, which might be best described as oxymoronic, is followed by another that at least suggests a change in attitude:

> Notre langue, en effet, comme toute langue parlée, ne peut rester stationnaire. Certes elle a son génie bien fixé, sa marche arrêtée, ses formes constantes. Mais dans tout idiome il se trouve une partie, pour ainsi dire, vivante, animée, progressive; il y a certaines locutions qui naissent et qui meurent tour à tour [...] Que d'idées et, par suite, que de mots ne crée pas chaque jour le progrès de l'industrie et de la science! Combien dans notre âge même la langue oratoire n'a-t-elle pas ressenti l'influence des révolutions! (1: iii–iv [1853])

These observations, as promising as they may seem, are followed directly, however, by Girault-Duvivier's preface in its original form; and the "Remarques détachées" section has been increased to two hundred forty pages.

3.2.1 Noël and Chapsal: a new grammar for a new market

The numerous editions of the *Grammaire des grammaires* over such an extended time frame (three quarters of a century) attest to the unrelenting commercial viability of its precepts. Both "grammaire générale" and "grammaire particulière," it promoted logical analysis and proper usage based on the atavistic formula articulated by Delesalle and Chevalier in their 1986 study:

"Ce qui est imposé comme idéal, c'est le discours de la classe dominante dont la littérature offre un modèle envahissant, valorisé par la référence au latin" (108). Unlike the Lhomond grammar, however, the use of Latin as universalizing agent is subsumed as a given. That modification suited the needs of the market share the producers of the *Grammaire des grammaires* had targeted: would-be writers and non-scholastics interested in improving their language skills for economic or social gain. It was far too bulky and cumbersome to be adopted or adapted as a textbook. The successor to the Lhomond grammar presented a very different format. Published in 1823, its descriptive title leaves little to the imagination: *Nouvelle grammaire française, sur un plan très-méthodique, avec de nombreux exercices d'orthographe, de syntaxe et de prononciation, tirés de nos meilleurs auteurs, et distribués dans l'ordre des règles.* The announced authors and their credentials combine authority of accomplishment, institutional recognition, and mainstream linguistic philosophy: "par M. Noël, chevalier de la Légion d'Honneur, Inspecteur-général de l'université et M. Chapsal, professeur de grammaire générale." Moreover, the grammar had received the *nihil obstat* of the Conseil royal de l'université, meaning that it had been approved for use as a textbook in an expanding marketplace that promised a lucrative return for author and publisher alike. Indeed, according to E. Weber, the number of schools in France would grow to 31,420 and would accommodate 1,200,000 students by 1833 and 60,000 schools and three million students by 1847 (307). By all accounts the *Nouvelle grammaire* cornered the market—to the tune of eighty editions as of 1889 (Chervel).

Smaller than the in-octavo format, it numbers a mere 197 pages of text and four of pre-text (approximately one-sixth the length of the Girault-Duvivier grammar.) A commercial emphasis stands out from the beginning. The preface is as much an advertisement as a foreword. The grammar is presented as unique in its field. Its authors have addressed a youthful audience in need of a more practical tool than those that have been heretofore available. As enticement, they claim to have avoided the "prolixité," the "sécheresse," and the "obscurité ou d'autres défauts" of their predecessors. As primary attributes they cite an unprecedented feature and an innovative, fail-safe methodology. The text is accompanied by a book of exercises ("cahier d'exercices") consisting of incorrect utterances (those baneful "phrases vicieuses") that can be set right by consulting the alphabetical (or analytical) table of contents. The methodology purports to generate clearer and more precise definitions, which are easier to retain, and to present the rules of grammar

> sous un nouveau jour; d'expliquer la raison des choses d'une manière proportionnée à la logique naturelle d'un âge où le jugement peut avoir déjà de la rectitude, mais n'a pas encore pris tout son développement; de ramener les principes de la grammaire française à ceux de la grammaire générale, et cela sans se perdre dans les subtilités de la métaphysique.

In their appeal the authors have adhered to the principles of mass marketing. They have been careful to include all segments of society in a position to buy or promote their product: the youthful users themselves, parents mindful of their youngsters' needs, the non-student neophyte in search of a guide, teachers whose practical requirements have received prioritized attention, and sanctioning institutions for which the philosophical underpinnings are a *sine qua non*. Hence, they can boast, the *Nouvelle grammaire* satisfies all the conditions of a "bon livre élémentaire," including its non-discriminatory affordability: "la modicité du prix [. . .] qui rend les ouvrages accessibles à toutes les fortunes." If the price itself is not indicated (a later development), the title page contains the usual self-promotional place of sale reference: "A Paris, chez Aumont Vve Nyon Jeune, Libraire, Quai Conti, No 13." Should that location not be convenient, another is listed, tellingly, on the facing page: "Cet ouvrage se trouve aussi chez M. Chapsal, rue de la Cerisaie, No 5, près de l'Arsenal."

Pedagogically, Noël and Chapsal would set a standard that would endure until the 1870s (the *cahier d'exercices* is still common today). The prescribed approach—which in reality owed much to both Quintilien and the Jesuit *praelectio* method—entailed the following: 1) reading the text, 2) declaiming the text, 3) clarification of the text by means of philosophical observations and examination of language difficulties, 4) identification of historical references, 5) extrapolation of principles of morality. Compositions could be assigned on topics such as literature, history, or ethics (Chevalier 137). As innovative as the grammar may have appeared, the ideology it promoted had changed little. So-called bourgeois mores once again dominate model phrases penned by the "bons auteurs" (authorship is not always identified): "Dieu est juste" (1); "Les cieux annoncent la gloire de Dieu" (7); "Servir Dieu est le premier de nos devoirs" (88); "Le roi et le berger sont égaux devant Dieu" (107); "Endormi sur le trône, au sein de la mollesse,/Le poids de sa couronne accablait sa faiblesse" ([Voltaire] 106); "Ils n'ont d'autre gloire que celle de leurs aïeux" ([Massillon] 7); "Que votre âme et vos mœurs, peintres dans vos ouvrages,/N'offrent jamais de vous que de nobles images" ([Boileau] 107); "Les passions, qui sont des maladies de l'âme, viennent de notre révolte contre la raison" (89); "Là gît la sombre Envie à l'œil timide et louche" ([*La Henriade*] 78); "La gloire de l'homme consiste dans la vertu" (87); "Le peu d'instruction qu'il a eu, le fait tomber dans mille erreurs" ([Marmontel] 158); "Rien ne nous appartient, tout est à la patrie" ([Gresset] 130). As for gender, entrenched stereotypes suffered no compromise:

> Les substantifs représentant des êtres inanimés ne devraient point avoir de genre; cependant, par analogie, on leur a donné le genre masculin et le genre féminin, selon qu'ils paraissent imiter la force, le courage des êtres mâles, ou la faiblesse, la douceur des femelles. C'est ainsi que le *soleil* a été fait du genre masculin, et la *lune* du genre féminin." (5)

3.2.2 The *Journal Grammatical*: Guardian of the "sacred flame"

If, in addition to educating youths in matters of language, the *Nouvelle grammaire* could be marketed as a means of fostering in them a "healthy" respect for religion, moral integrity, and civic responsibility, it was because of the belief that the dangers (political and linguistic) issue of the Revolution had not subsided. Four years later, in 1827, a monthly review was founded partly in response to a related threat: the activities of a group of the nation's youths who seemed bent on systematically altering both mother tongue and prosody. These young people, some of them very well born indeed, were of course the Romantics. The review, destined to be known by various titles through three series until 1840, was initially called *Journal Didactique de la Langue Française*. It was founded by "une société de grammairiens" directed by MM. Marle and Boniface, old-line disciplinarians committed to the principles of Condillac, Dumarsais, Domergue, and Beauzée, and to whom was entrusted "la garde du feu sacré." The need to preserve the "sacred flame" had become especially pressing, Marle aîné wrote in his introduction to the initial volume: "C'est bien après une révolution politique qui a prodigieusement accru le domaine de notre néologie et enfanté le dangereux Romantisme, qu'il devient nécessaire d'opposer de nouvelles barrières au Néologisme."

The program, announced formally in the first issue, divided its format into five discrete parts: solutions to language problems submitted by subscribers; a series of lessons constituting a complete course on French language; the didactics of the art of teaching; in-depth analysis of new grammars; and, finally, "une critique grammaticale principalement exercée contre les écarts du Romantisme [dont] nous ferons passer sans pitié les parties défectueuses au creuset de l'analyse grammaticale" (Marle aîné "Introduction"). As for pedagogical innovation, the very first lesson serves notice. It is titled "Notions métaphysiques" and separates cognition into the language of sensory perception, abstract and concrete ideas, gender, space, individual, judgment, precept, and reasoning, which the author identifies as "la science idéologique" (21).

By 1835, however, the situation had grown more complex. Saint-Gérand has written a poignant article on the sociolinguistic function of this review as it appeared in that year under the title *Journal Grammatical* and under the direction of C. Redler. As Saint-Gérand points out, the date is important for several reasons. The devastation of the worker revolt in Lyon in 1834 had left the nation unnerved; the July Monarchy had consolidated the transfer of power to a bourgeoisie ardently in search of further political and capital gain; the Romantics were gaining the upper hand in literature; and the sixth edition of the Academy's dictionary appeared that year (1835)—its preface calling for rigid conservatism in the face of nothing short of a language crisis. To the journal's editors and many of its subscribers the "sacred flame" and the nation thus appeared increasingly imperiled. Moreover, in an environment of unbridled commercial speculation and economic upturn, language publications of all descriptions had flooded onto the marketplace. (The review itself was widely distributed, not only throughout France, but to numerous foreign destinations as well: Brussels, London, Leipzig, Naples, Florence, Saint Petersburg.). Contributors, pen in hand, came to the rescue; they extolled or denounced grammarians, both present and past; they assailed even the moderate Lamartine and championed the (mediocre) Béranger. The zeal of certain writings chronicled in its pages would surely surprise today's unsuspecting reader, the theories of one P.-R. Auguis, for instance (a *député* no less), who postulated the historical primacy of Gaullois in the formation of the French language, degenerate Latin having only served to contaminate it (Saint-Gérand [1981]).

3.2.3 The Bescherelle brothers: patriotism for profit

It was in this context of political and social instability—fueled also by railway mania, technological advances, and the rising tide of capitalism— that the Bescherelle brothers published their *Grammaire nationale* (1834). The name Bescherelle remains familiar to students of the French language around the world today owing to the proliferation of the slim book of conjugations known, simply, as the *Bescherelle*. If this vestige of their work continues to experience commercial success, it is only one in a long list of titles to their credit, and hardly the most significant one. The mastermind of the pair was Louis-Nicolas (aîné). According to the anonymous "Notice biographique" published in the *Revue des contemporains* (1847), Louis-Nicolas (1802–1883) was born in Paris, studied at the collège Bourbon, and learned Italian under the tutelage of Giosaphat Biagioli before enrolling in law school. Having received his degree and having embarked on a career as notary, like so many others of his day he was drawn to books and to literature. Those interests led to his nomination for a position at the Bibliothèque du Louvre, which he accepted in 1828. The following year he was admitted to the Société grammaticale, closely aligned with the *Journal Didactique de la Langue Française/Journal Grammatical*. He quickly established himself in the field of education by founding the Société pour la Propagation de l'Instruction Primaire and by producing two texts on the teaching of grammar in 1829, both of which he published himself: *Le participe ramené à sa véritable origine* and *Revue grammaticale ou Réfutation des principales erreurs des grammairiens*. Ultimately, he would produce more than a score of related works, often in collaboration with his younger brother, Henri-Honoré (attaché au Conseil d'Etat). Their range reflects the breadth of the language market in the middle third of the nineteenth century: grammars and dictionaries—large and small—of varying descriptions and targeting various professions or socio-economic groups, an exercise book, a pedagogical journal, two polemical treatises (one denigrating the Noël/Chapsal grammar and another taking on the dictionary of the Academy of 1835), a teachers' almanac, a verb book, a book on the subjunctive and tense sequences, a complete French course in seven volumes—in addition to the two titles previously mentioned and numerous minor works or works of uncertain attribution.

In this extensive bibliography both the *Grammaire nationale* and the *Dictionnaire national* assume particular prominence. Although published a decade apart, they function as complements, the first supplying the holistic framework for the second. The *Grammaire* was destined to enjoy enormous popularity both in France and abroad. It underwent fifteen successive editions between 1834 and 1877. The dictionary, published in 1846, was touted as being truly universal—that is, compiled for use by all segments of French society: a lexicographic democratization to interface with the "national grammar" in such a way that their combined use would guarantee language mastery for all and would make for a healthier, wealthier, and better citizenry. If such a claim would enhance marketing prospects, the very titles of these "language tools" advertised their ideological agendas overtly. Indeed, the grammar's title page depicts language learning as a patriotic act and proper language usage as a civic duty. The model writers have scarcely changed over the years. Only the most moderate of the new generation of authors merit mention:

> *Grammaire Nationale ou Grammaire de Voltaire, de Racine, de Fénelon, de*
> *J.-J. Rousseau, de Buffon, de Bernardin de Saint-Pierre, de Chateaubriand, de*
> *Lamartine, et de tous les écrivains les plus distingués de la France; Renfermant*
> *plus de cent mille exemples qui servent à fonder LE CODE DE LA LANGUE*
> *FRANÇAISE. Ouvrage éminemment classique, publié sous les auspices de*
> *MM. Casimir Delavigne, De Jouy, Villemain, Tissot, Nodier, de Gérande, E.*
> *Johanneau, Boniface, Levi et Sabatie. (Grammaire nationale* [1835–36])[10]

So initially the work is billed as "le code de la langue française," that is, a book of laws tantamount to the Justinian code or the Napoleonic code, founded on "classical" principles (meaning pre-Revolution), and designed to restore or maintain order in matters relating to the nation's idiom (and therefore to the nation as a whole—a goal of the early reign of Louis-Philippe). The authors are listed as the Bescherelle brothers and Litais de Gaux (a professor of literature and member of the Société Grammaticale de Paris). Whatever may have been omitted in the title itself comes to the fore in the lengthy epigraph written by Tissot:

> Dans un état libre, c'est une obligation pour tous les citoyens de connaître
> leur propre langue, de savoir la parler et l'écrire correctement. La carrière

---

[10] Interestingly, later editions would add Bossuet to the list of authors and shift Casimir Delavigne to the front line while eliminating Lamartine altogether. Similarly, the term code is replaced by "les règles" (*Grammaire nationale* [4e édition 1847]). Lamartine had of course entered the political arena by that time.

des emplois est ouverte à tous; qui sait ce que la fortune réserve au plus humble des membres de la grande famille? La base de la connaissance de toute langue est la *Grammaire*...et en fait de grammaire, ce sont les écrivains qui font autorité. (*Grammaire nationale* [1835–36])

The preface further describes the grammar as a "manuel moral." Beyond the bombast and patriotic pretensions, then, the work presents itself as being very much in line with Girault-Duvivier's prescriptive *Grammaire des grammaires* and others like it: "les grands auteurs," edifying model phrases of political, religious, or ethical relevance, fixity as counter-agent to contaminating elements, and so on. The difference, as Saint-Gérand has indicated, stems from the transition from eighteenth-century rationalism to a nineteenth-century moralizing aestheticism in need of a "français de reference," a socio-semantic homogeneity capable of conveying linguistically a uniform (or standard) image of France as a nation (Saint-Gérand [2000]: 57–59). The means to that end lay in the schools. Thus the Bescherelles were careful to publicize their grammar as pedagogically sound and superior to other grammars. Its simple, methodical, active, hands-on approach would keep students alert and interested, they said; its lessons would be useful in everyday life; and its contents would train young minds in all the desired disciplines, especially citizenship. Their goal, it should be obvious, was to garner institutional approval, thereby gaining access to the vast textbook market.

The sources cited within the text reflect a certain updating. Napoleon, banished since the early editions of the *Grammaire des grammaires*, makes a reappearance, perhaps in response to calls for his remains to be enshrined in France. Hugo, Sainte-Beuve, Madame de Staël, Lamartine, and Chateaubriand find their way into occasional citations amidst the many "classical" references, including several gleaned from Girault-Duvivier or Boiste. Some quotations exhibit in tandem a certain ambiguity or irony that may have been selected as springboards to discussion: "Une de mes chances était d'avoir toujours dans mes liaisons des femmes AUTEURS" (Rousseau [37]), followed closely by "Les femmes poètes sont mauvaises ménagères. La rime s'accorde mal avec l'économie"(Boiste [38]), for example. Despite such improvements, the Bescherelle grammar fell short of a complete success. The anonymous author of the previously cited "Notice biographique" concluded his remarks by lamenting the work's misfortune with regard to officialdom. "C'est à l'aide de sa grammaire que les plus jeunes des fils du roi ont étudié le français," one reads, "et cependant, ces ouvrages ne sont pas approvés par l'Université! Jamais leur auteur n'a reçu aucune de ces récompenses dont on est si prodigue envers les personnes dont les titres sont souvent bien équivoques" (8).

The Bescherelles' hopes that the *Grammaire nationale* would replace the Noël and Chapsal *Nouvelle grammaire* as textbook in the public schools thus remained thwarted as late as 1847, that is to say even after the publication of the companion *Dictionnaire national*. They had therefore missed out on a financial return of considerable proportions. Their failure to gain institutional favor had not come about without a fight, however. As early as 1838 Louis-Nicole had gathered his forces and mounted a frontal attack in the form of a vituperative publication entitled: *Réfutation complète de la grammaire de MM. Noël et Chapsal, Appuyé sur plus de 3000 exemples tirés de nos grands écrivains; ou Grammaire des Ecoles primaires supérieures, des pensions, des colléges et des gens du monde; conçue sur un plan plus simple, plus méthodique, plus complet et plus propre à l'instruction que tous les ouvrages du même genre publiés jusqu'à ce jour.*

This publication reveals a good deal about the marketing psychology of the period. Both its sophistication and the acrimony of competition are surprising. Today the title itself is immediately recognizable as competitor specific. Its hype lays claim to product superiority based on the merits of exhaustive research, innovation, and universal consumer utility. Its authors are identified as "MM. Charles Martin, Bescherelle aîné, Edouard Braconnier et plusieurs membres de la Société grammaticale de Paris." Although the members of the Society remain unidentified, the reference has the effect of adding the authority and sanction of a rival institution, as does the publisher, which is cited as: "Librairie de la Société d'Emulation pour le perfection-nement de l'instruction primaire en France." Conveniently, from a commercial standpoint, the product cost and purchase options (1 fr. 75 c. et 2 fr. 25 c. par la poste) are prominently displayed next to the name and place of purchase: "Braconnier et Compagnie, rue Saint-Jacques, 38."

The preface documents the target product as primary or dominant, the number one on the market, so to speak—the Noël et Chapsal grammar being in its thirty-second edition—and the rival product as worthy successor. The ploy of false praise explains the competitor's success. The *Nouvelle grammaire française* was introduced amidst a widespread call for a non-traditional grammar. "Les temps étaient favorables à un pareil succès," one reads. "Depuis longtemps la foule était fatiguée des règles incomplètes de

Lhomond, des abstractions de Wailly, de l'obscurité et de la diffusion de Letellier. On fut séduit par la simplicité du plan de la grammaire Noël et Chapsal; on sut gré aux auteurs [. . .] de l'économie des détails, de l'élégance des règles, de la généralité des principes" (vi). But the work is irreparably flawed. Despite appearances, it is too abstract, too vague, and above all, not grounded in the principles established by France's finest writers. Of course, as Bescherelle et al. note, the work dates from the early-1820s when the public, especially the purchasing public, was not nearly so sophisticated. The continued success over the years, the Preface claims, is due to subterfuge and to institutionalized proprietorship. In fact, it is claimed, the original edition which was M. Chapsal's alone, is nowhere to be found. "La Bibliothèque Royale elle-même possède la seconde édition, mais elle ne peut pas présenter la première" (v). That is because it was pulled off the market in order to add Noël's name as co-author and to take advantage of his position as Inspecteur-général de l'Université, thereby garnering a hegemonic monopoly, which it has enjoyed since 1823.

Of course Louis-Nicole's brother's position as attaché au Conseil-d'Etat does not bear mentioning. Such innuendo and pot-and-kettlism render the commercial intent unmistakable. Too, the volume itself is used as publicity vehicle for two of the authors: Braconnier's *Théorie du genre des noms français* (3 fr. 50c.) and Charles Martin's *Rhétorique pratique* (1 fr. 75 for the teacher's edition and only 50 c. for the student version).

By the time the sixth edition of the *Réfutation* appeared, bearing the date 1853, the tome had changed significantly. The names Braconnier and Martin had disappeared from the title page. The authors are identified as MM. Bescherelle frères. The edition had been updated to compensate for fifteen years of continued institutional monopoly ("entièrement refondue et mise en rapport avec les changements faits par MM. Noël et Chapsal depuis la publication de la première édition de la Réfutation"). The title had also undergone an expansive evolution: *Réfutation de la grammaire de MM. Noël et Chapsal et de toutes les grammaires adoptées par l'université*. The Bescherelle brothers had thus taken on the entire French language establishment, and could do so using the name of their own publishing house (Chez Bescherelle jeune, Rue de Rivoli No 10), all for the price of 3 fr. 75 c.

The expanded version had become especially necessary, the authors say, both because of the continued national monopoly and because of the market proliferation of defective and incompetent grammars seeking to profit unscrupulously from increased literacy, evolved scholastic exigencies, and the needs of an ever-growing middle class. In support of their claims the Bescherelles cite an article published in the educational periodical *L'Instituteur*. Behind the scenes lurks a familiar Balzacian theme:

> Le charlatanisme est sans contredit la plaie la plus profonde et la plus honteuse de notre commerce et de notre industrie nationale. D'avides spéculateurs ont envahi toutes les professions, la librairie surtout, et n'ont pas craint, pour faire des dupes, de débiter des ouvrages informes, rédigés sans art et sans talent, mais parés de titres pompeux et de riches promesses. [...] Ils ont fait fructifier le mensonge et la déception. Tous les moyens leur sont bons pourvu qu'ils parviennent à tirer de l'argent. (*Réfutation* [1853]:165)

As noble as the Bescherelles intended their position to appear, however, the identity of very first *grammairien* taken to task sends another message. It is a matter of the former co-author of the *Réfutation*, Monsieur Charles Martin, who has enjoyed enviable success in the provinces since the parting of the ways. "Voilà un ouvrage entièrement ignoré à Paris," the Bescherelles write of their erstwhile cohort,

> mais qui jouit dans la province d'une immense popularité, du moins s'il faut en croire M. Charles Martin et ses pompeux prospectus, avis, catalogues, réclames, *pallas*, rapports, etc., etc.; car M. Martin n'a rien épargné pour arriver à cette prétendue popularité dans nos campagnes (*Réfutation* [1853]:167)

But there were even bigger fish to fry: Monsieur Guizot, for example (who, subsequent to reshaping the law on public education, arranged to have his five manuals officially adopted for use in French primary schools) and, most prominently, the Academy itself in a scathing section titled: "galerie critique de la plupart des barbarismes, solécismes, fautes d'orthographe, définitions fausses, décisions ridicules, remarques absurdes, [...] etc., etc. dont formule la sixième et dernière édition du dictionnaire de l'Académie" (*Réfutation* [1853]: 261, 264).

If competition in the world of French language textbooks had become so ruthless, it was because of their enormous profitability. Whereas a general accounting would be difficult to reconstitute, financial figures for the *Dictionnaire national* are available for the period 22 June 1843 to 30 April

1846, owing to a liquidation action brought in the Court of Appeals (4e chambre) in 1849. The document is titled "Tableau des dépenses et recettes du DICTIONNAIRE NATIONAL." It concerns the partnership of "MM. Simon, Mayer et Bescherelle" that was dissolved on December 31, 1845 and the adjudication of the dictionary which took place on April 30, 1846. The partners, a subsequent document reveals ("MM. Simon, et Garnier frères contre M. Mayer"), began to squabble almost from the beginning. The "dissolution" did not put an end to the dictionary; it was published subsequently without interruption by Garnier frères. The documents list the vital statistics for the period (1843–1846), including nearly 13,000 francs expended for a vigorous publicity campaign in various newspapers:

Number of tomes ("livraisons") sold to subscribers or bookshops:
  2,267,000 or 1,133,500 two-volume sets

Total sales (including returns, etc):	306,697 fr.
Total expenses:	234,415 fr.
Profit	72,281 fr.

Over a million sold, without benefit of institutional approval. One can only wonder what the totals would have been, had the Bescherelles been able to acquire the necessary certification for their national grammar to be used in schools in tandem with their national dictionary. Their railing and their ire are certainly more understandable in that light. The French language had become big business, indeed, "un bon objet marchand," as Saint-Gérand puts it in an understatement (Saint-Gérand [1981]: 342). The language market had adapted both commercially and ideologically to the times; it had adopted as its own the program of promoting the French nation as an all-embracing hegemonic entity devoted to the betterment of all its citizens; it had recast itself as the primary means to the "universal" inclusion of all its constituents. Universality had thus evolved from the elitist, geopolitical construct of French as the vehicular language of the Republic of Letters to that of universal fixing agent in the drive toward political, social, and economic cohesion. Increasingly, the marketing platform excluded antiquated meta-physical underpinnings in favor of a self-sufficient domestic generalization whose parameters encompassed every stratum of French society and whose commercial potential grew with the expansion of the education system. By the end of the fourth decade, the mission of the French language had been largely determined for the remainder of the nineteenth century. Its function as homogenizing/fixing agent was destined to be reconfirmed time and time again despite the many challenges to come: the Revolution of 1848 and the burst of linguistic enthusiasm that would "enfranchise" the lower classes to the point of fostering a network of male and female worker poets; the censorship and volatility of the Second Empire; the tribulations of the Third Republic following the fiasco of the Franco-Prussian war, the Commune, and the ominous shadow cast by the emergence of Germany as a militarily, politically—and intellectually—superior power; the technological advances that accrued exponentially as the century approached its end.

4

Overcoming Impairments:
Braille, LSF, ASL

LANGUAGE ISSUES THAT EMERGED during the French Revolution stem from basic ideological conflicts that persist to the present day. On the one hand, as the previous chapter has stressed, the perceived relationship of "mother tongue" and patrimony expanded to allow for inclusion of all of France's inhabitants, that is to say the entirety of the new social order. This egalitarian emphasis had its underside, however, for on the other hand the hegemonic needs of the newly conferred status of nation produced programs designed to relegate popular speech to the catacombs and to eradicate free speech in the form of "minor" languages, dialects, and patois. The nefarious paradox of egalitarianism as abrogation of basic rights—associated most prominently with the Terror—looms as an unfortunate legacy of the Revolution. Detractors were and are quick to point out the reprehensibility. Yet such views often neglect the fact that the Revolution also "nationalized" humanitarian institutions that would impact the language community far beyond the scope of the French national idiom. Indeed, in the long term and despite the many obstacles, the founding of separate national schools for the blind and the deaf would grant official standing to two classes of individuals that, until the end of the eighteenth century, had been marginalized socially and disparaged by many as inferiors unworthy of anything other than pity. These institutions would ultimately transform perceptions around the world. Within their midst and owing to the persistence of the devoted individuals who nurtured them (sometimes against great odds), Braille was born and would be successfully promoted as universal scripting vehicle for the visually impaired; likewise, with the return to order, the hearing impaired found new hope in the state-provided premises and an innovative state-financed language program conceived to sustain and enhance a model that was already being imitated widely abroad.

4.1 Louis Braille: an accident become marvel

Behind the eponymous term "Braille" lies a tragic quirk of fate turned marvel.[1] Louis Braille was born into a working-class family in 1809. His father, a prosperous harness and saddle maker in the Seine-et-Marne village of Coupvray east of Paris, operated a shop occupying a portion of the ground floor of the family residence. There, in the work area outfitted for tooling, Louis, nearing his fourth birthday, suffered a terrible accident. Endeavoring to imitate his father's skillful use of cutting instruments to pare and fashion bulk leather into finely crafted saddlery pieces, the child punctured one of his eyes with an awl. Treatment failed to save the eye and, in the process, the second eye became infected. Soon that eye failed as well; blindness would be his lot for the rest of his days.

Louis received instruction at the local school until the age of ten when his father, who had fallen fatally ill, enrolled him in the national school for the blind in Paris founded by Valentin Haüy. The school suited the boy well. Beyond the usual academic subjects (in which he excelled), the music program drew his particular attention. Dr. Sébastien Guillié, director at the time, had gained notoriety for the performances of his student chorus, the *Jeunes Aveugles*. Even Paganini extolled their merit (Ross 124). This emphasis permeated the curriculum. Louis responded by taking up the violoncello and the organ. Before long he had become the envy of his class. Recognized for his extraordinary "touch," though still a teenager he was engaged as organist at Saint Nicolas-des-Champs church and then at the well-known Saint Vincent-de-Paul.

Braille's academic success, talent, and popularity caused administrators to ask him to join the teaching staff at the school—which consisted of both

---

[1] The biographical and historical information pertaining to Braille and the founding and development of the French national institution for the blind, presented in this chapter, draws particularly on the following sources: C. Michael Mellor's *Louis Braille: A Touch of Genius*, Ishbel Ross's *Journey into Light*, Euclid J. Herie's "La maison natale de Louis Braille," Pamela Lorimer's "Origins of Braille," and Paula Kimbrough's "How Braille Began." Mellor's superb biography contains several letters written by Braille over the years and presents a detailed account of technical aspects of the writing system.

sighted and non-sighted personnel. Both Haüy and Guillié were sighted; their literacy program utilized a reading system (developed by Haüy) composed of embossed, raised-surface letters that had been used to the acclaim of educators for years. As useful as the system had been, Braille, as a blind student, quickly discerned its inefficiency. It compelled the reader to sense tactilely the complete contours of individual letters formed by a combination of straight edges and/or arcs. Whereas such could be accomplished, as the many successes had revealed, Braille realized that his fingers were much more adept at recognizing clusters of embossed points. For some time he had been puzzling over the matter when he discovered Charles Barbier's *écriture nocturne*. Barbier, an engineer and cavalry officer assigned to the Signal Corps, had devised a method of nighttime communication for the battlefield that avoided the need for perilous illumination. The method depended on a phonetic ciphering code consisting of a series of frames each of which contained twelve embossed points. The system had drawn both scientific and public interest (as would Jean-François Sudre's *téléphonie* in later years [see Chapter Five]). If Barbier's invention had a dim military future, its fortunes at the school for the blind would prove otherwise. Barbier approached Guillié in 1820. The director recognized its potential and approved its use on a trial basis. The initial results were deemed unsatisfactory. In spite of Barbier's modifications, the system was cumbersome for students: its phonetic code complicated the process and did nothing to reinforce conventional spelling and punctuation; moreover, the twelve point clusters were too broad for the fingertip.

Braille used the system with his pupils during the trial period. His own enthusiasm dampened, but the concept continued to fascinate him. Little by little the means of converting the method to a viable means of communication for the blind took form. It involved, primarily, a process of simplification. First, he reduced the twelve-point frame to a six-point oblong three points high and two points wide, thereby making it accessible to the fingertip. Second, he converted the phonetic code to a series of symbols consisting of one or more points and corresponding to the letters of the French alphabet. Third, he devised similar symbols for punctuation and contractions. Other material modifications followed: recessed points in the place of grooves to delineate frames and an improved stylus for writing, for instance. Barbier acquiesced to his request to use the altered system in his instruction. Braille's own reading and writing skills and those of his students improved dramatically. Indeed, they found they could read and "punch write" with virtually the same speed and proficiency as the sighted. Ultimately, in a labor of love, Braille expanded the system to include musical notation.

The genius of this invention lay in its absolute universality. It could be adapted to any language and applied to music, mathematics, or any other code. Yet, as so often is the case, acceptance was long in coming. The same institutional recalcitrance that continued to characterize the French Academy impeded its implementation. Sighted teachers remained skeptical. For a significant period Braille was allowed to teach the system only as an extracurricular activity after hours. Furthermore, the same commercial interests that had invaded the language textbook market blocked dissemination. As a national institution, the school (and others like it) relied on government funding. Private firms held government contracts to supply embossed books of the old order. Retooling would be costly. Politics and business, once again, imposed their will. It took some thirty years (1854, two year's after the originator's death from tuberculosis) for the Braille system to be fully accepted as the official print medium for the blind in France. As for dissemination beyond its borders, there would be other obstacles to overcome.

Whereas there are surely other gains to realize, those obstacles no longer exist at present. France would ultimately honor Louis Braille by placing his remains in the Pantheon in June of 1952 (where those of abbé Grégoire would also be interred in 1989). International recognition of another sort sprang forth on Wednesday, January 4, 2006: Google's main search page featured the company logo in Braille accompanied by the message "Happy Birthday Louis Braille." The commemoration, as altruistic as it may have been intended, was far from gratuitous. Technology has created talking computers and Braille printers that enable the blind to communicate in ways unthinkable until recently. Indeed, Google was addressing and recognizing a segment of its users, its non-sighted clientele. Today Braille and Braille-related products compose a considerable market worldwide. Enabling Technologies of Jensen Beach Florida, for example, bills itself as "the world's leading merchandisers of Braille embossers." The company's claims include development of the Plate Embossing Device (PED) that "changed Braille production forever" and has been responsible for the production of millions of pages of Braille text, many of them available in libraries everywhere. Capacities and designs have improved to the point that, in terms of print communication and the internet, the blind have unimpeded if not complete (visual) access.

4.1.1 France before Braille: Valentin Haüy

This fortunate state of affairs is the culmination of endeavors that date back centuries and involve France from the very beginning. The Florida company's link "How Braille Began" (http://www.brailler.com/braillehx.htm) identifies one of the first institutions for the blind as French; Louis IX, known as Saint Louis, established in Paris the Hôpital des Quinze-Vingts following the dreadful Sixth Crusade. Ishbel Ross (*Journey into Light*) provides details. Opened in 1254, it grounded a tradition for state, Church, and private assistance for the blind that has benefited thousands over the years. In fact the hospital has survived into our day as a treatment center for eye patients and a training center for ophthalmologists. In its original form it quickly garnered the attention and support of the aristocracy and the Church. It welcomed the blind from all walks of life—rich and poor alike. The institution offered the means of learning available at the time: blind scholars were welcomed and intellectual discourse encouraged, handicrafts were taught, and music was provided both for pleasure and therapy. As time wore on and financial support waned, administrators turned increasingly to charitable fundraising and residents were compelled to seek alms in the streets of the capital. A group of them were engaged in that activity when Valentin Haüy happened by St. Ovid's Café in 1771. The Café had become known, in effect, as Café des Aveugles, for the blind often came there to entertain the public by putting on shows of questionable taste. In this instance it was a group of would-be musicians performing a self-deprecating caricature. The hooting of the crowd and the distasteful pantomime repulsed Haüy to the point, it is said, that he was moved to undertake a mission of mercy for which he would become known throughout Europe (Ross 97–98, Lorimer 21).

Originally from Picardy, it was his brother René, a student in botany and mineralogy at the Jardin Royal, who had led him to Paris. While René was busy making a reputation for himself as the originator of crystallography, Valentin eked out a living by giving lessons in modern languages and by serving as translator for government agencies. Buoyed in his intent by a meeting with the internationally acclaimed blind musician Maria von Paradis who arrived in Paris on tour in 1784, he went into action. He began by undertaking to educate an illiterate seventeen-year-old blind youth, François Lesueur. Haüy had been reading the available literature on the blind, especially Diderot's

Lettre sur les aveugles. He was convinced that he could customize the learning processes to accommodate the specific needs of the blind, as abbé de L'Epée was doing for the deaf in his Rue des Moulins home. His initial experiment succeeded in part owing to the latest technology: a literacy program utilizing a set of letters carved onto thin wooden blocks originated by the Italian Rampazetto only a few years before. As Lesueur's education progressed, Haüy realized how awkward the blocks were to carve and to handle. It occurred to him to develop an improved medium. The results, produced in concert with Lesueur, took the form of the embossed lettering on heavy paper that Braille would encounter years later. Haüy designed a rudimentary hand press that, by means of typographical characters created specifically for the task, embossed letters from the underside and in reverse order. If the system was as yet to be perfected, an important step had been taken in the education of the blind—and with it the beginnings of the earliest library for the blind.

The young Lesueur responded favorably. Within six months he had mastered the process of reading and writing with the characters in relief. René's contacts in the scientific community proved useful at this point. An exhibition before members of the Royal Academy of Sciences generated enthusiasm and caught the attention of the recently formed Société Philanthropique—which had accepted the charge of several blind children. Arrangements were made to provide accommodation in a small dwelling on Rue Coquillière near the present-day Bourse and only a short distance from the site of abbé de L'Epée's residence. The "first school for blind children in recorded history" thus emerged under the aegis of the Ancien Régime in 1784 (Ross 101–02). A report summarizing the first year's operations received glowing reviews from members of the Academy. Like the good abbé across the way, Haüy organized public demonstrations in order to publicize his accomplishments and to garner wider support. His efforts resulted in the acquisition of expanded premises at 18 Rue Notre Dame des Victoires, closer still to Rue des Moulins. There, in their new quarters, the children fared even better; soon they were assisting Haüy in the printing and binding of embossed texts.

The road ahead lay strewn with peril. The political upheaval placed the school in particular jeopardy. The Société Philanthropique, the charitable organization upon which Haüy depended integrally for funding, had attracted a number of prominent aristocrats and was viewed by revolutionaries as subversive. In 1786 Haüy had dedicated to Louis XVI the published account of his methods and successes, *Essai sur l'éducation des aveugles.* That same year the children were invited to spend a week at Versailles for the Christmas festivities. Demonstrations were arranged for the Court. Moved by the children's proficiency, the king appointed Haüy Court interpreter and arranged for him to become professor of ancient inscriptions. Frequent performances of the blind children's chorus and musical ensemble in the intervening years kept the school in the news. As appropriate as they seemed at the time, these events aroused suspicion within the context of the gathering revolt.

As the Revolution unfolded, Haüy needed to look elsewhere for support. He went directly to the Constituent Assembly. It was decided that both a school for the blind and a school for the deaf should be officially recognized and supported. They would be forced to share quarters in the Convent of the Celestines, however, a less than ideal arrangement since the needs of the two groups varied so considerably. Money was scarce in the early going. Haüy rallied his minions in an effort to gain the Revolutionary regime's acceptance and increased support. Soon the chorus and ensemble were performing at various Revolutionary festivals instead of in local churches and at Court. In 1794 the Convention divided the two institutions, designating the Maison Sainte Catherine on Rue des Lombards (near the present-day Pompidou Center) as the new residence for the blind children. The following year (1795) the school was officially recognized as the "national institution for blind workers," a designation that reflected the ultra pragmatic attitude the Revolution had adopted with regard to such organizations. Nevertheless, now blind children from all of France could be housed and educated under its roof.

The entire spectrum of France's institutions suffered from the twists and jolts of politics in Paris. Support from both government and private sources experienced interruptions and reversals as power passed from one hand to another. The school for the blind fell to a low ebb under Napoleon. First, it was relegated once again to the Quinze-Vingts site, then Haüy was dismissed by the emperor for his association with political factions now in disfavor. Because his work had gained an international reputation, Haüy was able to take his expertise abroad. Russia, Great Britain, and Germany sought his assistance in establishing institutions for the blind. He traveled initially to Berlin in 1806 where his methods and literacy program had won particular favor. His reception and success there led him to believe he could duplicate the feat in Russia. Unfortunately, protracted negotiations with the czar produced only limited results. Finally, after several years of lobbying, he was able to open an institution whose mission—sadly—had been reduced to the sole function of caretaker.

4.1.2 The Braille system in France

The Restoration returned the Paris institution to favor. Louis XVIII provided both funding and new premises in the Saint Firmin Seminary. Dr. Guillié, an ophthalmologist who had founded the first eye clinic in Paris, was selected to head the school, now known as the Institut Royal des Jeunes Aveugles. Guillié was a harsh taskmaster, but his love of music proved to be ample compensation. Louis Braille, of course, would excel in that portion of the curriculum. Guillié was replaced by André Pignier in 1821. Pignier brought new resolve and commitment to the position. He succeeded in obtaining funds for both expansion and renovation and fashioned a publicity campaign that brought in additional monies. It was Pignier who appointed Braille to his teaching position.

Braille's efforts to publicize his writing system outside the Paris institution met with little success. By 1829 he felt he had perfected the method to the point that he could publish the results. His book on writing words, music, and songs for the blind attracted little attention. In 1837 his students produced the first Braille textbook, a three-volume history of France, a signal accomplishment that suffered a similar fate. In fact competition was to emerge from within the institution itself. Armand Dufau, assistant director and an opponent of the Braille system, published in 1837 a book awarded the year's prize by the French Academy: *Les aveugles. Considérations sur leur état physique, moral et intellectuel.* The Braille system had no place in his vision of how the blind should be instructed. Indeed, when he became director and sought to replace Haüy's method, he turned instead to a similar British embossed-type system developed by John Alston for use in Glasgow's Asylum for the Blind. So adamant was the sighted Dufau that he removed the library of books produced by Haüy and Braille. Students revolted and kept the Braille system alive underground in defiance of threats of punishment or expulsion. By 1843, at wit's end owing to insubordination and the lack of results, Dufau gave in. Braille had finally become the school's medium, although political concerns would keep the measure under hat for the time being (Lorimer 35). Another decade would pass before it would receive French government certification. Competing systems would continue to vie for prominence elsewhere for years to come.

4.1.3 Braille: a long road to acceptance

As in Paris the rifts of sighted and non-sighted teachers reverberate throughout the institutional history of literacy programs for the blind in other countries. John T. Sibley, Superintendent of the Missouri School for the Blind in the 1880s and 1890s and a leader of the Braille movement in the United States, praised the French for finally heeding the voice and needs of the non-sighted and encouraged others to follow their lead (Tobe 41). Resistance stemming from bureaucratic perceptions of efficacy and those who believed in the replication of print alphabets (so difficult for the blind to produce in relief) hindered acceptance almost everywhere. It is true that Switzerland soon adopted the Braille system (Kimbrough), but Switzerland almost always proves the exception. Samuel Gridley Howe's success with the legendary blind deaf-mute Laura Bridgman earlier in the century spurred and prolonged print alphabet usage in the U.S. for decades. Aware of Thomas Hopkins Gallaudet's recruitment of Laurent Clerc (the deaf instructor from Paris) in the founding of the American Asylum for the Deaf, Howe visited the Paris institution for the blind and in 1832 brought back to Boston Emile Trenchéri who was schooled in relief writing. In 1842 when Charles Dickens came to the Perkins Institution (founded by Howe), he was amazed by what he found—especially Bridgman's diary, "written in a legible, square hand" (Ross 165). His glowing portrait of the girl's accomplishments in his *American Notes* did much to further embed in Britain the "triangular" print alphabet that had been developed by Edinburgh's James Gall and modified, respectively, by Howe, Edmund Frye, and John Alston (Tobe 42–43). It would take nearly a century of fending off challenges from these and other newly devised forms of relief writing before Braille would be officially adopted by the U.S. and Great Britain in 1932. Modification, standardization, and improvements have ensued in the intervening years, all in the interest of efficacy and universality.

In Austria Johann Wilhelm Klein began his instruction of the blind in 1804 with a single student, as had Haüy. His initial methods, developed independently, resemble those of his French counterpart; he fashioned a raised letter system featuring frames and emphasized music, both instrumental and voice. As his interest swelled and the number of students increased, he investigated Haüy's system, experimented with embossed type, and produced printed texts. He informed himself on the status of blind education elsewhere and modified his procedures and system according to local needs. His success was tempered by lack of government support, but through his own fundraising efforts he was able to maintain both a school and a museum in Vienna. When the Braille system came to his attention, he rejected it for virtually the same reasons as others had. Nevertheless, Klein had made his mark. By the 1880s half a dozen schools for the blind had opened in Austria.

Braille would eventually make its way into the German language community, nevertheless. Haüy's charge of establishing a school for the blind in Berlin included staffing. He chose August Zeune who, after a hiatus of several years, decided to travel broadly in order to view first hand practices being followed in institutions in France, Switzerland, England, and Holland. His findings resulted in a work-related emphasis designed to make the blind as financially independent as their condition would allow. By the mid-1880s Germany could count some thirty institutions for the blind. The hands-on method led to the production of rope, knitted and woven goods, pieces of furniture, shoes, small appliances, and so on. The goal was to integrate graduates of the schools into society at large. Government took an active part in placement, marketing, and finance. As elsewhere, Braille made serious headway following World War I. By the 1930s libraries in Hamburg and Leipzig could boast 65,000 Braille texts (Ross 178). From Scandinavia to Italy and Spain, similar successes followed throughout Europe and the Soviet Union. Gradually, the system gained footholds in India, Africa, and beyond.

Work continues on "unifying the Braille codes," both nationally and internationally (Bogart 161–81). Given its status in today's world marketplace, the English language has received the greatest attention to date. Diversity survives as an impediment. Several technical codes have developed regionally over the years. A unification project jointly sponsored by the various governing organizations was undertaken in the early-1990s. The difficulties differ little from those Braille had encountered from the outset. Competing codes lack compatibility—the Computer Braille Code, the Nemeth Code for Mathematics and Science Notation, and the general literary code, for example:

> The BANA [Braille Authority of North America] codes for mathematics and computer notation, used mainly in North America and New Zealand, were both matched by codes, utterly different in design, used in the United Kingdom and among many other English-speaking populations in Africa, Australia, and elsewhere (sometimes with notable local variations). Not surprisingly, these two main systems for technical notation differed not

only from each other but also from the codes that had been adopted by
speakers of other languages for the same purposes—even though print
notation for mathematics and computer material is essentially the same
across language boundaries. (Bogart, Cranmer, Sullivan 165–66)

Headway has been made, but like "natural languages" the codes will
doubtlessly undergo constant evolution. What is clear is that the dominating
force in Braille today is English-language bound. The same factors that affect
language utilization on a global basis apply to the scripting medium of the
non-sighted. In this sense, the French origins of the Braille system, while
appreciated and even celebrated historically, have given way to external
imperatives. Yet if the French idiom is no longer the universal language of
Europe, Braille is the universal vehicle of communication of the blind, everywhere. Its continued codification in light of technical advances in so many
fields speaks both to its resilience and to the "vision" of its creator.

4.1.4 Blindness as impairment: Diderot as torchbearer

Higher mathematics, computer codes, access to the worldwide web,
the possibilities now seem almost endless. Non-sighted students have become
virtually commonplace in universities in many countries. Future technical
advances promise to integrate the blind to an even greater extent and to
contribute more meaningfully than ever to the realization of individual
potential and self-fulfillment. In slightly more than two centuries, then,
science and philanthropy have overcome great odds. Such progress was made
possible by an abrupt change in thinking, a byproduct—so to speak—of the
Enlightenment. Initially, empiricism concerned itself with the plight of the
blind only to the extent that the "missing sense" affected human understanding. Locke limited his interest to the relationship of tactile and ocular
perception, concluding that the congenitally blind skilled in discerning
geometric shapes tactilely could not make the transfer to ocular perceptions
should they suddenly gain their sight. In other words, a lack of ocular
experience would prevent them from recognizing the very cubes and globes
that had become familiar to their touch (Locke 2: 9 § 8). Voltaire supported
Locke in his findings ("Eléments de la philosophie de Newton," 1738).
Condillac's countering of Locke's notion of "innate ideas" by separating the
elements of cognition into stimulus, perception, and judgment tended to

steer such questions away from the pragmatics that would ultimately impact the blind favorably.

Such was the lay of the land when Diderot published his *Lettre sur les aveugles* in 1749. In search of another direction, the architect of the encyclopedia project turned to other sources, especially to the works of the iconoclastic physician Julien Offroy de la Mettrie whose theories derived from Descartes's "homme-machine" concept and emphasized the mechanics of physiology. He focused on the congenitally blind in order to comprehend how the other senses function in the absence of sight and how that absence would affect mnemonics. If such individuals learn to speak with somewhat greater difficulty than others, Diderot observed, it is only because the variety of sensations at their disposal is reduced, not because of any cognitive short-fall. History had made its case, from Homer to Milton. Indeed, Diderot's considerations posited the existence of a congenitally blind "philosophe" whose lack of sight enhanced his capacity for abstract thought and whose increased command of the other senses and meticulous interpretation of sensations might well make him less prone to error in matters of "pure speculation" (Diderot 97–98). In other words, if the semiotics are altered, the cognitive function itself remains intact and may even be improved.

In an Enlightenment society that extolled the written word, language—literacy, the means of communicating intelligence—posed the greatest challenge to increasing the potentialities of the blind. Diderot proposed a digital language ("fixed" and complete with a "grammar and dictionaries") based on the invention of the recently deceased blind mathematician Nicholas Saunderson (Diderot 100). The gifted Englishman had created the palpable ciphering board that allowed him to "calculate" at great speed and had gained him an international reputation as a scholar and lecturer. Diderot reproduced images of the Cambridge professor's invention, praised the concept, and called for a concerted effort to assist the blind of all walks of life.

Diderot's ideas were widely disseminated. When Haüy sought to open his school, the intellectual community had already accepted the premise that blindness did not represent a cognitive prohibition. The blind could function, learn, teach, and make meaningful contributions to society. All they needed in order to do so was a structured, assisted environment and an opportunity. After all, even in the absence of literacy, blindness does not affect speech physiologically; in that sense oral communication is not impeded to any greater extent than for the sighted illiterate. Intelligence and literacy thus remained separate issues in perceptions and determinations pertaining to the blind. The hearing impaired were not so fortunate in that respect. Centuries of misunderstanding lay in their path. Biases would prove deep-seated and resistant. As for France, where cognition and language were conjoined philosophically at an early date and measured in terms of "l'art de bien parler," one might anticipate inveterate aversion. There would be obstacles aplenty, to be sure, but owing to the resolve of a small group of individuals and basic—if limited—government support, France would serve as torchbearer long enough for the torch to be passed.[2]

4.2 Deafness as impairment: centuries of bias

From the very beginning, cultures as diverse as the Babylonians, the Greeks, and those of Judeo-Christian tradition marginalized the congenitally deaf, depicted them as aberrations, equated their inability to communicate orally as a sign either of imbecility or alienating deficiency. The earliest recorded references to the deaf describe a prohibitively debilitating condition, a pathological perspective destined to endure for centuries. In Babylonian society the rights of the congenitally deaf were restricted by law; Talmudic precepts would do as much by the second century BCE; and Saint Augustine would declare the deaf incapable of faith because they cannot "hear" the word of God (Groce 99, Roots 27). Plato's use of the word *logos* combined inextricably speech and reason. Aristotle, in his *History of Animals* (4: 9), held that speech and hearing are the cognitive channels through which

---

[2] Whereas biases and resistance posed major problems for both the blind and the deaf in France, it is also essential to add that at no time during its history did the French adopt the radical eugenic policies that led to sterilization laws in the United States, Sweden, parts of Switzerland, and Nazi Germany. Humanitarian and religious concerns limited such measures to hygienics, despite the strong influence exerted by neo-Lamarckists of the late-nineteenth and early-twentieth centuries. (See, especially, Schneider and Weiss). If B. A. Morel in his classic *Traité des dégénérescences physiques, intellectuelles et morales de l'espèce humaine* (1857) classified congenital blindness and deafness ("surdi-mutité") alongside other pathologically degenerative conditions capable of producing imbecility (alcoholism, disorders of the nervous system, toxicosis), he recognized that such degeneration results from extreme neglect ("abandon extême") rather than from pathology. Moreover, aware that his opinion was not universally shared, he challenged the medical profession to devote greater resources to the study of the problem and to find the means to nurture the "regeneration" to which those afflicted had the "uncontestable right" ("droits incontestables" [Morel 59–60]).

thought flows to knowledge and (in *Politics*) that by law no deformed child incapable of being schooled in literacy should be allowed to survive (Lang 10). The Justinian code distinguished between the deafened and the (congenitally) deaf, limiting the rights of the latter owing to their lack of speech (Roots 28). Hence there arose the characterizations "deaf-mute" and "deaf and dumb" and the pervasive prejudices that would accompany them into the modern era.

At the same time there is early evidence of the sporadic development of sign systems to compensate for lack of speech. In Plato's *Cratylus* Socrates speculates about the effectiveness of such a system; in his *Natural History*, Pliny the Elder reports on the education of a deaf child; in his translation of the *Vulgate*, Saint Jerome poses the hypothesis of attaining salvation through a signed language; and Augustine (his contemporary), in somewhat of a turn-about, addresses the same possibility as an alternative means of receiving the "Good News" (*De Quantitate* and *De Magistro* [Lang 10, Winzer 13]). Attention increased and views began to diversify during the Early Modern period. Both Rudolphus Agricola in Holland (late-fifteenth century) and Girolamo Cardano in Italy some forty years later defended the proposition that the deaf could learn and communicate by means of signs and/or a written language (Lang 10). In Italy Leonardo da Vinci mentored the son of a deaf artist (Christoforo de Predis) who communicated by means of signs. Leonardo's studies of hands and gesture are well known, and he may well have influenced Raphael's painting entitled *La Muta*. Furthermore, Raphael had known the deaf artist Betto di Biagio (known as Pinturicchio) as a student. The predilection of the deaf for the plastic arts would meet with success in artist communities elsewhere as well: most notably the Dutchman Hendrick von Avercamp of the Pieter Brueghel school and Juan Fernández Navarette (also known by the name El Mudo) in the Spain of Philip II (Mirzoeff 13–15).

Recent scholarship makes a compelling case for recognizing Navarette (1526–1579) as the first truly educated deaf person. Having lost his hearing to disease at the age of two and a half, he never learned to speak. That improvidence did not prevent him from developing his many talents, however. At the monastery of La Estrella in Logroño where he was sent for care, he began to communicate with the monks by means of signs. He progressed rapidly, was taught to read and write, displayed a gift for drawing, and was afforded the means to study in Italy where he resided for nearly two decades.

Upon his return he was heralded for his artwork and for his intelligence, despite his lack of speech. For those who came in contact with him, the notion that the deaf cannot receive instruction must have seemed spurious:

> No one could have concluded that he was lacking in reason, however, for he communicated clearly by way of signs; he could read and write; and he was well versed in history and the Scriptures. Indeed, Fernández Navarette's intelligence was renowned at the Spanish court, as were his talents at gambling and the skill with which he kept account of wins and losses, according to the testimony of the king's chaplain. (Plann 9)

4.2.1 Spanish precursors: Pedro Ponce de León and Juan Pablo Bonet

Spain has long occupied a salient position in the history of deaf education. Pedro Ponce de León (1520–1584), a Benedictine monk, is usually credited with being the first educator of deaf children. If that distinction is placed in doubt owing to the education acquired by Navarette at the monastery in Logroño, two other distinctions of consequence remain: 1) it would be to the church and its subordinates that the charge of educating the deaf would fall in the centuries to come; 2) the cleavage between the proponents of signed language (both "natural" and "artificial") and "oralists" that would rack deaf communities in the nineteenth century has its origins in sixteenth-century Spain—Ponce de León taught his students to speak. Moreover, as it now seems likely, the two deaf children who first came under his tutelage, Francisco and Pedro de Velasco, arrived having developed their own manual system, as rudimentary as it may have been (Plann 8). Hence this "natural language," coupled with the monks' own hand signals developed for communication during hours of silence, would have formed the initial means of interlocution. The incidental dichotomy, "natural manual language" (created spontaneously by the deaf) and "artificial manual language" (created by the hearing for the deaf)—as innocuous as it may seem in sixteenth-century Spain—is also full of portent. It would eventually evolve into the full-fledged theoretical polemics that would face future manualists.

The path seemed clear for the time being, nevertheless. In 1620 Juan Pablo Bonet published in Madrid a source book that would inspire educators for years to come: *Reducción de las letras y arte para enseñar a hablar a los mudos.*[3] The book promotes a philosophy and a method. The author holds that the goal of deaf education is to teach students to read, write, and speak Spanish, thereby allowing them to integrate into society to the extent that they are able. No status is granted natural manual languages that may have been developed in hereditary deaf families or communities such as they may have been formed. In order to facilitate instruction, Bonet devised an "abecedario," a series of one-hand manual signs representing the letters of the Spanish alphabet. With these signs individual words could be spelled manually, finger spellings to be used by teacher and student alike in the instruction process. Each letter had its own pronunciation in which the student was also to be schooled. Manual signs thus calqued the vernacular down to the letter. In terms of the overall dynamics of signed languages as they would develop into the twentieth century, this event may seem of little consequence. Yet it was to these basic signs that abbé de L'Epée would turn a century and a half later when he was faced with the task of improving instruction for his deaf charges. He adopted them virtually wholesale, abandoning a two-handed manual alphabet. Indeed, although somewhat evolved, many of Bonet's signs are recognizable in the LSF (langue des signes française) and the ASL (American Sign Language) manual alphabets of today (the alphabet of BSL, British Sign Language, remains two-handed). Historically, the publication of Bonet's manual alphabet, promoted by the hearing for the betterment of the deaf, leant at least a basic standing to a form of communication that would receive increasing consideration as Europe inched its way toward the Enlightenment.

4.2.2 Early Modern France: Montaigne

Manual signing, as a natural language, would seem to have been developed to a high degree by at least some of France's deaf in the sixteenth century. Montaigne marveled at the facility they had acquired and the breadth of subjects they were able to address. "Nos muets disputent,

---

[3] This rare document has been made available on the web under the rubric Biblioteca de Signos at http://www.cervantesviryual.com. Those responsible are due the gratitude of all those interested in the history of deaf education. As important as Bonet's contribution would be, he was not the first to initiate finger spelling. Its existence dates from Antiquity. Indeed, Montaigne speaks of "les alphabets des doigts et grammaires en gestes" (1: 499) in his *Apologie de Raimond Sebond*. See below.

argumentent et content des histoires par signes," he wrote in the *Apologie de Raimond Sebond.* "J'en ay veu de si souples et formez à cela qu'à la verité, il ne leur manquoit rien à la perfection de se sçavoir faire entendre" (Montaigne 1: 498). Montaigne would have savored the irony of these words, for "entendre," semantically, constitutes a "double entendre": it may denote at once "to hear" and "to understand." Hence the Renaissance sage, knowingly, smites the equation "mutism therefore imbecility."

Montaigne's appreciation of such means of communication derived in part from his own language experience. From an early date he was struck by the linguistic variations that surrounded him: the Gascon spoken by the region's peasantry, the Latin imposed artificially as vernacular by both preceptors and servants in the family château, the Greek he would learn, the French he would write, the incomprehensible Languedocien spoken by the commoners of Toulouse where he would study law, the legalese he had to master as student and use as magistrate, the many languages of the merchants and sailors attracted to the port city of Bordeaux. This awareness spawned a certain linguistic sensitivity, to be sure, but at the same time it led him to consider "the speech act" as a phenomenon in and of itself—that is to say in its broadest terms, as a means of conveyance of that which the senses perceive, the cognitive process that categorizes, interprets, and relates the perceptions, and the mode of conveyance which, itself, is sensory bound. In the course of events it occurred to Montaigne to examine cases of sensory impairment, namely the congenitally blind and deaf. As would Diderot two centuries later, Montaigne concluded that although the perceptions of the blind depend on senses other than sight, they are no more limited in matters of judgment than the sighted. Whereas blindness for Montaigne is certainly a disability and may lead to errors that sight would otherwise prevent, such errors emanate from a lack of information not from a lack of cognitive capacity. There does exist an essential difference, however. Owing to language convention, the blind may use "sighted/visual" terms to describe perceptions, but the perceptions themselves, being unique to the other senses, activate a different (and not necessarily inferior) mode of judgment. Montaigne presents the case in narrative form in the *Apologie*:

J'ay veu un gentil-homme de bonne maison, aveugle nay, au moins aveugle de tel aage qu'il ne sçait que c'est que de veuë; il entend si peu ce qui luy manque, qu'il use et se sert comme nous des paroles propres au voir et les applique d'une mode toute sienne et particuliere. (Montaigne 1: 663)

As for "the speech act" as it relates to the deaf, in recognizing manual signing as a complete and authentic linguistic medium, Montaigne discerned an element that would be neglected by hearing deaf educators far into the future and that, for him, represented the "natural," humanizing link between the deaf and the hearing. He emphasized that in addition to the hands, everyone—the deaf and the hearing alike—uses parts of the body other than the tongue to communicate: gestures involving the head, face, eyes, eyebrows, and the shoulders. "Body language," both sign and gesture, is thus common to all humanity, "le propre de l'humaine nature" (Montaigne 1: 499). It is language itself that is universal, then. The particular form of language, in that sense—whether spoken or unspoken—does not rank as determinant in his view.

Montaigne's voice in seventeenth-century France, as noted earlier, would fade amidst the swell of support for the promotion, regulation, and institutionalization of the French language and the elaboration of the "classical" literary frame. The rhetorical attributes associated with the vernacular, the "art of speaking" equating to the "art of thinking" and the monopolistic position the French language would come to occupy in higher circles in France and elsewhere left little room for progress in non-verbal communication. Indeed, gestures accompanying speech went into decline as logocentrism ascended the language scale and "corporal decorum" became fashion.

4.2.3 The Enlightenment: Diderot (again)

In the long term, it would be thinkers concerned with the theory of language origins who would provide the intellectual basis upon which practitioners could build—socially, pedagogically, institutionally. Adam Kendon provides a cogent overview and chronology in his "Historical Observations on the Relationship between Research on Sign Languages and Language Origins Theory." Whereas he traces the phenomenon all the way to Chomsky and William Stokoe's seminal works relating to ASL in the twentieth century, he is careful not to neglect foundations. For him, contributing developments begin with Giambattista Vico's *Scienza nuova* in 1744. Vico believed that spoken language evolved from the imaginative capacities of humans, their ability to conceptualize and to project first in the form of symbolic action (gesture) and then in the form of image (cave drawings and the like), prior to the advent of aural signs. Ultimately, representational image advanced to metaphor and nurtured the development of abstraction. According to the theory, then, thinking originates as an "iconic" phenomenon whose initial modes of expression are forms of "visual mimesis" (gesture followed by pictorial representation). Marcel Danesi depicts the advent of speech in this process as the "aural-oral osmosis hypothesis":

> The third in the Vichian scenario signals the passage from *Homo sapiens* to *Homo sapiens sapiens* (= *Homo loquens*). The main feature of this event is audio-aural osmosis—the tendency to emit sounds that reflect or reproduce some property of the referent (onomatopoeia), or to associate an interjectional emission with some affective state, urge, or response. (Danesi 105)

Within this theoretical context, the primacy granted to visual signs did much to bolster the hypothesis that gesture, not oral speech, constituted the original, and therefore, "natural" language of humankind.

Condillac's *Essai sur l'origine des connaissances humaines* (1746) followed on the heels of Vico's *Scienza nuova*. Its author's notoriety lent credence to his theory of "language of action," according to which the first language was a "natural," gestural language that evolved in time into a system of arbitrary signs. Condillac, like Montaigne, was aware of the manual language developed spontaneously by groups of deaf people. He drew on this knowledge and anecdotal evidence; he cited the case of a young man from Chartres—deaf, mute and reared in a speaking community—who miraculously gained his hearing at the beginning of the eighteenth century. When the young man had acquired the ability to communicate orally, it became obvious that he did not comprehend abstractions such as God, religion, death, and so on. The reason for this state, Condillac conjectured, had nothing to do with his mental capacities. Rather, because he had spent his twenty-odd years within a speaking culture to which he did not have access, the arbitrary signs that would have served as vehicle were unavailable to him. In other words, he lacked the socialization that constitutes a linguistic community, not the wherewithal to think abstractly:

> Ce n'est pas qu'il eût naturellement de l'esprit; mais l'esprit d'un homme privé du commerce des autres est si peu exercé et si peu cultivé, qu'il ne pense qu'autant qu'il est indispensablement forcé par les objets extérieurs. Le plus grand fonds des idées des hommes est dans leur commerce réciproque. (Condillac 122)

It is not difficult to imagine how gratifying such recognition would appear to abbé de L'Epée when, some years later, he would seek to found a school for the deaf that would supply both the community and the "arbitrary signs" for its students. In 1751 Diderot would bring further authority to such thinking. In that year he published *Lettre sur les sourds et muets à l'usage de ceux qui entendent et qui parlent* in response to the aesthetic and epistemological theories of abbé Charles Batteux (Chouillet, "Introduction," Diderot 1751/1978: 111). In presenting his own position on the relationship of sensation to language, Diderot imagines a deaf and mute man ("un sourd et muet de convention"), a prototype of those he had observed communicating by means of signs. ("J'en connais un [sourd et muet] dont on pourrait se servir d'autant plus utilement, qu'il ne manque pas d'esprit, et qu'il a le geste expressif, comme vous l'allez voir" [Diderot 1751/1978: 144]. To this individual he suggests a project: the translation of a text written in French into "natural signs" (as determined by convention among the deaf) in their "natural order," followed by a retranslation back into French. Diderot believed that gesture and sign preceded speech on the originary calendar and that, with regard to cognition and syntax [signs or words], such an exercise would allow him to determine "les véritables notions de la formation du langage" (Diderot 1751/1978: 142). His projected findings not only attest to the intelligence of the "sourd et muet," but also to the capacity of manual signs to express beauty. The retranslation holds a surprise: "On parviendrait à substituer aux gestes à peu près leur équivalent en mots, je dis à peu près, parce qu'il y a des gestes sublimes que toute l'éloquence oratoire ne rendra jamais" (Diderot 1751/1978: 142).

Thus visual signs are elevated to the highest ranks of human expression: hieroglyphs which, when offered in concert, compose a tableau of sublimity unknown to the hearing world. This determination leads to the aesthetic import of the inquiry. In addition to theater as spectacle and the relationship of serious theater to pantomime, Diderot selects pictorial art as medium, painting in particular, which translates as the aestheticization of the second stage of development on Vico's language scale. As an aside, he also relates an oft-cited anecdote according to which a deaf acquaintance comments by way of gesture, idiomatically and humorously, on the end game of a chess match (Diderot 1751/1978: 144–145). The incident "integrates" the real-life "sourd de naissance" socially as well as intellectually and has meaning beyond its "comic relief": it documents Diderot's recognition of the difference between the "sign language" used to translate the French text and the "gestures" used to communicate with the hearing assembly of chess player and onlookers.[4]

4.3 Divergent methods: Etienne de Fay and Jacob (Jean) Rodrigue Pereire

Beyond the theories that would promote support within France's intellectual community, those interested in the well-being of the deaf could look to the practical experience and divergent methods of instruction of two practitioners: the deaf and mute Etienne de Fay and the hearing and speaking Jacob (Jean) Rodrigue Pereire. Recent scholarship has unearthed significant information pertaining to the legend of de Fay, long known only as the "vieux sourd-muet d'Amiens." Maryse Bézagu-Deluy (1990, 1993) and Bernard Truffaut have published enlightening accounts of the accomplishments of the deaf architect and the lives of his students in eighteenth-century France. De Fay, born deaf circa 1669, received instruction at the Abbey Saint-Jean in Amiens from the age of five. There, in addition to teaching him to read and write, the monks schooled him in the subjects of the day, including mathematics, history, drawing, and architecture. He would reside at the Abbey as live-in for the rest of his life, but not as ward. Indeed, although it would appear that he never learned to speak, the import of his duties would have exceeded by far the cost of his keep: procurator, librarian, architect, and teacher of deaf children in the only school for the deaf in France at the time (Bézagu-Deluy 1993: 29). As an architect, he was called upon to design the rebuilding of the Abbey. The results (the solidity of construction, the compelling facades, the stately entryways) elicited praise from monks and chroniclers alike (Truffaut 16–17). As a teacher, de Fay used the "natural language" of the deaf, manual language, to instruct his pupils. Little is known about the signs themselves, whether they were of de Fay's complete invention or whether he allowed for signs developed by the pupils, either prior to or after their arrival. Events in the lives of three of his charges provide particular insight into the difficulties the deaf faced in those days and the controversy concerning their method of instruction.

---

[4] At least one scholar has identified this "sourd de naissance" as Saboureux de Fontenay, the prize student of the oralist Jean Rodrigue Pereire (Presneau 416). If this is true, the episode loses significance because Saboureux could read, write—and speak.

The Meusnier brothers came to the Abbey Saint-Jean in 1728. Both were named François, the elder having been born in 1713 and the younger in 1715. Having come from a prominent family that counted among its ascendants the Prince of Carignan (Savoy) who was both deaf and mute, the teenagers arrived with a king's pension. They were taught the subjects in which de Fay was proficient and therefore were prepared academically to assume positions commensurate with their capacities. Outside the walls of the monastery school, society proved less accommodating. By law the non-speaking deaf could not attain "majority" status in France, that is to say, legal adulthood. Nor could they look forward to serving as Court Usher, as the boys' father had before them. Furthermore, when it came to the sizeable inheritance to which the sons would otherwise be entitled, the courts balked, recognized them only as perpetual minors in constant need of a court-appointed tutor, and turned over the inheritance to their tutor to dispense in their name and stead (Bézagu-Deluy, 1993: 26–30).

However effectively manual language could be used in the education of the deaf, the inability to speak presented a potentially devastating obstacle. Another of de Fay's students, Azy d'Etavigny, would play a pivotal role in the early development of the oralist approach to the education of the deaf in France. Etavigny spent several years under the tutelage of the aging de Fay at the Abbey. Accounts are scarce, but the young fellow eventually left Amiens and sought instruction from Jacob (Jean) Rodrigue Pereire in La Rochelle in order to learn to speak (Truffaut 18). Pereire, who was of Spanish origin, had adopted Bonet's manual alphabet and his goal of teaching the deaf to speak. His success was recorded in the *Journal des Savants* and in 1749 his paper presented before the Academy of Sciences was published by the prestigious *Mercure de France*. Public demonstrations followed to the delight of the scientific establishment. Pereire's prize student, Saboureux de Fontenay (god-son of the Duke of Chaulnes), caused people to marvel: more than an oddity, not only could he speak, he was intelligent, poised, charming, witty, at ease in polite society. These achievements eventually earned a state pension both for him and his teacher (Bézagu-Deluy, 1993: 138).

Saboureux de Fontenay found acceptance and a measure of notoriety in a society that would otherwise have been closed to him. Having been taught to speak opened doors, it is true; but other circumstances contributed as well: lineage, intelligence, and, especially, financial support. Such instruction came at a price that the vast majority of France's deaf could not afford. Instruction needed to be intense, hands on, in the form of individual tutoring rather than group activity. Few potential students would ever have the opportunity. Thus, in the early 1760s when abbé de L'Epée met the deaf and mute twins who would change his life as much as he would change theirs, he soon realized that the situation required a new approach. The solution he found would affect the lives of countless deaf people over more than two centuries. It would lead to the creation of two new languages that would both nurture and preserve the community and culture native to the deaf alone.

4.3.1 A miracle, a chance encounter, a calling: abbé de L'Epée

Bézagu-Deluy's 1990 biography (which builds on Ferdinand Berthier's 1852 work) provides a basic chronology in addition to a sympathetic and often stirring account of events leading to L'Epée's ultimate calling. Charles-Michel was born in Versailles into a well-heeled bourgeois family in 1712, the third son and fourth child of Charles-François Lespée (as the name was written at the time) and Françoise Marguerite Varignon. The father would distinguish himself as an architect credentialed by the Royal Academy of Architecture, as would his first-born son Jacques-François. Charles-Michel's education and ordination followed the usual sequence: courses in philosophy at the Collège des Quatre Nations in Paris (1728–30), law studies at the University of Paris (1730–33), reception into the clergy (1731), a series of clerical assignments that took him first to Feugues and then to Pougy in Champagne before his return to Paris. The late 1740s find him serving as titular chaplain and, in 1748, as honorary "chanoine" of the Eglise Saint-Louis du Louvre.

From an early date L'Epée revealed himself as a man of principle. A Jansenist of conviction, he opposed the 1713 "Unigenitus" papal bull condemning the Jansenist Pasquier Quesnel's 101 propositions and moral reflections. The 1730 Royal declaration making the bull law in France riled emotions and provoked controversy. In 1731 Charles-Michel refused to sign the cleric's formulary. In 1739 he filed an appeal of the bull and renewed it in 1744. Events became increasingly politicized. In 1753 Louis XV exiled the Parlement de Paris for its Jansenist sympathies. In the early-1760s the same king expelled the Jesuits (the Jansenists' redoubtable rivals) from France. Political maneuvering would continue into the Revolution and would pose a real danger for those caught in the middle. L'Epée did well to avoid the conflict during those years. A miraculous cure and a chance encounter would render that line of conduct easier, and necessary, to follow.

In June of 1759 L'Epée published anonymously his interpretation of a miracle involving a neighbor that had taken place at his parish church, Eglise Saint-Roch, the week before: "Relation de la maladie et de la guérison miraculeuse de Marie-Anne Pigalle." The woman, who had been afflicted with pulmonary tuberculosis and unable to speak for some time, experienced a complete recovery while in prayer. The event became the talk of Paris and caused L'Epée to reflect on the relationship of Providence, faith, and medical intervention. He reviewed accounts of other such cures and inferred divine complicity and a personal calling. Providence would soon intervene.

L'Epée himself describes his beginnings as instructor of the deaf in his well-known *Institution des sourds et muets, par la voie des signes méthodiques* (1776). He relates that one day he chanced upon twin girls, both of them deaf from birth. They had been undergoing instruction from a priest, abbé Simon Vanin, who had died, leaving them with no means to continue their religious education:

> Croyant donc que ces deux enfans vivroient & mourroient dans l'ignorance
> de leur religion, si je n'essayois pas quelque moyen de la leur apprendre, je
> fus touché de compassion pour elles, & je dis qu'on pouvoit me les amener,
> que j'y ferois tout mon possible.[5]

Once having accepted the charge, the question remained as to how he would go about it. If Vanin's method of devising lessons based on pictures seemed lacking to him, his own experience provided no immediate solutions. Although he had learned a French manual alphabet as a youngster, he knew that would only facilitate teaching the twins to read. Gestures of the most obvious sort could serve as basic communication, but he sought more: "Il s'agissait de les conduire à l'intelligence des mots" (L'Epée 1776: 9).

4.3.2 L'Epée: the language, the method, the opposition

The challenge led him to examine pertinent literature and the experience of his predecessors: Descartes, Condillac, Diderot, Ernaud, Pereire,

---

[5] L'Epée 1776: 8–9. The original spellings of the 1776 text have been retained in order to remind the reader of the state of French orthography prior to the Revolution, as depicted in earlier chapters.

Saboureux de Fontenay, among numerous others. Over time his readings, inquiries, and personal convictions spawned a dual project of monumental proportions: the creation of a universal sign language and the establishment of a school where the deaf could be educated free of charge. The subtitle of his 1776 *Institution des sourds et muets* provides insight as to methodology: *Ouvrage qui contient le Projet d'une Langue Universelle, par l'entremise des Signes naturels assujettis à une méthode.* A "universal language" of "natural signs" privileges theories espoused by Condillac and Diderot, it is obvious. But there is another dimension as well: the twins had created their own rather extensive set of signs, "naturally," with which they "conversed" in silence. These would serve as basis, to which L'Epée planned to add, "arbitrarily" and "methodically," as many more signs of his own invention as would be necessary to construct a complete language.

The success of the program L'Epée developed at the rue des Moulins residence he had inherited in his late forties has been chronicled by biographers and historians alike. The passing of his parents had left him in an enviable financial position, his means surpassing by far his needs. Hence the doors to his home opened to increasing numbers of deaf and mute children who were welcomed without regard for finances. Instruction and daily life transpired communally, fostered a sense of both individual and collective identity, stimulated the mind, just as Condillac had theorized. L'Epée logged lessons and progress in thick notebooks that would serve as manuals and to which he would return when seeking to review and refine the methodology. As the method took shape and acquired greater sophistication, the results improved commensurately. At this point, in search of added support, L'Epée began to exploit the publicity mechanisms used by predecessors. The first public demonstration took place in 1771, rue des Moulins. Two more drew greater interest the following year. In 1772 and periodically thereafter he published program descriptions, exercises, and a series of four letters in which he outlined his pedagogy, designs, and aspirations. The news traveled quickly. In 1775 the unthinkable occurred: Condillac himself showed up at the school. Exuberant at seeing his theory in action, the *philosophe* acclaimed the method in his 1775 *Cours d'étude pour l'instruction du prince de Parme.* By 1776 L'Epée felt he could bring all these materials together under a single title: *Institution des sourds et muets par la voie des signes méthodiques.* In May of 1777 the emperor Joseph II came to rue des Moulins to observe with his own eyes the marvel about which he had heard so much. Both delighted and moved, upon his return home he designated an envoy, Frederick Stork, to come to Paris to learn the method that, in turn, would be adopted for the Institute for the Deaf in Vienna. Other foreigners followed suit. In 1778 Louis XVI issued a decree recognizing the school. In August of 1783 a papal nuncio arrived to observe the wonderful work being done in the name of God. A second decree in 1785 provided funds from the royal coffers to alleviate the financial stress of teaching more than seventy students. That same year abbé Sicard, L'Epée's eventual successor, came to rue des Moulins to study the method. His enthusiasm and quick mastery earned him in 1786 the position of director of the newly established Institute for the Deaf in Bordeaux.

Praise came from near and far. Foreign admirers published papers and books outlining the method and urging its adoption in their own countries. But detractors did not fail to voice opposition, the oralists Pereire and Saboureux among them, as one might expect. Surprisingly, perhaps, Pierre Desloges, the first "deaf and mute" to author a book (*Observations d'un sourd et muet sur un cours élémentaire d'éducation des sourds et muets* [1779]), also criticized the method. The most heated debate arose with regard to Samuel Heinicke and the Leipzig institute. Heinicke had published a treatise on deaf education in 1775. He reacted with disdain upon learning of Stork's use of L'Epée's method in Vienna. Heinicke maintained that the deaf and mute are irreparably handicapped, that signs—manual or written—cannot compensate for lack of hearing and speech, and that such individuals do not have the intellectual means to conceptualize, to construct or comprehend abstractions (Bézagu-Deluy 219–22). The atavistic dragon had reared its head once again. It would not be easily slain.

4.3.3 Final rewards: the case of Joseph

To French officials of the 1780s L'Epée had proved his worth by means of demonstrations, testimonials, and in court. Judicial recognition came about in a strange and dramatic sequence of events that anticipate the case of Victor, the so-called "wild boy" of Aveyron. In 1773 an emaciated, deaf and mute male adolescent of unknown identity appeared on a doorstep in the village of Cuvilly in Picardy. He was taken in and cared for by locals for three years, during which time all attempts to learn his origins failed. L'Epée, summoned in early 1776, quickly established communication through signs. He learned that the boy had come from a well-to-do family, had brothers and sisters, and a father who limped, amongst numerous other details. Investigation pointed to the family of the Comte de Solar. Thus began a saga whose initial episodes would last five years and whose final chapter would not be written until 1792. Joseph, as L'Epée called him, was believed to be the deceased count's son. As such he could claim name and title and stood to inherit. Of course a legal battle ensued. Under the preceptorship of L'Epée, Joseph pled his case through signs that were translated by a court appointed interpreter, as would testimony in any language other than French. If that were not legitimization enough for the language of "methodical signs," the decision handed down in 1781 favored Joseph. Little did it matter that it would be overturned eleven years later. The notoriety had worked its magic.

Abbé de L'Epée died the twenty-third of December 1789. Revolutionaries did not hesitate. While on his deathbed, he was informed that henceforth the work of his school would continue as an institution of the State (Bézagu-Deluy 29). In 1790 abbé Sicard was called in from Bordeaux to assume duties as director. The following year the school was officially elevated to the status of "Institution Nationale" and L'Epée was awarded recognition as model citizen and humanitarian. Three years later, in 1794, the newly formed Institute moved to new premises, the former Seminary Saint-Magloire on today's rue Saint-Jacques in the Latin Quarter.

4.3.4 The methodical signs

To this point little has been said about the specific method and signs Sicard inherited from L'Epée. Their originator left two full-length publications on the subject, the aforementioned *Institution des sourds et muets par la voie des signes méthodiques* (1776) and a second revised and condensed edition that appeared in 1784 under the title *La véritable manière d'instruire les sourds et muets, confirmée par une longue expérience.*[6] The remarks that follow derive from the revised edition, since it benefits from nearly a decade of hindsight and documents the evolution of L'Epée's thinking. A concern arises regarding the signs themselves. Whereas L'Epée describes many of them, there exists

---

6 The edition of the latter text cited here is the 1984 Fayard bicentennial edition which modernizes most spellings. L'Epée did leave a dictionary of sorts that was published posthumously. Unfortunately, the signs do not accompany the definitions which are exemplified by moralizing phrases typical of the religious teachings of the period.

no pictorial representation. Nor does he address in a satisfactory manner the matter of origination, that is to say signs developed by the deaf and incorporated into the language either unchanged or altered as opposed to those of his own particular device. He simply declares the signs to be methodical because they are subject to rules, meaning his rules. Chapter Sixteen of Part One of *La véritable manière* ... is entitled "Réflexions sur une méthode et un dictionnaire à l'usage des sourds et muets." The frame of reference within which he situates his methodical signs seems all too familiar. Like the Academy before him, he assumes the arbitrary role of central authority: "dans toutes mes Leçons je suis moi-même le Dictionnaire vivant, qui explique tout ce qui est nécessaire pour l'intelligence des mots qui entrent dans le sujet que nous traitons, et que ce secours est pleinement suffisant" (L'Epée 1984: 102). L'Epée as "living dictionary" *fixes* meaning, determines proper usage, provides paradigms. Yet if one anticipates as a consequence a mere calquing of the French language, the individual chapters themselves dispel that notion. Calque proves to be the major reservoir from which L'Epée draws, but it is an unusual reservoir indeed. Gendering corresponds to the French system—as reflected by the articles *le, la, les*—and partitives do as well: *de, du, de la, de l', des*. So too verb tenses, voices, and modes calque their French counterparts in accordance with the linguistic taxonomy of the time: present, future, future perfect, imperfect, simple past, past indefinite, past anterior, and pluperfect; active and passive; indicative, subjunctive, imperative, infinitive, and past participle. Instructions for designating the various past tenses indicate how simply and efficaciously time frames could be conveyed:

> [L'étudiant] jettoit indifféremment sa main vers son épaule, pour exprimer une chose passée; nous lui disons, qu'il ne faut la jetter qu'une fois, quand il s'agit de l'Imparfait ; deux fois, quand il est question du Parfait ; et trois fois pour le plusque-Parfait. (L'Epée 1984: 49)

Once for the imperfect, twice for the perfect, and three times for the pluperfect. But simplicity does not always reign. Elsewhere the system takes the form of a complex amalgamation. There exists a six-case declension system, each case identifiable by a sign of "degree." The ablative is thus represented by the partitive sign accompanied by the sign for the sixth degree. The predominance of the case structure is confirmed by the lack of a preposition corresponding to the "dative" *à* so common to the French language. Other prepositions have designated signs: *avec, avant, après, devant, derrière,* and so on, twenty-four in all. Comparatives are analytical, as opposed to synthetic, but unlike French the adjective *grand*, for instance, is signed first, followed by the sign for *plus*, rather than the usual *plus grand*. French syntax has thus been regularized to reflect the noun/adjective (or base word/modifier) prevalence. (Examples of this sort are far too numerous to enumerate here.) L'Epée demonstrated publicly that his sign system could function within language environments other than French. Universality figured prominently in his goals. It is difficult to disagree with Renate Fischer's assessment:

> It is often said that methodical signs were a sort of signed French. [...] An analogy between de l'Epée's methodical signs and signed French, however, might only be assumed in those cases in which both methodical signs and signed French use certain traditional grammatical features. [...] The purpose of employing methodical signs was to aid deaf pupils in learning French, or any other spoken language, coupled with the aim of advancing cognitive development. De l'Epée started from the assumption that no one, hearing or deaf, learns a foreign language (which French was to persons born deaf) with the help of just the foreign language. Rather, people learn by means of the language they know—sign language in the case of deaf people. (Fischer 20, 23)

4.3.5 Adding sound and lip reading

L'Epée had rejected oralism initially because he felt that teaching the deaf to speak required too much time, did nothing to develop the cognitive process, and hindered the socialization that was essential to intellectual development. By 1784 and by his own account his attitude had altered. In the interim he had discovered Bonet's manual alphabet and had set about learning Spanish in order to be able to read his book on the subject. He then sought out other oralist literature, including Johan-Conrad Amman's *Dissertatio de loquela surdorum et mutorum* and reports of John Wallis's work in England. He discovered that a straightforward, self-evident methodology was common to each approach. So inspired, he devised his own program, to which the entirety of Part Two of *La véritable manière*...is devoted: Chapter One on the pronunciation of vowels, Chapter Two on sound and orthographic correspondences, and Chapter Three on lip reading. The final chapter constructs the pragmatics of visual phonetics for which L'Epée produced an "alphabet labial" to complement the "alphabet manuel." Dictation exercises akin to those used so successfully in French mainstream education served as testing instrument and reinforcement mechanism. L'Epée's depiction of the ease with which the children mastered the process reflects the satisfaction of all parties:

> Les Sourds et Muets acquérant cette facilité de très-bonne heure, et d'ailleurs étant curieux, comme le reste des hommes, de sçavoir ce que l'on dit, sur-tout lorsqu'ils supposent qu'on parle d'eux, ou de quelque chose qui les intéresse, ils nous dévorent des yeux (cette expression n'est pas trop forte), et devinent très-aisément tout ce que nous disons […] J'ai soin de recommander aux Personnes qui nous font l'honneur d'assister à nos Leçons, de ne point dire en leur présence ce qu'il n'est point à propos. (L'Epée 1984 : 134–35)

He is quick to add, however, that in the interest of the children's development, this process takes place only after they have become proficient at writing the dictations given to them in signs, "even though the signs represent neither words nor letters, but only the ideas they have learned through lengthy practice" (L'Epée 1984 : 135). Children are forewarned that people outside the school will not articulate labially with the precision of their instructors. As a courtesy, L'Epée advises, people should make the same effort to make themselves understood to lip readers as they make when speaking to foreigners.

In the end, and perhaps in spite of himself, abbé de L'Epée came to recognize speech as the primary bridge to the outside world. After lengthy consideration and while continuing to privilege sign over speech, he declared in favor of bilingualism.

4.3.6 Sicard: the tumult

Rising to any position of prominence in the midst of the Revolution meant courting danger. Being appointed director of the Institute for the Deaf proved no exception, especially for an ardently committed Jansenist priest such as Sicard. Jansenism had come under scrutiny at this juncture owing to the politicization it had undergone in previous decades. On the one hand, Jansenists had expressed strong opposition to the Crown's legitimization of the "Unigenitus" bull and to the Jesuits' views on the role of "good works" in the attainment of salvation. In so doing, they had supported change in the Old Regime status quo. On the other hand, the Civil Constitution of the Clergy of 1790 placed them under the direct auspices of the new temporal authority against which they might be expected to rebel. Suspicion arose on both sides of the aisle.

According to decree, Haüy, Sicard, and their blind and deaf charges had been directed to share quarters at the ill-suited Convent of the Celestines. In addition to the inconvenience and lack of space, the premises had been severely damaged during the conflict. Both directors complained formally. Sicard, who had openly supported the Revolutionary regime and had even made a sizeable monetary contribution from his personal funds, suddenly found himself arrested and incarcerated the 26th of August 1792. The official charge accused him of harboring refractory priests. Headed by Jean Massieu, Sicard's leading deaf pupil from Bordeaux and newly appointed teaching associate, a delegation of the Institute's students presented a petition in his favor to the Legislative Assembly. The widely admired rhetoric of the appeal, which gained further respect for the Institute, resulted in a directive ordering Sicard's immediate release. But the "September massacres" had begun. Prussia had invaded and troops had advanced to Verdun. The Revolutionary Commune had prevailed since August 10th and both Danton and Marat stirred foment. The massacres began the 2nd of September and would continue for four days. The rampage cost the lives of some eleven hundred prisoners deemed enemies of the Revolution. Sicard narrowly escaped their fate. At one point he was loaded into a carriage filled with prisoners headed for execution. The crowd attacked, killing some of them. The driver altered his route and delivered the rest, including Sicard, back into the hands of the Revolutionary Committee. His ultimate release came only after the Assembly issued a second decree. The drama did not end there, however. Newly returned to his directorship in 1796, appointed to the staff of the Lycée national, and received as a member of the recently formed Institut de France, Sicard felt he could safely express his political and religious beliefs in the journal *Annales Religieuses, Politiques et Littéraires*. The decision earned him an order of deportation. He went into hiding and did not emerge until his formal disavowal had been delivered to authorities by influential cohorts who lobbied in his favor. The director reassumed duties in 1799 and was reinstated to the Institut de France in 1801 by the First Consul himself.

4.3.7 From methodical signs to mimicry

In the following years deaf education continued largely in the mold L'Epée had shaped. Sicard simply improved the approach, modified signs and techniques. He published his version of the method in two books: *Cours d'instruction d'un sourd-muet de naissance* (1800) and *Traité des signes pour l'instruction des sourds-muets* (1808). Other changes began to take form as the institution matured. As with the institute for the blind, the school's own students were recruited to fill the ranks of instructors. The policy meant that teachers who had grown up in a world of silence were providing daily instruction with increasing frequency. Like their blind counterparts, they brought a new perspective to their pedagogy. Jean Massieu, Laurent Clerc, and Roch Ambroise Auguste Bébian (so named for his god-father, abbé Sicard) all recognized that as well as the methodical signs had served the deaf, their inherent artificiality posed undue limitations. They saw deaf language, in and of itself, as a unique and authentic language that develops naturally among the deaf and derives from their particular needs and innate ability to communicate communally. For these deaf teachers, at least theoretically since recognized alternatives did not yet exist, there was no necessity for any other language—or language system, for that matter—to intervene as intermediary. This thinking inspired Bébian to publish two works on the subject, *Essai sur les sourds-muets et sur le langage naturel* (1817) and *Mimographie ou Essai d'écriture mimique, propre à régulariser le langage des sourds-muets* (1822/1825). Bébian's concept of "natural signs" relates to the direct expression of ideas rather than translation into lexical surrogates. The dynamics are increased from manual to corporal: facial expression, shoulder movement, body position, and so on. The language thus gains in nuance and subtlety. The grammar arises from the system itself. Notions of parts of speech give way to visual components and phrasing. Syntax might be best described as sensorial. Bébian gives numerous examples in his Essai, the following for instance:

> Si l'on veut figurer l'impression qu'un objet a produit sur nous; après avoir désigné cet objet par un de ses caractères les plus essentiels, le geste indique l'action qu'il exerce sur tel ou tel sens: le visage, qui était auparavant dans le repos, s'éveille, s'anime, et montre que l'*impression* est sentie. On y voit en même temps si la *sensation* en est agréable ou désagréable. (Bébian 1817: 52)

This notion of "natural order," perception/action/perceiver, constitutes an inversion in terms of the subject/verb/object "natural order" precept espoused by traditional French grammarians. At a later date the divergence would be cited by oralists as yet another reason to prioritize the teaching of spoken French. For the moment Bébian concentrated on "regularizing" the language of "mimicry" and producing an instructional manual which was approved by the Conseil d'Administration de l'Institut Royal des Sourds-Muets de Paris in 1823, the year following Sicard's death. It is at this juncture, then, the second decade of the nineteenth century, that deaf language takes a turn toward becoming the Langue des Signes (LSF) that France knows today. It also marks an important point of gestation for the most studied and developed language of the sort: American Sign Language (ASL).

4.3.8 Laurent Clerc: LSF, ASL

In the year 2000 the MIT Press published the findings of the American Sign Language Lingustic Research Project under the title *The Syntax of American Sign Language*. The team of five scholars led by Carol Neidle identified as objective examination of the simultaneity of manual signing and the "crucial syntactic information [...] expressed nonmanually by specific movements of the face and upper body" (Neidle 1). Since syntax has been the primary focus of synchronists for some time, the team sought to determine how ASL compares with spoken languages in this respect. The results confirm a level of development that had been in question prior to this investigation. The team found that not only is there a full spectrum of tenses (past, recent-past, formerly, traditional past, up-to-now [since], immediate past, future) marked at the head of the clause, there is also tense agreement within the clause and, with regard to transitive and intransitive clauses, subjects and objects are marked nonmanually: "Agreement in ASL may be expressed not only by morphological inflections on the verbs but also nonmanually, through the use of head tilt and eye gaze. This use of the head is 'systematic'" (Neidle 64). Moreover, and in addition to numerous other observations, ASL syntax was seen to exhibit readily identifiable variations whose "skeletal structure" is represented in the form of a tree diagram (Neidle 3). Using Jean-Yves Pollock's widely recognized model (proposed in 1989 and published in the journal *Linguistic Inquiry*), the team concluded both that ASL has a "hierarchically organized phrase structure" and that nonmanual syntactic markings are key to its high-level sophistication.

If these features sound familiar, it is because ASL and LSF share a common past in the person of Laurent Clerc. Both deaf and lacking the sense of smell either from birth (1785) or resulting from an accident in infancy, Clerc came to Sicard's institute at the age of twelve. After a decade of schooling during which he often played the leading role in public demonstrations, his progress was such that he was appointed to assist Massieu as "répétiteur." His efforts earned immediate praise; his acumen and gentlemanly demeanor won the hearts and minds of pupils. His ability to communicate was such that he was frequently thought to be a "parlant instruit." Sent one day to retrieve a book from one of Sicard's cohorts at the Académie Française, Berthier relates in his biographical sketch, Clerc was questioned on all manner of subjects as a test of his intellect. His responses, especially on the topic of metaphysics, proved so auspicious that the learned questioner is said to have exclaimed: "Ma foi, Monsieur, je vous admire!" (Berthier 1873: 181–93).

Clerc's connection with the development of ASL is owed to Thomas Hopkins Gallaudet who, in 1815, accepted to direct the first school for the deaf in the United States: The American Asylum for the Deaf and Dumb in Hartford, Connecticut. The Congregational minister, like his counterparts L'Epée and Sicard in France, sought to guide the deaf along the road to salvation and to instruct them in matters of Christian morality.[7] Truly committed and benevolently paternalistic (Valentine 1993), Reverend Gallaudet went abroad to gather information and insight from directors of foreign institutions. He met both Sicard and Clerc, similarly engaged, in London where the Frenchmen invited him to Paris. He soon arrived on Sicard's doorstep. The American spent some three months observing and learning the French method of instruction. Duly impressed and convinced that its "universality" would lend itself to an English language setting, he offered Clerc a position at the newly established Asylum. To the dismay of French students and director alike, Clerc accepted and set sail with Gallaudet for America, taking with him the language of methodical signs (or Old French Sign Language [OFSL]) such as it existed in 1816. His intention was to stay for only a short time. He ended up learning English, marrying one of the deaf pupils, and remaining as a teacher until his retirement forty-one years later in 1858. Clerc left an

---

[7] It is of note that the evangelical Protestantism of Gallaudet's Connecticut had a good deal in common with L'Epée and Sicard's Jansenism (which has often been compared to a certain Protestant fundamentalism). The similarities would have eased Clerc's transition as he assumed duties in a foreign institution and society

indelible mark on deaf education in the United States. His success is legendary. Today the Laurent Clerc National Deaf Education Center at Gallaudet University stands as testimony to the gratitude of America's deaf. Tributes and honorary degrees abound, as do anecdotes, especially those emanating from his meetings with dignitaries such as Henry Clay and President Monroe. Estimates vary, but as many as "two-thirds of today's ASL signs have French origins."[8] Consultation of Webster's *American Sign Language Dictionary* and the *ABC...LSF Dictionnaire visuel bilingue* yields grudging evidence. A number of signs correspond identically or are very similar: wine/vin, woman/femme, hundred/cent, to look for/chercher, to eat/manger, to drink/boire, to sleep/dormir, house/maison. But others one might expect to correspond do not at all: God/Dieu, mother/mère, father/père, daughter/fille, son/fils, and so on. The reason is of course that the two languages share "origins." The same forces that were modifying the methodical signs in Paris at the time of Clerc's departure were already present when he arrived in Hartford, albeit in the form of a truly amazing sociolinguistic phenomenon. An unusual number of congenitally deaf children had been born into the community located on Martha's Vineyard. Over time those afflicted developed their own sign system to even greater extent than had L'Epée's twin girls. Indeed, it is not an exaggeration to speak in terms of the island's deaf culture in which everyone—the hearing included—participated by means of signs (Groce 1985). Hence, the children who entered the Asylum and who had knowledge of this language (Old American Sign Language [OASL]) brought with them the means of influencing the Asylum's language in the long term as that language matured. Maturation, of course, entails increasing abstraction and a commensurate distantiation from origins—in this case *la langue des signes méthodiques*.

Today's ASL serves a community several hundred thousand strong. Thanks to Gallaudet University (for which "clear visual communication is the norm in every University unit and department"[9]) and the energizing

---

[8] Anon. Gallaudet University's electronic "Laurent Clerc: Apostle to the Deaf People of the New World." The article contains an ample bibliography. Other sources to consult: Carroll, Cathryn, and Harlan Lane (1991) and Lane (1984). A particularly rich source for anecdotal material may be found in *Laurent Clerc papers* at the Yale University Library and which exist on microfilm.

[9] If visual communication is the norm, the University catalogue also recognizes that "Gallaudet University is a bilingual community in which both American Sign Language and English thrive."

efforts of William Stokoe beginning at the mid point of twentieth century, it presently enjoys an envious prestige. Those who "speak" it form a vibrant subculture that boasts deaf sports, social clubs, literary societies, and political action groups. The "collective memory" that had been handed down from generation to generation is now supported by histories and grammars as well as educational and social institutions of varying descriptions. ASL has thus "joined the family of 'natural languages,' including spoken languages, allowing it to claim a status of equality" (Padden and Rayman 248). The struggle for equality has been lengthy and difficult. ASL has had to overcome the same biases that have plagued deaf communities everywhere. Whereas it would be naïve to say that problems of perception no longer exist, its proponents have succeeded largely through strength of purpose and a belief in a collective identity defined and authenticated by a genuinely inherent language and culture.

4.3.9 LSF: an identity, a culture, a society

Despite the deplorable material conditions of Paris's Institute in the years following Clerc's departure for the United States, the many students who passed through its portals began to recognize a collective identity of their own. Within the school they improvised their sign language, created their own ludic "argot." Instructors were befuddled, to the delight of their charges. Youthful playfulness served a social purpose, to be sure, but more serious matters promoted kinship as well. The students' protests clamoring for increased government funding united them ideologically, formed permanent bonds, kept them in contact with one another once they had left the school, moved them to seek out deaf people from other communities. A sense of pride swelled with the successes of former classmates—in business, in government, in artisanship, in literature, and especially in the arts. The plastic arts meant to the deaf what music meant to the blind. Nicholas Mirzoeff (*Silent Poetry*) has outlined and contextualized the wealth of works produced by the deaf during the period: painters, sculptors, and eventually photographers. Their contributions raised the profile of the deaf, moved them toward the realm of respectability they all sought and deserved; their numbers are impressive: Marie-Pierre Ponce-Camus, Frédéric Peyson, René Princeteau, Félix Martin, Paul Choppin, Léopold Loustau, Ferdinand Hamar, Léon Cogniet—and, in Spain, a Goya whose genius came full bloom only after he had lost his hearing.

For all that, society remained recalcitrant. The hearing public could not understand. Suspicion continued to surround those who moved their hands and heads and eyes in such a strange fashion. Pathology judged them to be anatomically and functionally incomplete. Culturally, "mimicry" was viewed as a type of primitivism, the means by which the savage tribes of the Americas were compelled to communicate. To make matters worse, in the years following Sicard's death the Paris Institute began to re-emphasize oralism. The future seemed very much in jeopardy. The sense of pride and community among the deaf spawned a new awareness, self-awareness on the one hand, but also an awareness of the need to organize, to promote, to lobby, to "tell" their story and celebrate their history, to remember and commemorate—and to do so outside the walls of the Institute. What better way to start than with a tribute to the revered founding father, abbé de L'Epée? So reasoned Ferdinand Berthier and a committee of deaf representatives in 1834. Thus began the tradition of the banquet honoring the good priest annually on his birthday. The form these yearly affairs would assume over time says a good deal both about the status of the deaf community of Paris at this juncture and the frailties of human nature.

The banquets represented at once a political act and a social statement. They were the accepted means by which organizations fêted their accomplishments, announced their agendas, recognized individuals and groups, all the while partaking of the mediocre banquet fare spiced by drink and by the spates of the humor-laced eloquence and bits of poetry required for such occasions. From academicians to surgeons to artists and journalists, philosophers—and especially politicians—the banquet had become an institution. The first banquet for the deaf took place in a Place du Châtelet restaurant; fifty-four guests attended, and seventeen deaf artists were recognized in grateful tribute. The esteemed inventor of the daguerreotype, Louis Daguerre, was extended a special invitation and did attend (Mirzoeff 1995: 114). Needless to say, these banquets were like no others. Bernard Mottez has gleaned a number of salient passages from the minutes of the *Société Centrale des Sourds-Muets de Paris*, as the deaf organization came to be known. They include the following:

> A cinq heures, près de soixante membres de cette nation tout à part, étaient réunis dans les salons du restaurant de la place du Châtelet. Il y avait là des professeurs, des peintres, des graveurs, des employés de différentes

administrations, des imprimeurs, de simples ouvriers, qui, rejetés par la nature marâtre du sein de notre société, ont trouvé les moyens, par leur intelligence, d'y entrer et d'y conquérir des positions qui les font vivre honorablement.

[…] Il semblerait, que soixante hommes privés de l'ouïe et de la parole dussent former un ensemble pénible et affligeant; il n'en est rien. L'âme humaine anime tellement leurs fronts, pour la plupart fort beaux; elle se peint si vivement dans leurs yeux; elle se fraie un chemin si rapide jusqu'au bout de leurs doigts, qu'au lieu de les plaindre on serait tenté de leur porter envie. […] Ce n'est pas exagéré de dire qu'aucun des orateurs que nous admirons le plus ne pourrait lutter, même de loin, avec Berthier, Forrestier ou Lenoir, pour la grâce, la dignité et la propriété du geste. En vérité, quand on voit des discours comme ceux que ces trois jeunes hommes ont prononcés, on voudrait, je crois, désapprendre la parole. (qtd. in Mottez 153–54)

Such moving encomia call to mind Gautier's descriptions of the bastion of young Romantics gathered at the Théâtre Français in 1830 to cheer on Hugo's history altering *Hernani*. Both groups, having experienced marginalization, sought to nurture yet another new order. The Romantics would soon fragment, would follow separate paths into or out of the political arena. In the early years the deaf movement became more politically focused. Numbers grew and the invited guests reflected an increasingly liberal agenda; the leftist Ledru-Rollin attended in 1837, for example. Invitations went to leading journalists, assuring press coverage, and influential members of government, especially those who were positioned to aid the Institute (Mirzoeff 114). The banquets thus came to highlight an ongoing political campaign. For all the emphasis placed on its program of egalitarianism, however, the Société soon exhibited its own shortcomings. Guest lists could not be all inclusive; the growth in numbers of graduates from the Institute and the need to invite dignitaries imposed a selection process. The organization adopted society's inequitable standard: a set of elitist criteria based on prominence. But that was not the only measure that hierarchized deaf society, from the very beginning the organization defined itself as a fraternity: deaf women were not welcome.

4.3.10 LSF at the millennium

As the century marched on, numerous factors united to change the course of deaf education in France and elsewhere. The deaf movement as a political phenomenon proved all too human. Disagreement and fragmentation took their toll. As France bolted first to the left and then back to the right, deaf liberalism fell victim to the fray. The shifts from monarchy to republic to empire and back to republic left the deaf community in disarray. Atavistic biases sprang up anew. Evolving intellectual emphases tended to devalue mimicry as a valid or even desirable means of communication. Anthropology, in its probings and speculations concerning indigenous cultures, related gesture to primitivism (Baynton). Darwin's theory of natural selection did nothing to enhance the standing of the deaf; indeed, it was seen to support the taxonomy and praxis of medicalization; the abnormal strain was perceived as an aberration preserved by modern civilization rather than a product of the natural development of humankind. Eugenics, especially as understood by Alexander Graham Bell (whose father was an avowed oralist), branded the deaf as a pathological danger to the health and well-being of society (Mirzoeff 225).

The Third Republic, following the Franco-Prussian War and the Commune, prioritized reconstruction and reconsolidation, a reintegration of the various segments of society in the interest of the Nation. Policies affected all institutions, without exception. Education became mandatory, free, and secular. Deaf education, steeped in its Catholic origins, experienced a decisive reorientation. At the Milan Congress of 1880 it was mandated that henceforth in France and throughout Europe the deaf would be taught according to the oralist method, in the interest of integrating them as thoroughly as possible into their local and national communities. Only the delegation from the United States objected, to no avail. The deaf, as a first priority, would learn to speak. The congress adjourned with the cry "Vive la parole!"

Yet for all that, in France—as well as in Britain and the United States—Douglas Baynton writes:

> sign language continued to be used, and vigorously defended, by the deaf community. Deaf parents passed sign language on to their children, and those children who were deaf passed it on to their schoolmates. [. . .] Oral communication was too impractical for many deaf people, and sign language too cherished by the deaf community, for the latter to disappear completely. (94)

Nevertheless, oralism, as an official policy, would remain in place for nearly a hundred years and would be reinforced by the numerous medical and technical advances benefiting the hearing impaired. It took two congresses of the World Federation of the Deaf (Paris 1971 and Washington, D.C. 1975) to begin to turn matters around. The sign language that had persisted and evolved in France received the official designation Langue des Signes Française at the end of the 1970s. The advent of Cued Speech (developed by R. Orin Cornett in the United States in 1967) and its subsequent adoption as le Langage Parlé Complété (LPC) in France has virtually eliminated the uncertainties of lip reading. The European Parliament, at the end of the 1980s, passed a resolution supporting the teaching of sign language for the deaf and encouraging its financing (although it has as yet to recognize these languages as "minority languages"). The French education system has responded by making some accommodation for the deaf within its structure. On June 30, 1999, advocates joined together in a Marche Nationale des Sourds whose aim was official recognition of LSF as a "langue vivante" ([modern language]. The real goal, as Fabrice Bertin explains, is recognition of deaf culture:

> si aujourd'hui la L.S.F. est présente dans beaucoup d'établissements scolaires, elle n'est toujours pas respectée dans ses modalités propres. [. . .] Car la L.S.F. est rattachée à cette culture de façon importante. [. . .] Une langue n'est pas seulement un outil de communication, on ne peut ignorer les représentations qu'elle véhicule. (Bertin 2003)

What is needed for this culture to receive its due, according to Bertin, is a larger interpretation of the concept of integration that includes LSF as a living entity in the classroom, not a fragmenting mixture of French, LPC, and LSF. Unfortunately, in that respect, France has no Gallaudet University.

Bertin makes his point convincingly. National politics notwithstanding, LSF is now considered by linguists to be a "natural language"—alongside ASL, British Sign Language, and others. Universals no longer apply, of course, except perhaps in the sense of Chomsky's notion of universal grammar; each sign language has its own history and its own identity, as do spoken languages. Today LSF can boast numerous journals, dictionaries, grammars, and organizations devoted to its study and promotion. The late Paul Jouison picked up where Stokoe left off. Using videos, he studied LSF manualists and determined, as had his predecessor, that the head, the eyes, the upper torso, indeed the entire body, contribute holistically to the communication process. As a consequence, and based on the language as it exists today, he revived Bébian's concept of mimography and devised D'Sign, a system of graphic transcription that "writes" LSF body speak. Moreover, his *Ecrits sur la langue des signes française* (edited by Brigitte Garcia in 1998) provides an in-depth analysis both of the morphology and syntax of LSF as well as the "role of the body in the organization of gestural discourse." According to his determinations, LSF, as a language, has finally come of age.

5

From Jones to Martinet:
Language, Science, Nation

The final section of chapter eight of Michel Foucault's *Les mots et les choses* bears the heading "Le langage devenu objet." It is the culmination of Foucault's presentation of the opposition between the universalism that produced the *Grammaire générale* and the subsequent particularism that came to recognize individual, interrelated languages within discrete language families. These two phases, Foucault observes, are followed by a third phase, the "reification" of language: that is to say, the concept of language as "object" to be subjected to the rigors of scientific inquiry without regard for external factors. Each of these phases/strata supports, of course, a distinct conceptual mode germane to the history and development of linguistics: 1) the philosophy of language, 2) philology/comparative philology, 3) diachrony/synchrony. The third-phase reifying act, Foucault maintains, removes the "humane" from the "humane sciences": anthropology, ethnology, sociology, psychology, and so on, including linguistics. It is an isolating/extracting mechanism that treats a body of knowledge as independent from the very subjects from whom it derives. The result is both a dehumanization and a deculturation. Identifying dynamics and hierarchies are nullified and replaced by the egalitarian systemics of science that induce a state of parity. Henceforth not only are all sciences equal, but also equality reigns within each science. Thus, under the gaze of linguistic science, languages, dialects, patois, slang, and the like are democratized, so to speak, stripped of their non-linguistic attributes and pretensions, equally naked for all to see and to hear (Foucault 307–13).

5.1 France's linguistic narcissism

At the beginning of the nineteenth century, France's linguistic gaze was turned inward, narcissistically. The Revolution and its immediate successors sought to reinvigorate the French language, to standardize it and to consolidate it within its borders before exporting it once again as universal. Its future was seen to lie in a storied past that only needed to be reconstrued and reconfigured. The myth of Nation and its national idiom needed only to be rewritten. To this end Champollion's successful deciphering of the Rosetta Stone would be quickly promoted as evidence of the superiority of the French mind. The Duke of Orleans staked the following claim in April of 1823—in the name of France:

> La brillante découverte de l'alphabet hiéroglyphique est honorable non seulement pour le savant qui l'a faite, mais pour la Nation. Elle doit s'enorgueillir qu'un Français ait commencé à pénétrer ces mystères que les Anciens ne dévoilaient qu'à quelques adeptes bien éprouvés, et à déchiffrer ces emblèmes dont tous les peuples modernes désespéraient de découvrir la signification. (qtd. in Dewachter 1)

Despite this and other contributions, it would be decades before France would truly join an international community mesmerized by discoveries of a common linguistic past. When it did, it would have a great deal to offer. In the meantime Germany would seize the opportunity and would apply the knowledge gained to the elaboration of its own myth of Nation.

5.1.1 The Berlin Academy: Schwab and Rivarol

The 1782–1784 essay contest sponsored by the Berlin Academy of Sciences and Letters may be seen as a barometer of the state of linguistics at that point in history. In order to support French or another language as the rightful owner of or pretender to the title of "universal language of Europe," essayists were compelled to treat languages comparatively. Their findings could not have been more mixed. Whereas the dual prize-winners Schwab and Rivarol both predicted the French language would continue its reign, fully half of the entrants envisaged German in that position in the future (Storost 432–33). One might expect that, given the interest generated, the quality of the participants, and the prestige at stake, at least a trace of innovation would be found in the methods used to arrive at such a dichotomy of opinions—in other words at least a suggestion of the advent of historical linguistics to come. No such indication is to be found, however, for the reasons that Gerda Haßler underscores:

> L'utilisation des faits linguistiques dans une classification des peuples dépend nettement du but assigné à cette classification avant que ne s'engage la recherche empirique. [...] On est loin des méthodes d'une linguistique historico-comparative. Les jugements sur les langues et les explications de leurs différences n'étaient pas libres de stéréotypes et ces derniers ont une stabilité remarquable. (Haßler 38)

Thus, in spite of the general tenets outlined by Locke and Condillac, the goals of participants did not conform to the empirical imperatives that would come to dominate perspectives in the nineteenth century. Politics, religion, commerce, culture, fashion, agriculture, achievement in the arts, the sciences and industry, style, elegance and manners, geography, climate, all of these found a place as determinants in the contributions penned by the score of essayists. If these aspects might relate to philology in its broadest sense, they have nothing to do with linguistics as the discipline has come to be practiced. That is not to say that the essays were devoid of erudition. It is true that some of them contained rather silly notions and pronouncements, but others drew on an impressive breadth of knowledge and extensive research. Schwab's essay in particular has been deemed as an exemplary blend of the meticulous scholarship and acumen that would serve his countrymen so well the in the following century (Henry 2005). Two years later, in 1786, a pair of events would occur simultaneously that would change the course of German intellectual history and the history of linguistics: the death of Frederick the Great and the revelations of Sir William Jones.

5.1.2 Deconstructing the French paradigm

Schwab maintained that it was the civilizing process that had saved Europe from the marauding barbarians. Within that context, he insisted, the French language as vehicular idiom and the culture that produced and sustained it formed the nucleus of European identity. As such, both its language and its culture warranted recognition as universals and as guarantors.

Opponents in Germany, both inside Prussia and elsewhere, were at a loss to find compelling arguments to the contrary—as long as Frederick II remained as supreme arbiter of his Academy of Sciences. With his death in 1786, however, germanophiles seized control and quickly instituted German as the official language of the institution. The step was both a culmination and a beginning: the culmination of a phase of resistance and the beginning of the "linguistic construction of German identity," as Harold Mah writes in his essay "The Epistemology of the Sentence: Language, Civility, and Identity in France and Germany, Diderot to Nietzsche." Mah credits opponents such as Herder and Goethe with deconstructing the French paradigm and framing German epistemology: "Germans drew on the epistemological criticism of the French language both as dissembling rhetorical excess and dislocating abstract reason. On the epistemological locations where the legitimations of the French language collapsed Germans made their own assertions of identity" (73). Paramount in his argumentation is a quotation gleaned from Herder's travel journal to France (1769) in which the young German identifies the French speech act as a self-referential contortion of social performance:

> Whoever knows French in this way knows it in the depths of its nature, knows it as the art of shining and of pleasing in our present-day world, knows it as the logic of a whole way of life. Its turns of phrase, in particular, must be taken into account here. They are always twisted around: they never express what they say, but always form a relationship between the speaker and the one spoken to, and thus relegate the main issue to a subordinate position. The relationship itself becomes the principal concern—and is this not the etiquette of social intercourse? (qtd. in Mah 73)

Nearly thirty years later, Mah continues, Aurelie's condemnation of French as the language of elegant deceit in Goethe's *Wilhelm Meister's Apprenticeship* echoes the position and underscores Herder's notion of German as a language that maintains "a continuous direct connection to primary sense experience," whereas French relies on "second-order abstraction." The inversions native to German and decried by francophiles thus reflect the role of "brute perception" in arriving at "higher reason." Accordingly, they imbue the German language with an innate superiority that Fichte, in his *Addresses to the German Nation* beginning in 1807, would extol and would promote as political/cultural cohesive in the rising tide of German nationalism (Mah 75).

5.1.3 William Jones: the eighteenth-century context

Less directly but just as meaningfully, the second event of 1786 would shape Germany's self-perception and drive for self-determination. The search for origins that had generated so much speculation in the eighteenth century took a decisive turn in that year. In a series of discourses before the newly founded Asiatic Society of Calcutta, William Jones outlined mechanisms and objectives, staked out ethnological territories (the Indians, the Chinese, the Tartars, the Arabs, the Persians), and concluded with discourses devoted to each of these peoples. The third discourse focused on India and included the historic pronouncement on methodology that would shape philology far into the future. Jones approached problematics from the perspective of a comparative anthropologist. Empirical principles, he reasoned, could well be applied to etymology. In consequence, subsequent to the collection of verified data, hypotheses could be drawn, tested against the data, and probable affinities between various languages could be ascertained. Building on the phonological and morphological analyses of the Indian grammarian Panini and others, Jones established such a high incidence of similarities between Sanskrit and Greek that the only reasonable inference was a genetic connection (Cannon 241–45). His findings resound in the third discourse:

> The Sanskrit language, whatever its antiquity, is of a wonderful structure; more perfect than *Greek*; more copious than *Latin*, and more exquisitely refined than either, yet bearing to both a stronger affinity, both in the roots of verbs and in the forms of grammar, than could possibly have been produced by accident; so strong indeed, that no philologer could examine all three, without believing them to have sprung from some common source, which, perhaps, no longer exists; there is a similar reason, though not quite so forcible, for supposing that both the *Gothic* and the *Celtick*, though blended with a very different idiom, had the same origin with the *Sanskrit*, and the old *Persian* might be added to the family. (qtd. in Cannon 245)

The pronouncement contains, of course, the basic tenet of Indo-European comparative grammar. But as monumental as it appears today, its effects were not immediate. Jones presented his theories and observations over the decade stretching from 1784 until his death in 1794. His principal motivation involved promoting the study of Oriental cultures and languages. That objective met with quick response: interest in Sanskrit swelled as a consequence. Chairs in that language would become commonplace in universities around Europe and America in the early decades of the nineteenth century. But broader impact was slower in coming. When Denis Robelot sought to bring to the French a translation of Schwab's wonderfully documented essay, he added numerous notes of his own device to the 1803 work as well as a hefty appendix on the antiquity of the French language. None of Robelot's additions suggest acquaintance with the emerging theory. Indeed, Robelot repeats, willfully, common misconceptions in an attempt to bolster French resolve following the Revolution. Maintaining that *langue d'oc* and *langue d'oïl* were one and the same language in order to increase French cultural and linguistic prestige in the Middle Ages, for example, was an error Schwab had been careful to avoid. Yet such thinking must be considered within an eighteenth-century historical framework, as R. H. Robins reminds us:

> It is Jones's contemporary context, not in our contemporary context, that his linguistic work and his famous paragraph should be understood and evaluated. We must remember that historical etymology in the eighteenth century was still, as Jones remarked, "conjectural" [. . .] The achievement of a rigorous and therefore reliable discipline of lexical correspondences was the product of a succession of nineteenth-century linguists: Grimm, Pott, Schleicher, and finally the Juggrammatiker (Neogrammarians). (85–86)

5.1.4 Germany takes control

The list of names Robins evokes and a chronology that runs virtually to the end of the nineteenth century also remind us that if the Germans were Jones's most immediate beneficiaries, the process of distilling the theory and instituting the praxis was lengthy and involved (politically, culturally, and philosophically) on both sides of the Rhine. Rationalism, romanticism, mysticism, "Naturphilosophie," as well as the advent of Darwinism—framed by the search for identity and the arduous process of nation building—generated the volatile dynamics that have proved to be such a challenge for German historians. Ironically, in 1803 as Robelot's translation rolled off the Lamy presses, Friedrich von Schlegel arrived in Paris to study Sanskrit texts unavailable elsewhere. His experience there led him to coin the term "Vergleichende Grammatik" (comparative grammar) and to publish an important book on Indian language and culture, *Über die Sprache und Weisheit de Indier* (1808), in which (despite inaccuracies and some confusion) he outlined the task of unraveling the "genealogy of languages" (Pedersen 19). It was a Dane, however, that first had a clear vision of the great Indo-European language family. Rasmus Rask's work on Nordic languages and Zend-Avest expanded parameters linguistically and geographically. Yet Rask's vision, as broad and as governed by scientific principle as it was, lacked the historical underpinnings that would anchor the discipline. A major step in that direction was accomplished by Franz Bopp in 1816: the first comparative linguistic analysis of Sanskrit: *Über das Conjugationssystem der Sansskritsprache in Vergleichung mit jenem der griechischen, persischen und germanischen Sprache*. His later works, published between 1833 and 1852, firmly established historical Indo-European parentage. Bopp's perspective included only morphology, however. It was the second and subsequent editions of Jacob Grimm's *Deutche Grammatik* (1819, 1822, 1826, 1831, 1837) that provided the key to reconstructing languages of the past. Known as Grimm's Law, his formulation of the theory of sound shifts—which built on Rask's observations on consonant shifts in Germanic—identified phonologically correspondences between all the Germanic languages and dialects. Moreover, he explained the process of "umlaut" that characterizes the alteration of sounds induced by particular and predictable phonetic environments. Grimm thus provided a new barometer by which to gauge both the relationship and the antiquity of Germanic languages and dialects.

Phonology emerged, then, as the primary spectrum within which to examine languages of the past. August Pott's *Etymologische Forschungen auf dem Gebiete der indergermanischen Sprachen* (1833–1836) advanced understanding considerably. Pott provided both a comparative Indo-European grammar and a common Indo-European phonology that expanded Grimm's concept to include all the Indo-European languages. The numerous parallels Pott brought to light would serve as a basis for further investigation, but even he did not recognize the immutable regularity of the sound shift phenomenon. It would be several decades before scholars such as Georg Curtius, August Schleicher, and August Fick would sort out and substantiate the theory.

It is useful to pause here, however, to consider an element of Pott's title: "indergermanischen Sprachen." The origin and appropriateness of the term commonly used in German and Dutch has been long debated. It was thought to have originated in Julius von Klaproth's 1823 *Asia Polyglotta*. Bopp opposed its use, Pedersen informs us (262). In a 1981 study Fred R. Shapiro added important clarifications. First, Shapiro documented the initial use of "Indoeuropean" designating a language grouping as having appeared in 1813 in the *Quarterly Review*, penned anonymously by the English "physician and physicist" Thomas Young. His search for the origin of "Indo-Germanic" took him to French texts. He was rewarded when he located the phrase "family of the Indo-Germanic tongues" (Shapiro's translation, ostensibly "famille des langues indo-germaniques") in volume two of Conrad Malte-Brun's *Précis de la géographie universelle* (1810). According to this observation, "Indo-Germanic" predates "Indo-European" by at least three years. Moreover, since Malte-Brun was a Danish-French geographer and secretary of the Société de Géographie de Paris, Shapiro interprets the term "geographically," that is to say as representing an east to west longitudinal designation beginning with Sanskrit in the east and ending with Germanic in the west. Rather than crediting Malte-Brun with coining the term, Shapiro believes that it was already in use in geographical circles. It is important to emphasize that even though Malte-Brun failed to include several "Indo-Germanic" languages in his grouping, he excluded specifically the Semitic languages:

> Comme la plupart des nations qui parlent ces langues descendent, selon Moïse, de *Sem*, on a voulu désigner cette famille sous le nom général de *langues sémitiques*; on a également voulu donner aux langues indo-germaniques le nom de langues japhétiques. (qtd. in Shapiro 167)

Although the Biblical dichotomy referenced by Malte-Brun exhibited no undue ethnic overtones within the context of his geographical representation of the world's languages, that situation would change as Germany strove to write the history of its people and to define its place in nineteenth-century Europe. Soon the very notion of "indergermanischen Sprachen" would prove all too inviting for those whose designs exceeded the reconstruction of a linguistic past.

5.1.5 France: reconstruction and misconceptions

In France reaction to these multifarious developments ranged from fascination to misunderstanding to total disregard. The rebuilding of the early years of the nineteenth century called for new foundations. They were sought out on native soil in a cultural past that had been largely repudiated by Ancien Régime scriptors of patrimony. The Middle Ages, heretofore viewed as impervious, impetuous, indomitable, suddenly arose from the mist as a "vital metaphor." Jules Michelet would cast Jeanne d'Arc as the personification of the nation's will to sacrifice. Augustin Thierry, in the manner of Walter Scott, would add dialogue to history. The primary philological beneficiary was "la littérature d'oc, qu'on assimile globalement aujourd'hui à la poésie des troubadours, [qui] a été pendant très longtemps un trésor enseveli" (Saint-Gérand 1999b: 474). The dramatist/philologist largely responsible was François Raynouard (1761–1836). Known as the "father of Romance philology," he produced works that remain indispensable to the Old Provençal scholar today: an anthology of troubadour poetry (1816–1821), a dictionary and a comparative grammar—both published posthumously in a multi-volume opus, 1838–1844. His work was completed by his German successor Friedrich Diez, the pioneer of Romance linguistics, who published *Grammatik der romanischen Sprachen*, 1836–1843, and *Wörterbuch der romanischen Sprachen*, 1854 (Hall 234–35, Malmberg 435–39).

For all the linguistic acumen Raynouard brought to the study of Old Provençal, his understanding of the evolution of Indo-European languages was based on the faulty premise of the direct derivation involving Sanskrit, Greek, and Latin, a misconception, it is fair to add, that was shared by early German philologists. Misconceptions of another sort also enjoyed favor in France and elsewhere. The exuberance of the age of Romanticism and the desire to valorize the medieval period as the wellspring of national identity fostered fantasies that rivaled those avid that readers encountered in tales of chivalry. Some went so far as to posit the antiquity of Gaulois as parent of the vernacular of invading Roman soldiers. Diez himself fell prey to temptation. In a 1980 study Aldo Manichetti characterized the pitfalls to which he and others were subject. Diez, he observed, was seduced by the myth of the "people as creator" that led him to portray the art of the troubadours as "primitive, spontaneous, and relatively simple in form." When other philologists discovered that, to the contrary, the works in question exhibited an unsuspected "stylized sophistication and refinement," they were induced to suppose that there must exist an earlier, more basic form, a popular "roman" from which the later versions were drawn. Such wishful thinking did little to advance the science of language (Manichetti 52–53).

5.2 France: science, hegemony, and learned societies

None of this should detract from the persistence of intellectual activity in France following the Revolution. Indeed, with the restructurings that created the National Institute and the National Museum of Natural History and revitalized research already underway at the newly named Jardin des Plantes, France was poised to lead the way in the "natural sciences." The heirs of Buffon and Linneus—Lacépède, Lamarck, Geoffroy Saint-Hilaire, Cuvier, Gay-Lussac, Thenard, Arago, Jussieu, Mirbel, Chevreul, among others—forged ahead in areas as diverse as geology, paleontology, botany, biology, physics, chemistry, and astronomy, supported by a mechanism of dissemination that made findings accessible (in French) throughout the scientific world: the widely read proceedings of the various units of the Institute. What is more, an institutionalized intellectual fervor seized the country as a whole and fostered an unprecedented spike in the formation of local and provincial learned societies. Jean-Pierre Chaline's *Sociabilité et érudition: les sociétés savantes en France, XIXe–XXe siècles* provides an essential overview of a phenomenon common to several European countries of the nineteenth century but which acquired special status in France.

Learned societies modeled on the French Academy had sprung up across France during the Ancien Régime. For the year 1789 Chaline lists thirty-seven provincial academies and a total of between sixty and one hundred learned societies of various descriptions: medical, agricultural, and literary societies, for instance, a dozen of which held forth in Paris. The Law of August 8, 1793, ardently pursued by Marat, suppressed all such societies and stipulated the confiscation of their holdings. Three years of turmoil and readjustment later, the Constitution of 5 Fructador of the year III (22 August 1795) reinstated the citizens' right to found and administer organizations promoting progress in the sciences and the arts. Two months later the Institut National des Sciences et des Arts received official approval. By 1799 the number of societies had climbed back to fifty, a dozen or so located in Paris. The number continued to expand into the new century. In 1810 the Empire imposed its will and, by means of article 291 of the Penal Code, mandated that no group larger than twenty members could be formed or operate without the express permission of and according to the conditions specified by the government. Henceforth, what had been a tendency to align with the central authority for monetary support and official recognition became the standard that would persist across the decades even as laws were relaxed. Truly independent organizations fought desperately to sustain themselves, but—more often than not—fell victim to financial shortfall or political maneuverings. Centripetal force would thus prove to be a national determinant in the intellectual and scientific arenas in France throughout the nineteenth century and well into the twentieth century. Directly in some instances but most often indirectly by means of a finely tuned system of rewards, the country's homogenizing faculty would shape—according to national interests—projects undertaken if not results achieved (Crosland). The "conspiracy of silence" in reaction to Darwinism is but one case in point (Conry, Henry 1999).

Chaline's statistics reveal, however, that government regulation did little to slow the growth of learned societies. The numbers rose significantly decade after decade, in good times and in bad: 1810: 100 societies, 17 in Paris; 1820: 130 societies, some 20 in Paris; 1830: 160 societies, 35 in Paris; 1846: 310 societies, some 50 in Paris. By 1869, and despite the repression of the Second Empire, the number of societies had grown to 470 (76 in Paris); by 1885, the numbers were 680 societies (120 in Paris), and by the turn of the century 758 societies (130 in Paris). (These figures exclude the five national Academies, the "fifth class" [Les Sciences Morales et Politiques] having been reinstated in 1846.) It is abundantly clear from this accounting that public interest in intellectual matters increased as more and more French gained access to the expanding education system. It is equally clear that such growth placed budgetary constraints on the government and produced greater and greater competition for available funds. Consequently, individual societies were moved to seek special status and curry favor, a point to keep in mind with regard to the politics of these institutions across the century.

Another aspect to keep in mind involves the evolving character of the societies themselves. Under the Ancien Régime and well into the Restoration, societies formed around general interests, be they agricultural, commercial, literary, or scientific. As the century progressed they became increasingly specialized, reflecting both the expertise needed as disciplines acquired greater sophistication and the narrowing focus that would cause them to divide and subdivide. Chaline indicates for instance that the number of newly established societies devoted to pharmaceutics and medicine declined after the July Monarchy owing to mutations within the sciences—the emergence of toxicology, psychiatrics, and the like, for example, and the formation of societies related to them.

5.2.1 The original linguistic societies of Paris

Thus what is reportedly the world's first linguistic society came into being within the context of narrowing intellectual perspectives. That particular society, erroneously identified by Joseph Vendryes in 1955, Emile Beneviste in 1971, and others as the Société de Linguistique de Paris established in the 1860s (which turns out to be the third such society), was actually founded in 1837, predating its famous descendant by nearly thirty years. This stirring discovery is owed to Sylvain Auroux who published his findings in *Historiographia Linguistica* in 1983. Auroux's study confirms the society's existence and provides pertinent information concerning the circumstances into which it was born and the legacy it fostered. In reality nineteenth-century France had witnessed the advent of various language-related societies as early as 1804. The Académie Celtique, founded in that year, sought to explore the country's Gaulois origins, including inscriptions and other philological materials. Inherited from the eighteenth century, the newly reconstituted Académie Grammaticale (1807) turned its attention to "the science of ideas and the science of words." Nearly forty years after the initiation of Jones's Asiatic Society in Calcutta (1783), Europe's first such organization appeared as the Société Asiatique de Paris in 1821. It attracted an impressive international membership: Antoine-Isaac Silvestre de Sacy, Jean Pierre Abel Rémusat, Charles Wilkins, Thomas Colebrook, Julius Klaproth, the Humboldt brothers, Franz Bopp, August Wilhelm Schlegel (Auroux 244). Numerous language journals sprang up as well and either disappeared or evolved in response to changing exigencies and emphases. One of those journals, the *Journal de la Langue Française*, associated with the Société Grammaticale, published in 1837 the following announcement:

> Une société de grammairiens et de linguistes vient d'être constituée sous le titre d'*Institut des Langues*. Nous sommes heureux de pouvoir annoncer à nos lecteurs que le *Journal de la Langue Française* publiera les travaux les plus importants de cette société. (qtd. in Auroux 242)

The society, which would acquire the title Société de Linguistique in 1839, listed as an essential function the examination of "les ouvrages de *linguistique* qui lui sont remis" (emphasis Auroux). Its initial bylaws included a prohibition that would be reiterated thirty years later: "Toute lecture et toute discussion étrangères à la science qui est le but des travaux de l'Institut des Langues sont formellement interdites." Its first president, the author of the series "Introduction aux notions élémentaires de linguistique" published in *Le Temps*, was none other than Charles Nodier. Its adherents included honorary members Grimm and Bopp, as well as Eugène Burnouf (Chair in Sanskrit at the Collège de France) and the comparative grammarian Charles Hase (although none of them contributed studies). Despite these considerable assets, as Auroux has determined, the society soon fell victim to infighting, financial stress, and—especially—ill timing: neither public interest nor the state of "linguistic science" in France was of such magnitude to support the first linguistic society of Paris beyond 1840.

The second linguistic society of Paris came into being some fifteen years later in the mid-1850s. Known as the Société Internationale de Linguistique, it persisted until 1860 when it too fell victim to financial woes. If the prohibition of the former society would prove to be a harbinger for its third version, so too would the emphases of the second; for its structure provided for a "Comité de la Langue Universelle." Louis Couturat and Léopold Leau have outlined the society's program in their invaluable *Histoire de la langue universelle*. They quote the organization's statement of purpose as containing the following: in addition to examining all matters "qui se rattachent à la philologie et à la linguistique considérées dans leur plus grande extension," the society proposed to actively pursue "une réforme plus ou moins radicale de l'orthographe" and to

> répandre dans les esprits l'idée d'une langue universelle, dont le besoin commence à se faire généralement sentir, de chercher les bases de cette langue, d'en définir les conditions, d'en grouper les éléments, et de préparer les voies à son établissement. (Couturat and Leau 71)

The Committee itself was charged with formulating the theory governing the creation of a universal language, whether it should be an a priori language or an a posteriori language and, in the latter case, which extant languages might be called upon to contribute. Having rejected any and all a posteriori languages, the Committee opted for an ideal "langue philosophique" and set about studying the various philosophical language schemes that had been devised since the seventeenth century. Ultimately, those of Letellier and Sotos Ochando attained the rank of finalists. The Committee opted for the Sotos Ochando version, finding it more attuned to the theory advanced by Le Mesl which it had adopted as its own (Couturat and Leau 71–76). Of course nothing came of the project; the society and its Committee soon disappeared leaving behind little to show for their efforts. But for framers of its successor there were lessons to be drawn.

5.2.2 Article 2 of the 1865 Society: language origins and universal language schemes

Virtually every scholar who has written about the institutional history of the French language or about the history of linguistics as it relates to France has found the opportunity, however contrived, to cite Article 2 of the original statutes of the (third) Société de Linguistique de Paris. The Society, which had been in the planning stages since 1863, was formally constituted in 1865 and its statutes approved by ministerial decree March 8, 1866. Article 1 of the statutes, published in the first pages of volume 1 (27 March 1869) of its now famous journal, *Bulletin de la Société de Linguistique de Paris*, reads as follows:

> Article premier.—La Société de Linguistique a pour but l'étude des langues, celle des légendes, traditions, coutumes, documents, pouvant éclairer la science ethnographique. Tout autre objet d'études est rigoureusement interdit.

The breadth of the discipline so defined exceeds the boundaries of modern linguistics (including sociolinguistics), to be sure. The debt to the philological/anthropological tradition that had emerged from the eighteenth century finds ample expression in the concept of "ethnographic science." Yet that tradition, in the view of the Society's framers, should not be all accommodating. Article 2 listed two distinct prohibitions:

> Article 2.—La Société n'admet aucune communication concernant, soit l'origine du langage, soit la création d'une langue universelle.

From the very beginning the Society's commitment to empiricism steered it away from the speculative and prescriptive emphases of the past. The abundance of theories relating to language origins (none of them provable) and the numerous universal language schemes being devised at home and abroad (including the versions created by L'Epée and Sicard) made it imperative, the founders believed, that the Society avoid filling its meetings and the pages of its bulletin with conjecture and improbable invention. This no-nonsense attitude, which would be maintained over the decades in spite of pressures to compromise, served to create a solid foundation for linguistic studies that would influence and attract serious minded researchers from around the world, including Ferdinand de Saussure. The late Gordon Winant Hewes provided an orienting perspective in the foreword to his indispensable two-volume *Language Origins: A Bibliography* he published in the 1970s:

> This bibliography of about 11,000 items is intended to cover all works on the origins of language, and related topics, to the middle of 1972. The literature on this subject is scattered through many disciplines besides linguistics, including psychology, anthropology, philosophy, speech pathology, animal communication behavior, anatomy of the larynx, and anatomy and neurophysiology of the brain. Although there are many references from the field of linguistics, it is well known that modern linguistic scholars have tended to avoid speculation about language origins, in the spirit of the rule adopted by the 1866 Société de Linguistique de Paris. The effect of this taboo was never complete, especially in German-speaking lands, where publications on the origin of language came out regularly during the period when glottogenesis was an unfashionable subject in France, Great Britain, and the United States. Quite recently, serious interest in the problem of language origins has been revived.

Indeed, although this area of investigation has never completely overcome its speculative proclivities (witness such outpourings as Derrida's 1967 *De la grammatologie* and Eric Gans's 1981 *The Origin of Language* [origin qua violence], among numerous others), the discovery of DNA and other scientific advances have brought new light to the search for origins. The Language Origins Society and its journal (*LOS Forum*) contribute annually to the stock of scientifically validated research; and the post-structuralist return of diachrony to academe has spurred related studies, Oxford's recent (2003) broad-spectrum collection of essays, *Language Evolution* (edited by Morten H. Christiansen and Simon Kirby), for instance.[1]

5.2.3 Language origins: competing paradigms from Cuvier to Pictet

Hewes's reference to the "glottogenesis" of "German-speaking lands" is particularly relevant to the concern Article 2 expresses. As recognizably elucidating as German contributions were, cultural/intellectual relations between

---

[1] Many thanks to Bernard H. Bichakjan, editor of *LOS Forum*, for his assistance in tracking down material pertaining to the famous Society and for pointing out Jean Perrot's review article in volume 59.2 (1964) of the *Bulletin de la Société Linguistique de Paris*.

France and Germany had been antagonistic for many years; and now other differences were on the verge of being politicized to the point of belligerence. The antagonism dated back at least to the controversial 1830 Cuvier-Geoffroy Saint-Hilaire debate on pre-Darwin transformism before the Academy of Sciences in Paris. Cuvier, the conservative (if somewhat misguided) defender of empiricism squared off against the Lamarckian-fueled chain of life "speculations" of Geoffroy. German interest was manifest in the presence of the sometime naturalist Johann Wolfgang Goethe who supported Geoffroy and progress in the sciences in two articles penned for the German press. Cuvier and his supporters did not fail to associate Geoffroy's theory with the quasi-mystical *Naturphilosophie* and its proponents from across the Rhine: Meckel, Oken, Spix, Bojanus, Carus. Such thinking, they insisted, inferred spontaneous generation and aligned itself not only in opposition to empirical science but also to the teachings of the Church (Corsi 242–49, Henry 2007).

More recent language-related developments gave further pause to the architects of Paris's latest linguistic society. Since the 1830s August Comte's formulation of "positivist principles" had institutionalized empiricism as the sole means to progress in the sciences. Government support depended increasingly on adherence to that model. Comte's theory of language, published within his sweeping four-volume 1852 elaboration of the systemics of scientism (*Système de politique positive instituant la religion de l'humanité*), defined language "biologically" as a "natural" phenomenon and thus legitimized "linguistics" as a science (Delesalle and Chevalier: Chapter 3). How to make the Society fit the mold was a subject of debate. That process would require modification and accommodation as the years passed and as new developments in the field came to light. Tradition held forth in that the French language itself was never challenged as appropriate vehicle of dissemination. From the outset, however, it was agreed that the Society should be spared occurrences the likes of the divisive Cuvier-Geoffroy confrontations and the polarizing chauvinism that "romantic folk theory" had fostered in Germany and that had found twisted (anti-Semitic) favor in France in Gobineau's *Essai sur l'inégalité des races humaines* (1853–1855)—not to mention an unexpected measure of acceptance in the views of Ernest Renan, a respected member of the Institut and future president of the Society. The very paradigm of linguistics as science was seen as being exploited to questionable, teleological ends. Max Müller, who viewed speech as a divine gift, divided languages according to race and, based on findings he believed in good conscience to be accurate, expounded a so-called "scientific" version of the Aryan myth. Other renditions appeared much less innocent. The religiously inspired theory of monogenesis according to which Hebrew was the matrix language had been brought into disrepute by Jones's findings. The formal separation of Semitic and Indo-European into discrete language groups provided fodder for other causes. Léon Poliakov, in his stirring account, *The Aryan Myth: A History of Racist Ideas in Europe*, cites a frighteningly ominous passage from the Swiss philologist Adolphe Pictet's *Les origines indo-européennes ou les Ayras primitifs: essai de paléontologie linguistique* (1859):

> This was the race of the Aryas, who were endowed from the beginning with the very qualities which the Hebrews lacked, to become the civilizers of the world; and nowhere does the evidence for a providential plan emerge more clearly than in the parallel courses of these two contrasting streams, one of which was destined to absorb the other. The difference between the two races could not be more marked.... The religion of Christ, destined to be the torch of humanity, was adopted by the genius of Greece and propagated by the power of Rome, while Germanic energy gave it new strength, and the whole race of European Aryas, under its beneficent influence, and by means of endless conflict, raised itself little by little to the level of modern civilization... It is thus that Aryas, more favoured than any other, was to become the main instrument of God's plan for the destiny of mankind. (qtd. in Poliakov 260)

Umberto Eco quotes another telling passage from Pictet's work. The question it poses would be not answered until the following century.

> Is it not perhaps curious to see the Aryas of Europe, after a separation of four or five thousand years, close the circle once again, reach their unknown brothers in India, dominate them, bring to them the elements of a superior civilization, and then to find ancient evidence of a common origin? (qtd. in Eco 106)

Ideology and linguistics commingle here in another, strangely ironic fashion. Pictet was the first to serve as mentor for the young Saussure (1857–1913). At the age of fifteen the young man who would be largely responsible for paring philology from linguistic science in the twentieth century sent his first essays to the aging philologist. He would later (1878) publish a series of articles on Pictet's theories in the *Journal de Genève*. By that time his youthful admiration had been tempered by broader study. Yet if he was moved to question the motives of Pictet's Aryanism, he had not yet discarded the commonly held notion of a "mother tongue" (perhaps Sanskrit) nor the anthropological emphases of his own early work. Indeed, as Maurice Olender astutely observes, it would be "some thirty years later, when Saussure offered his 'Course in General Linguistics,'" that he would point out "how misleading it was to base prehistoric anthropology on the reconstruction of a lost language" (100–01).

5.2.4 Darwin and Schleicher

Other concerns guided the drafting of the Society's regulations. Darwin's *Origin of Species* (1859) as translated by Clémence Royer in 1862 (under the altered title *De l'origine des espèces, ou des lois du progrès chez les êtres organisés*) transformed the treatise into a theory of social Darwinism before it could be judged on its scientific merits. Royer, the first woman member of the Paris Anthropological Society, translated "natural selection" as "élection naturelle." Scientists scoffed and French officialdom viewed the work as a potential incentive to social upheaval (Henry 1999: 298, Clark). It is little wonder, then, that the theories of August Schleicher, the linguist who unabashedly claimed Darwinism as the means of unraveling the language origin and evolution enigma, should deepen the Society's resolve to exclude such questions from its proceedings.

Schleicher (1821–1868) entered the linguistics arena as a polyglot and a trained botanist. He perceived language as a living organism subject to the principles of biological science and evolutionary theory. Accordingly, inquiry in the science of linguistics, which he called "glottic," should be conducted exactly as in the natural sciences. If his approach seems to attune him to basic Comtean precepts, his theory submits, to the contrary, that that the evolution of language took place in prehistoric times, whereas historical times have been witness only to linguistic decay—meaning that language development reached its pinnacle with Sanskrit, Greek, and Latin (Pedersen 242, Malmberg 301). Schleicher's principal work, *Compendium der vergleichenden Grammatik der indo-germanischen Sprachen* (1861–1862), has the special merit of devising a method of phonetic and morphological reconstruction. His postulation of hypothetical (non-documented) forms bridges gaps that would otherwise thwart historical linguists in their attempt to follow the language trail into the distant past. For all that, Schleicher's unbridled enthusiasm raised eyebrows in

France. The Darwinian theory of linguistics he published in pamphlet form in 1863 (*Die darwinsche Theorie und die Sprachwissenschaft*) met the same incredulity that Darwin himself had encountered. Furthermore, his claim to have reconstituted proto-indo-European to the point of being able to compose tales in it provoked justifiable skepticism. As Malmberg rightly observes, Schleicher could not prove that the words he used and their particular form co-existed at any given moment in time (301–03). Moreover, Schleicher's notion that the acquisition of a foreign language could genetically alter physical traits as well as the physiology of the brain equated language and race/ethnicity in a way that served as a further deterrent to the Society's founders.

5.2.5 The statutes revised: William Whitney and language origins

If Article 2 seems very much a credit to the Society in terms of the principles of scientific inquiry, the prohibitions did not fail to produce controversy both within the Society and in the intellectual community at large. At the meeting of April 24, 1869, a proposal sponsored by a founding member named Difriche-Desgenettes asked that Article 2 be rescinded because he could not recall its formal adoption by the constituting committee. No action could be taken at the time because the committee to which the proposal was directed was charged with revising rules and regulations rather than the Society's statutes. The matter might have been resolved sooner had history not intervened: the Franco-Prussian War, the Commune, and the advent of the Third Republic. It was not until 1875 that the Society would address the question within the broader context of revising its statutes for approval by the new government. In the interim the Society had rethought and refined its objectives in light of new scientific developments in linguistics. Article 1 was refocused to exclude reference to legends, traditions, customs, and ethnographic science. (Moreover, other associations had been created to examine such areas of inquiry.)[2] The revised article read simply, as recorded in

---

[2] Gabriel Bergounioux published a meticulous account of the year to year activities, membership, emphases, and tribulations of the Society in sequel articles in the *Bulletin*: "Aux origines de la Société de Linguistique de Paris (1864–1876)" in 1996 and "La Société de Linguistique de Paris (1876–1914)" in 1997. The first article is especially insightful with regard to the Society's early efforts to determine its particular identity and to stake out its territory in a period of intellectual fervor and realignment in the scientific community.

the *Bulletin*: "La Société de Linguistique a pour objet l'étude des langues et l'histoire du langage. Tout autre sujet d'études est rigoureusement interdit" (15: 1875–76, lxxxi). As for Article 2, it had disappeared completely. Three years later, in his minutes of the meeting of December 21, 1878 (*Bulletin* 18: 1878, 95), Michel Bréal (the German-trained mythologist who taught comparative grammar at the Collège de France and whose theory of semantics would gain universal recognition in 1897) explained the fate of Article 2. It had fallen victim to criticism from the international community. Bréal began by praising the Society's reputation abroad acquired by means of its strict adherence to scientific principle.

> Mais si [...] nous avons pu rayonner au loin, jusqu'au point de recueillir à l'étranger des éloges que nous n'aurions jamais ambitionnés, cela vient de ce que nous aimons notre science pour elle-même, et de ce que nous en disons sans prétention, toujours prêts à nous instruire, à écouter la contradiction et à profiter des conseils.

He then elaborated on the elimination of Article 2:

> Un savant de l'autre côté de l'Atlantique nous a reproché un jour l'article de nos statuts qui interdisait la discussion sur l'origine du langage et sur la création d'une langue universelle. Nous avons laissé dire, quoique les motifs que nous attribuait M. Whitney ne fussent pas ceux qui avaient suggéré aux premiers fondateurs de la société l'idée de cette défense. Plus tard l'article en question a disparu de nos statuts, sans que pour cela les discussions sur les deux sujets, autrefois interdits, désormais permis, fussent venues envahir nos séances. C'est la preuve qu'un même esprit anime aujourd'hui notre société, qui ne veut pas des théories ambitieuses et des creuses généralisations dont la linguistique, à une autre époque, a été si prodigue.

So the decision to excise Article 2 produced no procedural effect whatsoever: the prohibition of discussions of language origins and universal languages remained intact as a de facto, rather than a statutory policy. The excision, then, was a matter of diplomatic maneuvering in the interest of fostering cooperation within the international scientific community. Indeed, Bréal's minutes conclude by inviting "les autres nations, et particulièrement l'Angleterre, à continuer de marcher avec nous dans cette voie où il y a place pour tous les travailleurs de bonne volonté."

William Whitney, it is obvious, fell into the category of scholars of "good will," despite his philosophical differences with the Society. Whitney, the brilliant Yale linguist who had studied both in the U.S. and in Germany, had been in correspondence with European scholars on questions pertaining to his preparation of a Sanskrit grammar. It was in fact he that Bréal identifies as the "savant de l'autre côté de l'Atlantique." Whitney, finding his own interests at variance with the Society's original statutes, first addressed the measure in the April 23rd 1868 issue of *The Nation*. "We have just received the first volume issued since the beginning of the year, of the Memoirs put forth by the Linguistic Society of Paris," he wrote.

> This new society, founded but two or three years ago, but numbering among its fourscore members some of whose names are well known all over the world. Its organization presents one peculiar feature. By its constitution, it "admits no communication concerning either the origin of language or the creation of a universal language." Here, it seems to us, is a very odd confusion of two heterogeneous matters under a common condemnation. (147)

Whitney dismissed the creation of universal languages as "utopian" and worthy of scientific reproof. But as for the language origins prohibition he voiced poignant opposition:

> What should justify such an association in setting an arbitrary limit to its researches among the past phases of human speech by declaring that it will allow no account to be taken of the earliest phase is more than we can discover. [...] There can be no denying that the origin of language is a perfectly legitimate scientific question, and one which even thrusts itself upon the attention of every profound linguistic student. (147)

He admitted that the question had generated much "windy debate" and a "vast deal of trash and nonsense" owing to a misunderstanding of history and the "nature of speech." But much had been learned in recent years and the Society, given its eminence, should lead the way. "We should, then, expect of a Parisian 'Société de Linguistique' that it would do all in its power to remedy this unfortunate condition of affairs by setting an example of discussion on the right basis and the right spirit" (147).

As an afterthought, unwittingly perhaps, Whitney compared the question to the turmoil Darwinism was causing in scientific circles. In fact the French scientific establishment was responding to both in exactly the same fashion—by turning its back, officially, institutionally—on theoretical speculation. As for individual Society members who might express other opinions, they were free to do so outside the parameters of the association, a fact Whitney did not fail to recognize in a subsequent article published in *Transactions of the American Philological Association* (1:1869–70). "This has given the whole question a bad repute among sober-minded philologists," he regretted. "The prohibition, however, has not worked very well; for there is no similar society a larger part of whose members have rushed into print upon the subject before the general public" (84).

Whitney could not have been more accurate in his accusation. Language origins figure prominently in the publications of several members of the Society. First and foremost, Ernest Renan—second president of the Society and known as the anti-Christ to conservative Catholics for his *Vie de Jésus* (1863)—had published *De l'origine du langage* in 1858. Léon Gautier, at the opposite end of the spectrum, had brought out his *Essai d'une théorie catholique sur l'origine du langage* the same year. In 1857 a similar study had been produced by Emile Littré: *De la civilisation et du monothéisme chez les peuples sémitiques*. Louis Benloew's *De quelques caractères du langage primitif* appeared in 1863. Bréal's own *Les idées latentes du langage* went to press in 1869 and his later (1897) *Essai de sémantique* dismisses altogether the ability to determine the origin of significations. Language origins and natural or gestural languages were also the topic of books by both Yves-Léonard Valade and Léon Vaïsse in the 1850s and 1860s. As for Whitney's request that these members hash out their differences in formal session in the interest of science, the enormous disparity of approaches reflected in the titles cited serve as an obvious, and lethal impediment.

The Society acted according to its needs and the requirements of a government that sanctioned and funded scientific organizations only if they were viewed as non-divisive and a credit to the Nation. Its continued good standing in the eyes of the Institut was essential to its success and durability (Crosland). Consultation of reports and minutes of early sessions underscores the care the Society took to establish and maintain legitimacy. The Society's first three presidents also held seats at the Institut: Egger (1866), Renan (1867), Brunet de Presle (1868). Of the thirty-seven new members recruited for 1868 (which increased membership to one hundred nineteen), two (Littré and Maury) belonged to the Institut, two (Pierron and Gautier) had been recognized as laureates by the Institut, and Wladimir de Schoenfeld presided as secretary general of the Botanical Society of France. The balance sheet of 19 December 1868 (*Bulletin* 1: 22) reports that the Society had remained solvent by only 402 francs 80 centimes. The figure is followed by a request to the Executive Committee to do all in its power to collect back dues and by the recognition of the potential danger such arrears posed for new organizations: "L'amoindrissement graduel du capital annuel fourni par les cotisations est l'obstacle contre lequel ont trop souvent sombré des sociétés naissantes." In order to keep from going under, efforts were increased to secure other funding. Modest success was reported for the following year: for 1869 the Ministry of Public Education awarded the Society 400 francs.

5.3 Universal language schemes: the history

The minutes of the Society's initial meetings contain repeated reference to discussions of the perceived boundaries of philology and linguistics. The very topics addressed indicate an interrelationship that would require time and reflection to dissolve. It is clear, however, that the Society embraced the egalitarian status of all "natural" languages. The following array of titles is listed in the *Bulletin*'s pages as having been presented between 1867 and 1869: "Le pronom dans la langue Maya-Quiché"; "Les lettres aspirées en Sanskrit, en grec et en latin"; "La légende de Gargantua"; "Le mythe de Prométhée dans le Macklembourg"; "Sur la définition de quelques termes mathématiques dans le Dictionnaire de M. Littré"; "Traduction du mémoire de Georg Curtius: *Zur Chronologie der indo-germanischen Sprachforschung*." This last title reveals that from the very beginning the prohibition pertaining to language origins did not prevent the Society from discussing paleolinguistic topics relating to verifiable linguistic developments such as the well-documented existence of Indo-European. As for the origin and nature of the very first language there is nary a trace in the proceedings. Nor is there discussion of any universal language scheme. In fact, despite the eradication of Article 2, the Society was still holding firm on that commitment through the end of the century (1899) when it refused categorically a request to consider Leon Bollack's *Langue Bleue*, the last to be proposed in a series of "mixed system" language projects (Pei 1958: 156).

The Society did well to avoid the temptation. Not only was there Whitney's admonition to take into account; the sheer number of language schemes and the maneuverings of proponents in their attempts to gain advantage and recognition have filled countless pages. Indeed, Couturat and Leau's 1979 history of universal languages numbers 576 pages and lists seventeen a priori systems, twelve mixed systems, and twenty-six a posteriori systems. That is to say fifty-five of them in all, forty-four of them dating from the nineteenth century, and thirty-five of them dating from the period 1860 to 1899—the years following the demise of the second Linguistic Society of Paris and its Universal Language Committee.[3] These were also the formative years of Esperanto and Volapük, two rival systems that would vie internationally for ascendancy. In France, the situation was further complicated both by the intransigent notion of French as universal language and by the notoriety of an unlikely yet formidable home-grown product: Jean-François Sudre's Solrésol (*langue musicale universelle*).

The concept of polygraphy or the "universal sign" is of course an ancient one. Historians often view the genesis of Egyptian hieroglyphics and Chinese ideographic writing in this way. The extensive production of both scholarly and popular accounts continues to increase in our day. In 1929 Petr E. Stojan produced a bibliography (written in Esperanto and using broader criteria than Couturat and Leau) that lists three hundred twenty-one attempts to formulate a solution to the world's language problems over the centuries. In an internet publication copyrighted between 1992 and 1997, Richard K. Harrison updated earlier tabulations to account for "planned languages" devised in the twentieth century and writings relating to them. Salient English-language titles that have appeared over the last half century include: *Philosophical Languages in the Seventeenth Century* (Jaap Maat, 2004); *The Dream of an Absolute Language* (Lynn R. Wilkinson, 1996); *The Search for the Perfect language* (Umberto Eco, 1995); *The Languages of Paradise* (Maurice Olender, 1992); *Lunatic Lovers of Language* (Marina Yaguello, 1991); *Universal Language Schemes in England and France 1600–1800* (James Knowlson, 1975); and *One Language for the World* (Mario Pei, 1958).

The history of universal language schemes originates in the seventeenth century. As noted in Chapter Two, Descartes's 1629 letter to Mersenne

---

[3] The newly formed Society also declined to embrace its predecessor's program of orthographic reform; in the coming years it would systematically reject government requests to undertake prescriptive projects.

is often cited as a point of departure. Serious efforts in this vein emanate from northern latitudes. An early theory for creating a universal language in which to communicate thought and philosophy was laid down by the Scot Thomas Urquhart in his *Ekskubalouron* (1652) and *Logopandecteison, or, an introduction to the universal language* (1653). Urquhart, using Aristotle and emerging botanical taxonomy as guides, suggested categorizing words according to subject groups. He regretted that, despite the oft-lamented difficulties of communication inherent in natural languages, "hath none hitherto considered of a mark, whereby words of the same Faculty, Art, Trade, or Science should be diagnosed from those of another by the very sound of the word at the first hearing (qtd. in Knowlson 73–74). This goal served as motivation for those who followed. Another Scot, George Dalgarno, soon answered the challenge. He claimed to have produced the language the world awaited: a new, artificial philosophical language for both writing and speaking. The title page of his *Ars Signorum, Vulgo Character Universalis et Lingua Philosophica* (1661) boldly asserts that after only two weeks of study the language of his invention would allow speakers to communicate as effectively as in their native tongue (Maat 32–33). His scheme featured a logical classi-fication of ideas into seventeen primary classes represented by the letters of the Greek alphabet, with Greek vowels providing subcases. Thus, for example, words beginning with the following letters denote the respective cognitive classes: G- (sensorial) T- (intellectual), N- (physical), K- (political). Subcases for all classes conform to the following paradigm: K epsilon (judicial affairs), K upsilon (crimes), K omicron (role of judge), and so on (Couturat and Leau 15–18). Dalgarno's announced time frame proved to be quite unrealistic. Mastering his scheme within a short period would require a phenomenal memory, an obvious impediment to most a priori universal language projects. Maat has delineated other shortcomings as well: the confusing similarity of "radical words," the meager grammatical apparatus, the extravagance of claims that his language was the perfect introduction to philosophy, among others (130–31).

Seven years later the Bishop of Chester and one of the founders of the Royal Society of London, John Wilkins (1614-1672), produced a highly developed system in the form of a work titled *An Essay towards a Real Character and a Philosophical Language*. Published by the Royal Society in 1668 after much of the original manuscript had to be reproduced owing to the great London fire, Wilkins's six hundred folio opus contains an extensive section classifying English words according to their "referentiality," a section on "natural grammar," a binary taxonomy differentiating between "real character" symbols and "philosophical language," as well as a lengthy lexical conversion guide for translating English words into both character and language. It was in a very real sense a collaborative effort: cohorts with expertise in the biological sciences and lexicography produced tables on plants, animals, and the conversion guide/dictionary (Maat 135).

If as a founding premise Wilkins relies on Biblical accounts for the explanation of language origins, that belief does not find its way into the scheme itself. Nor does any "natural language" benefit from privileged status. He sees defects in need of correction in all extant languages. Consequently, he is able to proceed "logically" and "objectively" in his presentations. The resulting system builds on Dalgarno's. The "logical" classification of ideas in forty categories is actualized by consonant and vowel tandems: Dx (God), Da (the world), De (the elements), Di (stone[s]), Do (metals); Gx (plants), Ga (flowers), Ge (fruit), and so on. The third letter introduces differentiation. De, for example, signifies "element"; Deb signifies "fire." The fourth letter differentiates further: Deb$x$ signifies first "species" fire or "flame." The system is regularized to a very high degree. Adjectives are formed by changing the second consonant of the "radical," diphthongs designate adverbs, active verbs carry an *l* following the first vowel and passive verbs an *m*. The extensive vocabulary, sophisticated grammar, and regularized structure are such that they earned this analytical system wide acclaim and the praise of Wilhelm Gotfried Leibniz.[4]

As useful to his own designs as Leibniz believed the systems produced by Dalgarno and Wilkins to be, the German philosopher sought to devise a language capable of communicating thought innately, a language transparent both phonetically and cognitively to the human mind and whose "algebraic" dynamic would make it an unfailing "instrument of reason." He was of course attuned to his age and to the thinking characterized by Port-Royal. His proposal, the first elements of which are contained in his *Dissertatio de Arte Combinatoria* (written in 1666 when he was only nineteen) entailed the use of mathematical "combinations." The underlying principle of this ideal

---

[4] Couturat and Leau 20–22. It is interesting to note that, for all the information Pierre Larousse's *Grand dictionnaire du XIXe siècle français* contains in its seventeen encyclopedic volumes (1865–1890), the great lexicographer found worthy of mention only Wilkins's construction under the heading "philosophical language."

philosophical language, "combinatorics," conceives of logic as a process of mathematical compositions and decompositions which can be accurately conveyed by symbolic language. Unfortunately, Leibniz did not present the scheme in a single work; it was a project to which he returned repeatedly throughout his life and must be pieced together by gleaning information from a variety of texts. He did realize, however, that a collaborative, "encyclopedic" effort would be required in order to bring such a language into existence. That goal was never realized. Maat presents the enormous complexity of the scheme over some one hundred thirty pages filled with tables, charts, and diagrams before concluding that the project was doomed owing to Leibniz's "underestimation of the problems involved and his failure to appreciate the diversity of linguistic practice" (394).

5.3.1 Universal language schemes: France

Leibniz's protracted endeavors aside, these initial attempts at devising an a priori language for international use date from the early days of Louis XIV's reign. As the Sun King's Court gained notoriety and as the French language gained status as vehicular idiom in Europe, the need for creating a universal language dissipated. Couturat and Leau chronicle no serious endeavors until Joachim Faiguet introduced his Langue Nouvelle in the pages of the *Encyclopédie* a century later in 1765. The Frenchman limited his designs, however, to a regularized and simplified recasting of the French language. This "first a posteriori language" proposed to eliminate articles and gender and to make both verbs and adjectives invariable. The personal pronouns *jo, to, lo, no, vo, zo* replace their French counterparts. Substantives derived from verbs utilize the suffix *–ou*, augmentatives the suffix *–le* and diminutives the suffix *–li*. Similar suffixes mark voice, mood, and tense. Numbers, to the contrary, are newly invented, from one to ten, for example: *ba, co, de, ga, ji, lu, ma, ni, pa, vu*; eleven, twenty, one hundred, one thousand: *vuba, covu, sinta, mila* (Couturat and Leau 239–40).

Thirty years later, in the midst of the Revolution, Grégoire's revelations as well as a humanitarian concern for communication among peoples prompted Citizen Jean Delormel to present his *Projet d'une Langue universelle* to the National Convention in 1795. Delormel adapted Faiguet's goal of simplification and the taxonomies of Dalgarno and Wilkins to his own ends. His a priori project reflects the basic restructuring undertaken by the

Revolution itself, for it employs the decimal system as a basis for the logical classification of vocabulary. The vowels number ten and the consonants number twenty. Beyond that, the system looks similar to those proposed the century before: Ave = Grammar, ave = letter, alve = vowel, avi = syllable, avo = accent, avau = word, etc. Intentions aside, the resulting scheme presented the familiar impediment of enormous complexity that required an extraordinary memory and constant deciphering. Couturat and Leau dismiss it as totally "impracticable" and of purely historical interest (31–32). Pei finds the endeavor to be singularly "unimpressive" and cites numerous defects, among them the following: "ten vowels were decided upon merely to conform to a preconceived decimal system, and no indication was given as to how four of these vowels, composed of two characters, were pronounced" (Pei 1958: 151). Clearly, the Convention made the right decision in placing its faith and its resources in the project to "universalize" the French language.

By 1855 attitudes and the linguistic environment had changed. Numerous schemes had been devised in the interim. The twenty-three members of the Universal Language Committee of Paris's Société Internationale de Linguistique had several options from which to choose. Unfortunately, most of them did not come close to meeting the Committee's requirements. Indeed, some of them must have brought a smirk to otherwise serious faces. Joseph de Maimieux (*Pasigraphie* [1797]) and Zalkind Hourwitz (*Polygraphie* [1801]) had offered universal writing schemes that attracted attention at the turn of the century. In 1836 A. Grosselin published *Système de langue universelle* and an accompanying grammar. This digital scheme consisted of fifteen hundred root words (*racines*) and one hundred derivational suffixes. As for scripting, Grosselin assigned to each root word category a corresponding digital interval: 101–200 (parts of animals), 201–300 (animal species), 301–500 (plants and their parts), and so on. Likewise, suffixes were numbered from 1 to 100. For speech Grosselin assigned a phonetic value to each number, either a vowel, a diphthong, or a consonant. The system, as Couturat and Leau point out (40–41), was nothing more than "spoken pasigraphy," and a highly impractical one at that. E.-T. Vidal, in 1844, produced an even more unlikely variation that included both letters and numerals. His *Langue universelle analytique* featured twenty-two consonants and thirteen vowels arranged vertically and to which a number was assigned according to its rank within the column. This "vertical stenography" equated letters and numbers in a system so mind-boggling that Eco excluded it completely from his study, "for the sake of brevity" (306). Examples of individual words, however systematically contrived, support his decision: gan2 = Europe, gané = Asia, gana = Africa, gani = America, garu = Russia, ginu = France, gin2 = Paris (Couturat and Leau 45).

The two a priori schemes selected as finalists by the 1855 Society's Universal Language Committee were both published in 1852: *Cours complet de langue universelle* by C.-L.-A. Letellier and *Projet d'une langue universelle* by Sotos Ochando. Both authors privileged the scientific import of their schemes over their potential of becoming universal vehicles of communication. Letellier, a teacher and school administrator from Calvados, based his system on the "theory of language," by which he meant all ideas classified according to logical analysis and assigned a corresponding nomenclature. He emphasized that its use was not to replace natural languages, but rather to better understand and analyze them. His concept was to provide the first stage—the principles of a system that could be employed subsequently as a basis for an academy of scholars in their development of a truly universal language. The individual volumes of his work address separate issues. Volume one covers grammatical elements (inflections); and volume two lists invariable semantic roots or "radicals." This binary structure permeates the entire system. Each of the fifteen vowels and sixteen consonants falls into one of the two categories. Open and closed vowels tend to represent roots, and nasal vowels represent inflections. As for consonants, occlusives and fricatives tend to represent roots, and sibilants, bilaterals, and nasals represent inflections. Couturat and Leau (53) offer the translation of a well-known line of poetry by Voltaire to illustrate the language. The French reads: "Qui sert bien son pays n'a pas besoin d'aïeux" (He who serves his country well does not need forebears). The translation (without diacritics) reads: "Dua gibeli ji ivae jeb ibae te elgai." The project was an ambitious one, a system capable of translating all languages word for word. Its resulting enormity, the two bibliographers conclude, render it unmanageable and its amorphous syntax falls prey to chaos.

Benefacio Sotos Ochando, a Spanish priest, published his work in his native language. The French translation (by Touzé) appeared in 1855. Ochando's goal was to create an international language in which scientific information could be disseminated directly (obviously replacing the French language monopoly of the previous century). His system privileged writing over speech to such a degree that it has been compared to the creation of a "dead" language. Its merits are numerous nonetheless. Eco writes the following about it:

> Its theoretical foundations are comparatively well reasoned and motivated; its logical structure could not be of greater simplicity and regularity; the project proposes—as usual—to establish a perfect correspondence between the order of things signified and the alphabetical order of things that express them. Unfortunately—here we go again—the arrangement is empirical: A refers to inorganic material things, B to the liberal arts, C to the mechanical arts, D to political society, E to living bodies, and so forth. (307)

Examples cited by Couturat and Leau (66–68) demonstrate the nature of the scheme. Scientific terms are readily recognizable as belonging to the same category: Ababa = oxygen, Ababe = hydrogen, Ababi = nitrogen, Ababo = sulfur, etc. The liberal arts are denoted by: Ba = teaching, Be = printing, Bi = bookshop, Bo = the fine arts, Bu = music. The language possesses the potential, the author claims, to form six million words. Be that as it may, the same challenge to the memory exists for this scheme as for those that preceded it. If the Society's committee had reason to be dissatisfied, it was the ordered structure of Ochando's version that gained favor in the end. Of course the Society's days were numbered, and a priori systems were destined to attract increasing skepticism as the century advanced. The future, such as it was, lay with mixed systems (such as Volapük) or a posteriori systems (such as Esperanto). These factors make it all the more difficult to explain the surprising success enjoyed by a universal language found unworthy by the Society and judged to be the "most artificial and impracticable of all the a priori systems" (Couturat and Leau 37), the strangely captivating musical language Solrésol which, despite its numerous liabilities, "continued to find followers [...] even on the eve of the First World War" (Pei 1958: 144).

5.3.2 Jean-François Sudre: téléphonie and the universal musical language

The second edition (1867) of the *Biographie universelle des musiciens et bibliographie générale de la musique*, compiled by F. J. Fétis (director of the Royal Conservatory of Music of Brussels), contains a full-page, double-column entry devoted to Jean-François Sudre (8: 165). It was not Sudre's credentials as a musician that warranted such a lengthy tribute. Some twenty lines encapsulate his career in music. Born in Albi (Tarn) in 1787, he learned music at home as a child, attended the Paris Conservatory beginning in 1806 where he studied violin under François Habneck and harmony under Charles-Simon Catel. Returning to the South of France following his studies, he taught voice, guitar, and violin in Sorèze before moving to Toulouse where he founded a school of music and published several songs and nocturnes. In 1822 he relocated to Paris where he operated a music shop for a few years and produced several minor compositions. That is all. Nearly ninety lines, however, outline Sudre's "communication inventions" developed between 1817 and his death in 1862: téléphonie and the musical language Solrésol.

The early years of the nineteenth century in France witnessed numerous attempts to improve communications—especially military communications. Beyond matters of national security, motivation stemmed from the market place. The government had both the need and the means to finance large-scale ventures. Claude Chappe's invention provides a noteworthy example: the semaphore telegraph (and signal code) that, by means of a system of towers within line-sight of each other, enabled a vigilant Napoleon to send a message as far as Lille—well over a hundred miles—in as little as five minutes. "Night writing," an invention of similar intention designed to allow night-time messages to be transmitted without risking the exposure of sound or light, was developed by Charles Barbier and served as inspiration for Louis Braille's remarkable writing system for the blind (see Chapter Four). Samuel Morse perfected his revolutionizing code in the 1830s. Sudre's expertise in music sent him in a different direction.

In addition to Fétis's columns, government records, and several news-paper accounts, three language sources document Sudre's endeavors: the *Langue musicale universelle inventée par François Sudre, également inventeur de la téléphonie* (published posthumously by Sudre's widow Marie-Joséphine in 1866); Marie-Joséphine's manual, *Théorie et pratique de la langue universelle inventée par Jean-François Sudre* (1883); and Boleslas Gajewski's *Grammaire du Solrésol* (1902). Sudre's training as a musician brought him in contact with solfège (solfeggio), the seven-step notation of the diatonic scale found in Vedic texts and adapted in the tenth century by Guido d'Arezzo in order to guide monks in their performance of Gregorian chants. Before long both the system and Guido's Hand, a diagram of the seven positions on the palm to which Guido would point while directing the chanting monks, became mainstays in much of Europe. Like Braille, Sudre would use the invention to other ends.

The particular order of events remains unknown, but it is likely that the times and the financial potential would have moved Sudre to think first in terms of military communications before expanding the system to full-fledged language status. The relative simplicity of the system called "téléphonie" (so named by the Institut de France) tends to confirm the assumption. "Téléphonie" differs from the inventions by Chappe and Barbier in that it can accommodate either visual signals (disks, lanterns, flares) or acoustical signals (bells, whistles, drums, cannons). The three-sign system as described in the 1866 publication touted its adaptability and capacity to overcome distance impediments and the unfavorable atmospheric conditions often encountered in naval maneuvers:

> La téléphonie pouvait dicter toute la tactique navale à l'aide des *trois notes*, sol, do, sol. 1, 2, 3, indiqués par *trois sons* ou *trois disques* pendant le jour, trois *fanaux* ou *trois* fusées pendant la nuit, l'une blanche, l'autre bleue, l'autre rouge. Pendant la brume: *trois* coups de sifflet, ou *trois* coups de tambour, ou de canon, ou de cloche, et permettant de transmettre tous les ordres de jour, de brume et de nuit de la tactique navale. (Sudre 1866: xix)

5.3.3 Sudre: kings, queens, and emperors

Whereas the language Solrésol itself exhibits greater complexity, it utilizes no more than the seven solfeggio designators—a condemning limitation according to Couturat and Leau, but an enticement for learners intent on mastery within a contracted time frame. Indeed, the system—holistically—is designed to promote basic communication across national language boundaries as opposed to serving as vehicle for scientific investigation and dissemination (a prioritization promoters of both Volapük and Esperanto would adopt subsequently). To Sudre's credit he produced a manageable project that did not require the memory of a Julien Sorel. The 1866 *Langue musicale universelle* advertises the program in the following fashion: "Langue musicale universelle au moyen de laquelle (après seulement trois mois d'étude) tous les peuples de la Terre, les aveugles, les sourds & les muets peuvent se comprendre réciproquement." Its diversity stems from the various mediums of communication the system was designed to accommodate. Oral communication may be effected by singing, humming, playing any musical instrument, or by speaking the seven "musical syllables" of solfeggio. The written language can be in the form of musical notation or the "solfeggio alphabet," as in "solrésol" (the word for "language"). Finger spelling, represented in diagram by drawings reminiscent of Guido's Hand, functioned similarly (there is no indication of acceptance in this domain, nor of any contact with L'Epée or Sicard or knowledge of their systems).

Its success in France can be partially explained by the fact that although Solrésol qualifies as an a priori language, it simplifies and regularizes basic lexical and structural features inherent in the French system: its "direct" syntax (subject, verb, object), its prepositional and participial construction, its post-posed adjectival positioning, the lack of the numbers "seventy" and "ninety" (*pace* Belgium and Switzerland), its tense, mood and gender systems. Partitives disappear altogether, as do various other markers such as dissonances designating the various persons (represented by subject pronouns). As with other a priori schemes, logical/analytical classification systematizes the lexicon. Words beginning with *do* refer to human beings and food, *ré* to clothing and family, *mi* to actions and human frailties or faults, *fa* to nature or topography, *sol* to the arts and sciences, *la* to commerce and industry, *si* to cities and institutions.

Mastery is facilitated by the straightforward and readily internalized use of accentuation. The series of notes or syllables representing an object or concept changes in accentuation according to function. A four syllable/note word with no accent, for example, denotes the verb; accent on the first syllable denotes the abstract substantive, accent on the second syllable denotes the personal substantive, accent on the third syllable denotes the adjective, and on the fourth syllable the adverb. Accordingly, *sirelasi* is the infinitive *constituer*, *sírelasi* the substantive *constitution*, *sirélasi* the substantive *constituant*, *sirelási* the adjective *constitutionnel*, and *sirelasí* the adverb *constitutionnellement*. Antonyms have opposite musical notations (syllabifications): *Domisol* is *Dieu*, *Solmido* is *Satan*; *misol* is *le bien*, *solmi* is *le mal*, *solasi* is *monter*, *silaso* is *descendre*, and so on. Verbs tenses, reduced in number (the past definite and the imperfect are merged, for instance, and other markers are eliminated), use the infinitive as base unit. A double note prefix distinguishes them: *dodo* initiates the imperfect/past definite, *rere* the pluperfect, *mimi* the future, *fafa* the conditional, *solsol* the imperative, *lala* the present participle, *sisi* the past participle. The present (both indicative and subjunctive) utilizes the infinitve.

The "Historique" of the 1866 edition indicates that Sudre's initial success, a demonstration of *Solrésol* proficiency by a young student, was logged in the official newspaper, *Le Moniteur*, on October 29, 1823. By 1827

Sudre believed his system perfected to the point that he could submit a proposal to the Institute. The project was found to be of great potential value to society, especially to the military. Fétis reports that a series of tests were conducted on the Champ-de-Mars by order of the Ministry of War. The generals were particularly impressed with the adaptation to bugle and cited its efficacy both in transmitting field orders over large distances and the rapidity of responses. Perhaps the political turmoil of the intervening years hindered the project, for Sudre resubmitted in 1833. Once again the Institute issued a favorable report accompanied by a recommendation to the government to follow up and lamenting that the commission in charge had no funds for such purposes.

Undaunted, Sudre sought broader avenues. He had been perfecting his Solrésol system all the while. With the last of his inheritance he planned to have his artificial language translated into twelve dictionaries in order to promote it as truly international: French, German, English, Portuguese, Italian, Spanish, Dutch, Russian, Turkish, Arabic, Persian, and Chinese. (Only eight of them were completed, according to Marie-Joséphine, although it is not clear which ones.) Furthermore, he decided to take his program abroad. In 1835 he traveled to London where he gave demonstrations first at King's Theatre before a distinguished audience of scientists and officials, then in York before the Duke of Sussex (president of the Royal Society), the Duchess of Kent and Princess Victoria, and finally at Brighten in the presence of the King and Queen of England. The press in both countries celebrated the event: *The Times*, *The Morning Herald*, *The Morning Chronicle*, as well as *Le Moniteur*, *Le Constitutionnel*, *Le Journal des Débats*, *Le Siècle*, and so on. That same year, when Alfred de Vigny's *Servitude et grandeur militaires* went on sale, readers could appreciate in the section titled "La Veillée de Vincennes" the following tongue in cheek reference to Sudre's *Langue musicale universelle*:

> Que le ciel accorde de longs jours et toutes sortes de bénédictions à ceux qui ont le don de traduire la musique littéralement. [. . .] J'aurais le bonheur de dire mes idées fort clairement à tout l'univers avec mes sept notes. (110)

But notoriety did not translate into government subsidy. In 1839 Sudre submitted his project and dictionaries to yet another commission. Again the call was made for follow-up and compensation, with the same negative results. Sudre set off again on the campaign trail: Belgium, Holland, the French provinces. In 1841 and 1842 his efforts won for him medals awarded by Le Cercle des Arts and La Société Libre des Beaux-Arts. A turning point seemed to be in store in 1843. The Minister of War, Maréchal Soult, adopted téléphonie for the entire military: the cavalry, artillery, and corps of engineers alike. A commission recommended that Sudre should receive fifty thousand francs as compensation and an annual stipend of three thousand francs for his service as director of a school of téléphonie. Alas, implementation did not materialize and compensation was not forthcoming. Accolades continued to mount, nevertheless: recognition by the Académie Royale de Metz (1844), the Académie de Rouen (1845), and the Athenée des Arts (1845). In 1850 Victor Hugo wrote a letter in Sudre's behalf. In 1854 Sudre's demonstrations in Berlin won the support of the naturalist and explorer Alexander von Humboldt. Finally, in 1855, just as the second Linguistic Society of Paris was gearing up, Sudre received his first significant compensation: a ten-thousand franc recognition for excellence in language at the Exposition universelle.

After nearly thirty years Jean-François Sudre had arrived. The Academy acclaimed his now improved system once again in 1856. In 1857 he reached the pinnacle: an invitation to demonstrate Solrésol at tea before the Emperor and the Empress. Marie-Joséphine describes the July 17th event in the "Historique" (the lengthy passage has been translated to accommodate the general reader):

> A few minutes after our arrival, His Majesty asked Monsieur Sudre to tell him about La Langue Musicale and La Téléphonie. After a brief explanation [...] M. Sudre asked His Majesty to write any sentence whatsoever. The Emperor wrote the following: "Le premier qui fut roi fut un soldat heureux." ("The first to be king was a happy soldier.")
>
> Taking his violin, M. Sudre sounded a few notes and, scarcely had he finished when I repeated the sentence word for word. The surprise and astonishment that this experiment provoked were such that His Majesty exclaimed: "C'est inconcevable, c'est incroyable!"
>
> The second experiment consisted of speaking the seven notes instead of playing them on the volin. The Emperor wrote the following sentence: "Plombières est une ville charmante ce soir." ("Plombières is a charming town this evening.") M. Sudre pronounced several notes and, immediately, I got up and repeated the sentence straight away. The demonstration lasted more than an hour to the great delight and admiration of the assembly. (Sudre 1866: xiv–xv)

5.3.4 Marie-Joséphine carries on

In 1862 at the London Exposition the seventy-five year old Sudre exhibited the manuscripts of his eight dictionaries and four phrase books. He was rewarded by being presented the Medal of Honor. This jury's call for compensation and due recognition came too late, however. Jean-François died October 2, 1862. Marie-Joséphine would carry on in his place. She would continue to pressure the government to adopt téléphonie and would operate a Solrésol school well into the Third Republic. In 1883 she would write the final chapter, her improved version of the Solrésol manual: *Théorie et pratique de la langue universelle.*

At first glance Marie Joséphine's manual seems out of place in the Third Republic of the 1880s. The rival systems of Johann Martin Schleyer (Volapük) and Ludovic Zamenhof (Esperanto) were poised to spread their dominions and to attain a large measure of the success that had been Jean-François's dream. By 1886 free courses in Volapük were being sponsored in Paris by the Volapük Association and by the department store Le Printemps. By the end of the decade nearly three hundred Volapük organizations existed from San Francisco to Melbourne to Cape Town and beyond; the language supported two dozen newspapers worldwide, seven of them composed completely in Volapük (Couturat and Leau 142). In September of 1889 the first international Esperanto magazine, *La Esperantisto*, appeared in Nuremberg, marking the beginning of the prolific artificial language movement that subsists to this day (Boulton 49).

At first glance also the contents of Solrésol's new manual seem equally out of place. Grammar, syntax, and lexical variations are presented by means of the same moralizing examples common to grammars and dictionaries of the post-Revolutionary period. Marie-Jospéphine's lesson on gender, for instance, consists of three binary groupings imbued with unmistakable underlying messages:

> Dolâdo (l'homme charitable)/Dolaado (la femme charitable)
>
> Remîta (l'homme bienfaisant)/Remiita (la femme bienfaisante)
>
> Mirêla (l'homme dévoué)/Mireela (la femme dévouée).

In addition to charity, good works, and devotion, models of antonymic phraseology emphasize like humanitarian values: Dolàmido domilado (les muets parlent); Mirémido domiremi (les aveugles voient); Sirémido domiresi (les sourds entendent). Whole sentences define more specifically the veritable character of the ideology. Marie-Joséphine, like the good abbés before her, was on a proselytizing mission. (For the sake of brevity the following selections exclude the Solrésol phrasing):

> L'univers proclame la bonté infinie de la Providence, ce regard qui, de l'éternité, veille sur nos âmes immortelles.

> Prier Dieu, croire en lui, en Notre Seigneur Jésus-Christ et à la sainte Vierge, est la piété qui sanctifie.

Religious and moral aphorisms associated with conservative, "bourgeois" mores dominate the text. They militate against divorce, decadent literature, intrigue, libertinage, disingenuousness, pedantry, and occultism while promoting the family, justice, forthrightness, frugality, industriousness, technical progress, téléphonie, Solrésol, and appropriate compensation for authors and inventors—including the Légion d'Honneur for superior people (such as Jean-François, it is understood). Political pronouncements are not neglected, this warning pertaining to the dangers of popular uprising, for example:

> Le peuple en vraie démocratie ne devrait jamais conspirer ni se désunir, car de la dissonance des opinions naissent les révolutions;

or this advice about the true designs of politicians:

> Les diplomates en politique ne servent que leur esprit de parti, tout en feignant d'approuver les impérialistes, les monarchistes, les libéraux et les républicains;

or this admonition concerning voter responsibility:

> Le gouvernement ne force pas à voter: avant l'élection, il serait opportun de connaître en détail les aptitudes du Représentant.

Ironically, of course, Marie-Joséphine did not enjoy the right to vote. It would be an exaggeration to make a case for her as a "feminist," yet at least one statement she managed to insert innocuously suggests her leanings:

> Quel ennui d'être sans influence! Je suis condamné à balayer, à cirer, à brasser, et tous les jours il me faut continuer à nettoyer.

The masculine "condamné" instead of the feminine "condamnée" fools no one. The tedium and lack of empowerment the statement references would not be lost on her students, most of whom, the manual's foreword clarifies, were "jeunes filles."

5.4 The Third Republic: rebuilding (again) through language

Upon further reflection Marie-Joséphine's manual does not seem so out of place after all. The Third Republic had a good deal in common with Restoration France. It too was a period of restructuring and consolidation— albeit more bipolar, to be sure. Wounds needed to heal following the Franco-Prussian war and the Commune. The devastation spawned a fear of national decline to the point that some believed French civilization itself to be at stake. Many turned again to religion and traditional values as safeguards in the face of a smoldering anticlericalism and a nascent decadence in literature that courted the bizarre, the deviant, the outlandish. Matters took other peculiar turns. Catholicism, nationalism, and paranoia joined forces in the writings of Edouard Drumont. The xenophobic Dreyfus affair exploded into the international arena in 1894. By the late-1890s science would be drawn into the mix by Charles Maurras's strange appropriation of Comte's "positivism" in the name of Catholicism (Sutton).

For its part the government had the vision to designate education as an essential component in the rebuilding. Curricula re-emphasized the classics of the glory days of France; Corneille, Racine, Molière, Voltaire, and their cohorts would enjoy monopolistic status well into the twentieth century. Reform sought to integrate diverse elements of the socio-economic spectrum: the urban poor, the peasantry, women. Illiteracy had to be eliminated. As late as 1866, 45.6 percent of males and 55 percent of females were unable to read and write (Compagnon and Thévenin 51). In effect change had been underway since the latter days of the Second Empire. Victor Duruy, as Ministre de l'Instruction Publique from 1863 to 1869, encouraged local funding of free schools and mandated that all communities of a population above five hundred maintain a school for girls. A secondary school curriculum for girls was drafted in 1868. In the early days of the Third Republic, both Renan (*La réforme intellectuelle et morale*, 1871) and Bréal (*Quelques mots sur l'instruction publique en France*, 1872) emphasized the need for a concerted national program. In 1877 G. Bruno published *Le tour de France par deux enfants*, a "national" reader that would introduce millions of children to France, its regions, and its heritage (three million copies were sold over its first decade [Albertini 175]). Jules Ferry assumed the position of Minister of Public Education in February of 1879. Under his watch events escalated: establishment of the Ecole Normale Supérieure at Fontenay, revisions of the secondary school curriculum and the "licence" program, all three in 1880; the creation of the Ecole Normale Supérieure de Jeunes Filles (1881), the Loi Ferry—compulsory, free, secular primary education for all French children (1881–1882); creation of the Ecole Normale Supérieure at Saint-Cloud (1882).

5.4.1 The Alliance Française: language to the rescue

A related development destined to assume global proportions began to take form in 1883. In July of that year a group of dignitaries met to discuss the state of affairs in France and in the colonies. Their concerns were political, to be sure; the recent loss of Alsace and Lorraine to the Germans and plummeting prestige abroad troubled them deeply. What was needed, they concluded, was a strategy that would raise self-esteem at home and exert a proselytizing influence abroad—beyond the colonies: a worldwide patriotic campaign that would enlist French citizens everywhere as ambassadors. Their solution entailed creating an organization independent of government but supported by it and attuned to national goals and needs. That organization, initially titled Association Nationale pour la Propagation de la Langue Française dans les Colonies et à l'Etranger, would become the Alliance Française. Its originators—Paul Cambon (the then-Resident General of Tunisia and future Ambassador to Spain), Pierre Foncin (geographer, then-Inspector General of Public Instruction, future Secretary General, and President of the AF), Paul Bert (former Minister of Public Instruction), among others—realized that they would need to recruit supporters of standing in order to gain notoriety and attract government approval and funding. Their ranks soon swelled to include religious leaders, diplomats, members of the Institute, and the very recognizable names of Ferdinand Lesseps, Gaston Paris, Ernest Renan, Hippolyte Taine, Louis Pasteur, Armand Colin.

Less than a year later, in January 1884, the Association received official approval to function from the Ministry of Interior. In June of 1885 another pressing argument for the formation of the organization came to light: the threat of universal language schemes. In June of that year Charles Gide, the noted economist and uncle of the novelist-to-be, made a presentation titled "Lutte des langues du globe: role de l'Alliance Française." He made light of the gains artificial languages had made, especially Volapük whose growing popularity was causing concern among his cohorts in Paris, but resolutely urged his fellow citizens to carry the language of France to all corners of the globe (in tacit recognition of the threat [Bruézière 20]). The message was clear. In 1886 the organization attained the goal of being accredited by the State as the Alliance Française. The statutes ratified by the organization's General Assembly in March of 1884 proposed various activities pertaining to the propagation of French language and culture and contained the following provisions: 1) founding and funding French language schools in addition to developing French language courses for extant schools; 2) training teachers and creating normal schools; 3) providing compensation that would attract and retain students; 4) distributing prizes and travel awards to the best students; 5) encouraging publicity in journals and the press, especially in the area of pedagogy; 6) sponsoring a professional journal; 7) organizing conferences and other forms of "propaganda" (Bruézière 11). If the Alliance drew members from a broad social and religious spectrum and made claim to non-partisanship and federative principles, its internal organization reflected an unmistakable ideological model. The Comité General de Propagande and the multitude of Comités d'Action and Comités de Propagande that soon formed in Paris, the provinces, and abroad descend from their Revolutionary predecessors. As far as language is concerned, the relationship to the Regional Jacobin Clubs that assisted Grégoire in conducting his language survey is apparent. Indeed, as the Alliance evolved, especially under the direction of Pierre Foncin, it would adopt the same moral prescripts observable in dictionaries and grammars from Girault-Duvivier to Marie-Joséphine Sudre. It is not surprising that in our day of political correctness and post-colonial retrospection there should be accusations of linguistic (and cultural) imperialism. In fact as early as 1917 Georges Hardy authored a study to that effect (ironically, produced by the publishing house of Armand Colin): *Une conquête morale: l'enseignement en A.O.F (Afrique Occidentale Française)*. Foncin's role in the development of the ideology has been addressed by Numa Broc among others, and the whole question has been amply contextualized by Robert Phillipson in his 1992 *Linguistic Imperialism*.

Perhaps as much as anything else the Alliance's success has made it a target. In France the first year alone the organization attracted well over 2000 members: 1200 in Paris and even more distributed throughout the provinces, 431 in the East, 379 in the South-East, 340 in the Midi, 314 in the South West (Bruézière 13). By 1889 the Alliance had expanded beyond Africa to India. The following year it opened its doors in Melbourne. By 1904 it could count 150 chapters in France and 450 abroad. At its centenary in 1983 it had spread to eighty countries; twenty years later (2003) that figure had increased to 130 countries and 1072 chapters.[5] In France, from the very beginning, the press supported efforts with releases that announced events, lauded activities, and touted literary and cultural productions of all sorts. Alliance sponsored fund-raisers—conferences, lectures, exhibits, concerts, and festivals—drew crowds, sparked enthusiasm, and motivated the civic-minded to contribute to its expanding coffers. In 1919 the boulevard Raspail center opened its doors and by 1930 welcomed 4800 students. By 1982 Alliance Française centers around the world were teaching French to well over a quarter of a million students (Bruézière 246). These are impressive statistics, to say the least. Yet the struggle to "universalize" the French language within the country's borders faced constant challenges even as the Alliance Française was spreading its wings abroad.

5.4.2 At long last: French throughout the land

Eugen Weber's *Peasants to Frenchman* (1976) remains the most authoritative study of the programs designed to institutionalize the French language from 1870 to 1914. More recent works have enlarged the perspective, R. Anthony Lodge's *French: From Dialect to Standard* (1993), for example, which proceeds from the Latinization of Gaul; or James R. Lehning's *Peasant and French* (1995), which echoes Félix Pécaut's (1828–1898) views on the sacrifice of regional languages to national unity and questions Weber's notion of nationalism in light of recent developments.[6] Despite certain questionable interpretations, Weber's research—much of it drawn from primary evidence

---

[5] These statistics have been gathered from the official web site of the Alliance Française.

[6] Félix Pécaut's *Quinze ans d'éducation* laments the cultural loss stemming from the drive to institutionalize the French language throughout the realm. The title refers to the fifteen years he spent at the training school for women at Fontenay-aux-Roses which he organized. For a concise survey of recent opinions, concerns, and literature pertaining to regionalism in France, see Pierre Barral's "Depuis quand les paysans se sentent-ils français?" It is not possible to undertake any sort of meaningful analysis of regional language differences in this study. Those interested in the question would do well to begin with Roger Hawkins's "Regional Variation in France" in Carol Sanders's *French Today*. Non-standard French is treated with aplomb in the same volume (Ken George's "Alternative French"). See also Part 5 of Battye et al. ("Variations of French"). Sociolinguistic variations in general are amply treated by both Dennis Ager (*Sociolinguistics and Contemporary French*, 1990) and Nigel Armstrong (*Social and Stylistic Variation in Spoken French*).

of folk culture ("the songs, dances, proverbs, tales, and pictures of the country folk" [E. Weber xiv]) as a base from which to gauge alterations from region to region—and his presentation of evidence with a preponderance of charts, diagrams, maps, and statistics make his account indispensable. Over more than six hundred pages Weber isolates and analyzes the ways and means utilized and the results obtained throughout the various regions of France. The picture that emerges is of a composite homogeneity that required nearly half a century to effect. Weber explains in the Introduction how daunting the task was in rural France:

> A France where many did not speak French or know (let alone use) the metric system, where *pistoles* and *écus* were better known than francs, where roads were few and markers distant, and where a subsistence economy reflected the most common prudence. This book is about how all this changed, and about how mentalities altered in the process; in a word, about how undeveloped France was integrated into a modern world and official culture of Paris, of the cities. (xii)

That the task was accomplished at all is impressive. That it was accomplished without violence or insurrection is more impressive still, language being the heart and soul of cultural identity. The administrative departments imposed as a primary measure in the restructuring of Ancien Régime France had no history, offered no status beyond the convenience of economic and bureaucratic function. Gabriel Bergounioux, in *Aux origines de la linguistique française*, marvels at the feat. "L'unification linguistique se poursuit," Bergounioux writes,

> sans coercition ni répression—du moins physique—, le français, langue de l'administration, de l'école, des échanges, bref de la promotion sociale, s'impose progressivement [. . .] Le cas est unique en Europe: une minorité impose sa langue à des populations allophones, s'exprimant dans des langues celte (breton), romane (occitan, catalan, corse), germanique (flamand, dialectes alémaniques), basque et tsigane, sans rencontrer de véritable résistance, populaire ou savante. (18)

The feat is all the more striking given the central administration's attitude toward the provinces. Seventy years after Grégoire's report to the Convention, rural France continued to be viewed as alien territory where witchcraft and superstition reigned among unkempt, non-French speaking country folk. Reports of school inspectors often referred to the acquisition of the French language as a "civilizing process." The statistics of 1863 reflect the magnitude of the problem for the Ministry of Public Education:

> According to official figures, 8,381 of France's 37,510 communes spoke no French: about a quarter of the population. [...] 448,328 of 4,018,427 schoolchildren (ages seven to thirteen) spoke no French at all, and another 1,490,269 spoke or understood it but could not write it. [...] In 24 of the country's 89 departments, more than half the communes did not speak French, and in six others a significant proportion of the communes were in the same position. In short, French was a foreign language for a substantial number of Frenchmen, including almost half the children who would reach adulthood in the last quarter of the century. (E. Weber 67)

Progress was slow, regionalism resilient. At mid-century Peasant culture itself received a boost from the Félibrige movement that promoted Occitan and the poet Mistral who identified with the common folk. Other areas, especially where Breton, Flemish, and Catalan were spoken, proved equally recalcitrant. The government's comprehensive program began to make headway, nevertheless. Under Ferry and his successors school facilities were improved and professionally trained teachers were hired to replace the part-time and often religiously oriented teaching corps. Formal knowledge of the French language was enhanced through curricular adjustments at the Normal Schools. Inspectors traveled the entire country in order to ensure curricular and pedagogical uniformity. Military training included language instruction. The campaign was psychological as well as ideological and logistical. Changes in attitude during the Third Republic began to occur as a consequence of the same "civilizing" forces that Norbert Elias identifies in *Power and Civility*. By 1885, those who were unable to speak French began to feel ashamed and excluded from the benefit of a national identity. "Once patois became widely scorned, its fate was sealed," Weber observes. "The greatest function of the modern school: to teach not so much useful skills as a new patriotism," he adds; the *instituteur* "was intended to institute the nation" (88, 332). Be that as it may, as late as 1911 Arnold Van Gennep could write that peasants and workers still considered their patois to be their mother tongue (14). It was in fact World War I that completed the program. Combatants were drawn from all parts of France. The magnitude of the conflict, the need for national resolve, and the requirements of battlefield communication superseded regional allegiances.

How has the situation evolved in the interim? Polarities have not been effaced. Regional identities and regional languages persist yet today. Like proponents of LSF and its inherent culture, many supporters have rallied to protect their heritage from a central authority whose ideology privileges France as an abstraction, a political construct whose "national culture" mandates a "national language," that is to say the French language since the enactment of the constitutional amendment (Article 2) of 1992. Recent discord revolves around the 1994 "Loi Toubon" (examined in depth in the following chapter), France's refusal first to sign and then to ratify the Charter of Regional or Minority Languages adopted by the European Union, and the November 2002 decision by the Conseil d'Etat to block Diwan schools (Breton language schools) from being included in the public education sector.[7] It is difficult not to conclude, then, that the regional/minority language policies of the Fifth Republic differ little from those of the Third Republic—or the Convention, for that matter.

5.4.3 Lexis, grammar, syntax: chaos and the search for order

Of course the French of Grégoire's era was not the French taught in schools at the beginning of the twentieth century. Technical, scientific, and industrial innovations generated a flood of new vocabulary: the steam engine, the steamship, the railway, the automobile, photography, cinema, industrial and agricultural machinery (including the tractor), advances in engineering

---

[7] Leigh Oakes outlines the statutes governing regional and immigrant languages: "The teaching of regional and immigrant languages in state schools in France is governed by two separate provisions. Regional languages are covered by law 51-46 of 11 January 1951 relating to the teaching of local languages and dialects (a.k.a. Deixonne Law). In the beginning, this law only applied to four languages, but at the time of writing [2001] includes Basque, Breton, Catalan, Corsican, Gallo, Occitan (Auvergnat, Gascon, Languedocien, Limousin, Nissart, Provençal, and Vivaro-Alpin), Alsatian and Lorrain, Tahitian, and four Melanesian languages (Aije, Drehu, Nengone, Paicî). Immigrant languages are predominantly covered by programmes for teaching languages and cultures of origin (*enseignement des langues et cultures d'origine* or ELCO). These programmes are financed by foreign governments and established through bilateral agreement" (117). Oakes does not address the Conseil d'Etat's decision because it would occur the year following the publication of the study.

and medicine (especially following Claude Bernard's *Introduction à l'étude de la médecine expérimentale* [1865]), the rise of the behavioral sciences, the recognition of linguistics as a bona fide field of inquiry. Saint-Gérand, in his chapter "La langue française au XIXe siècle" (1999b), measures alterations and proclivities. Many of the lexical newcomers bore their origin in their nomenclature, he observes. Early industrial development in England produced a significant contribution. Railroad terms, for example, were often drawn directly from English. *Chemin de fer* translates the English *Railway*, and other terms such as *rail, dérailler, tunnel,* and *wagon* are similarly derived. Once again the arts, especially opera, were fecundated by Italianisms: *diva, fantasia, libretto, presto, trémolo, modérato,* and so on. Professionalism in music, a product of affluence and the increasing numbers of middle class concert-goers, spawned specific designations for its specialists: *violoniste, hautboïste, corniste, trompettiste, tromboniste.* Genres, sub-genres, and their practitioners across the arts became specifically identified: *concertino, polonaise, requiem, oratorio, paysage, paysagiste, caricature, caricaturiste, aquarelle, aquarelliste, miniature, miniaturiste.* Scientific terms often reflected the new-found complexity of organisms and their systemics by means of juxtapositions or compounds: *éroticomanie, bactériologie, hématographie, néphro-thromboïde, pancréatico-duodénal.*

The multitude of neologisms that were finding their way into French at an ever quickening pace caused a good deal of lexical confusion. Archaisms and neologisms coexisted, fought for survival, subsisted or disappeared according to the forces of usage and official recognition. So too—due especially to the journalistic liberalism of editors bent on selling newspapers to an avid, broad-based public—"popularisms" and "formalisms" struggled to gain or retain acceptance, further complicating the task of the lexicographer. Lines of demarcation became increasingly blurred. Indeed, the logocentrism long touted as being preeminently served by the French language seemed to erode progressively in light of an enhanced understanding of language and its inherent shortcomings as well as the commercialization of the press whose paid advertisements utilized vacuous superlatives to hawk everything from can't-miss investments to elixirs and hair restorers. Following in the footsteps of Aloysius Bertrand and Charles Baudelaire, Arthur Rimbaud and Stéphane Mallarmé blurred lines further by creating aesthetic hybrids that conjoined prose and poetry. Mallarmé, the consummate master of polysemy, went so far as to claim that prose did not exist at all: prose being in reality nothing more than fragmented verse.[8] In 1896 Théodore Joran published *Le péril de la syntaxe et la crise de l'orthographe*. Concerns about syntax arose as the rigid structures of controlled reform gave way to the expanding dynamics of language as an historically situated sociolinguistic phenomenon. Already by the 1870s traditional grammar according to Noël and Chapsal was disappearing from schools. Chervel explains that the new grammar (and its liberal syntax) owed its sanction in part to the university's espousal of the latest developments in "linguistic science":

> Une nouvelle science linguistique apparaît à l'horizon universitaire vers 1870: la grammaire historique et comparée, qui bouleverse les perspectives sur la langue. Le français que nous parlons est l'aboutissement d'une longue histoire. Les sons, les formes, la syntaxe, le sens des mots, l'orthographe même ont évolué au cours des siècles conformément à des "lois" que les spécialistes dégagent, et qui "expliquent" le présent. (Chervel 1977: 257)

Alexandre Hovelacque summed up the theory in *La linguistique* (1876): "Les langues [. . .] naissent, croissent, dépérissent et meurent comme tous les êtres vivants" (9). The works and reputation of Gaston Paris played a decisive role in this change of emphasis. A member of the Linguistic Society of Paris alongside Bréal, his probing scholarship brought the medieval period to life in the form of literary texts that bore witness to the birth of the French nation and established the foundations of future greatness. *La vie de Saint-Alexis* (1872), *Les plus anciens monuments de la langue française* (1875), *Manuel d'ancien français* (1888), and numerous other titles caught the public eye and earned Paris the directorship of the Collège de France in 1895 and a seat at the Académie des Inscriptions in 1896. The advent and recognition of

---

8 The fourth section of Barbara Johnson's seminal *Défigurations du langage poétique* is titled "Crise de prose" and is superseded by two epigraphs from Mallarmé: "La littérature ici subit une exquise crise, fondamentale"; "En vérité il n'y a pas de prose." The latter is worth citing in context: "Le vers est partout dans la langue [. . .] Dans le genre appelé prose, il y a des vers, quelquefois admirables, de tous rythmes. Mais en vérité, il n'y a pas de prose: il y a l'alphabet et puis des vers plus ou moins serrés: plus ou moins diffus" (Mallarmé 867). Walter Benjamin, Michel Foucault, Jacques Derrida, and others have written forcefully about the commercialization and fragmentation of language. Benjamin points a reproving finger at capitalism, journalism, and the bourgeoisie—while extolling Baudelaire's "technique du putsch" (Benjamin 143).

historical linguistics led to new approaches in language pedagogy. The notion of evolution, of change, thus found its justification in the form of a natural dynamic that could (and should) be represented in language instruction. In response, in 1874, Auguste Brachet published *Nouvelle grammaire française fondée sur l'histoire de la langue* in which the prescriptive tenets of the past were denounced as outmoded authoritarianism. New manuals based on revised linguistic premises soon appeared in schools, as did a Noël and Chapsal grammar in 1884, appended and remodeled to fit the mold. The administrative decisions to acquiesce to trend took a toll, however. The historical method was found to be ineffective in teaching basic grammar, syntax, and orthography. The historical dimension did not enhance the learning process, but rather served only to distract and to deter mastery. Not only did the failure leave students ill-prepared and the conservative wing of the language establishment disgruntled, it tended to undermine the authority of philology/ historical linguistics and to accentuate the need for reform within the scientific establishment (a conclusion Ferdinand de Saussure had already reached).

5.4.4 Into the twentieth century: Bédier, Lanson, Bréal, Saussure

At the beginning of the twentieth century, even as inroads were being made in the countryside, language policies, texts, and pedagogy lacked direction. The return of atavistic precepts produced no panacea. The resulting amorphous compendium of grammatical principles amounted to "un bricolage assez monstrueux" that defied analysis, Chervel observes (1977: 259). The functions of the various parts of speech, as presented, overlapped; clauses and their interrelationships were ill-defined and presented inconsistently, ellipses (inevitable and practical) were disdained. Moreover, both the need to master orthography and the sanctity of the written language narrowed linguistic vision. Thus the failure of the historical method was closely followed by the failure of the grammatical method: "l'échec de la grammaire comme mode de connaissance de la langue" (Chervel 1977: 263). Although manuals would continue to emphasize the traditional values of clarity, eloquence, and articulacy, methodology would remain in question for the remainder of the century.

Yet for all the misgivings about pedagogical theory and method, neither language learning nor the emphasis on history waned in France. To the contrary, (French) literacy made strides year after year. Joseph Bédier,

Paris's successor in the chair of medieval literature at the Collège de France, rekindled interest in the Middle Ages and produced an edition of the *Chanson de Roland* (1921) that would make that *chanson de geste* known to school children throughout the country. Gustave Lanson, whose *Histoire de la littérature française* (1894) did much to bolster the Third Republic's program of national rehabilitation, founded a form of literary criticism (literary sociology) that would endure for half a century. Owing in large part to his influence in the Reform of 1902, the exegesis method of textual analysis (the famous "explication de textes") turned students' attention to short texts to be subjected to close readings and holistic interpretations derived from a deterministic environment of social, political, psychological, and aesthetic factors.

Events in "linguistic science" had begun to take an opposite direction in Paris, however. Saussure's "theory of a systematic, synchronic linguistics [...] which marks the beginning of European linguistics and which helped to launch structuralism in a wider arena," writes Carol Sanders, was "shaped and articulated in his Paris lectures" (30). Saussure (1857–1913), while still a student studying historical linguistics at Leipzig, first journeyed to the French capital in 1879 in order to present a paper on the Indo-European vowel system at a meeting of the Linguistic Society of Paris. (He had been a member since 1876.) The experience and the contacts he made, most particularly his burgeoning relationship with Bréal (the Society's *secrétaire adjoint*), led him to relocate. He would spend the following decade (1880–1891) as Bréal's protégé at the Ecole Pratique des Hautes Etudes where the Frenchman had set up the first phonetics laboratory. In addition to lectures as "maître de conférences de gothique et vieux haut allemand," he was an active member of the Society. By 1883 he had risen from the position of assistant to the secretary to succeed Bréal as *secrétaire adjoint*. He presented numerous papers at the biweekly meetings, primarily on Greek and Sanskrit; one title stands out as being an obvious consequence of his association with Bréal: "Phonétique du patois fribourgeois."

Bréal's conception of language differed from the historically oriented theories offered by the most recent German school, the Neogrammarians (Brugmann, Paul, Osthoff, Leskin) for whom phonetic laws (sound changes) admitted no exceptions. Bréal, in his *Essai de sémantique* (1897), for which he is primarily known, describes language as a human phenomenon subject to human volition as opposed to a discrete phenomenon subject only to auto-induced (non-human) alteration. According to Bréal, speakers and listeners interact on a linguistic continuum in "synchrony" with which they simultaneously relate meaning to circumstance. If Bréal fails to recognize the interaction as a "logical step" toward studying "meaning from a synchronic perspective," Sanders observes adroitly, he "seems to be working with an implicit and embryonic version of what would become the Saussurean concepts of *langue and parole*" (33–34).

Saussure's subsequent abstract/ideosyncratic bifurcation of concepts (*langue*: the study of the structure [not history] as an end in and of itself; *parole*: the way individuals speak and use language) recognizes language as a social phenomenon, on the one hand, but, on the other hand, proscribes its study as such. It thus distances linguistics from the humanities, aligning it with the sciences in a new and integral way. The posthumous dissemination of Saussure's theories, owed to his French students who reproduced and published the *Cours de linguistique générale* in 1916, changed the landscape in linguistics and emerging semiology. Historical linguistics, as a discipline henceforth, would be forced to exist apart; sociolinguistics would emerge as its synchronic counterpart, would embrace the entire spectrum of language (granting status to oral language), and would bring new focuses to the study of polylingualism, dialects/patois, popularisms, and slang. By mid-century and by way of formalism, Noam Chomsky, a synchronist for whom syntax is the defining property of language, would stake his claim as heir to Saussure's paradigms and become the dominant linguist of the second half of the twentieth century. His notion of grammar as "a purely formal schema, without speakers, without a history, and without an origin" maintains the ahistorical stance formalized by Saussure and intuited by Bréal (Beaken 7).

5.4.5 Phonocentrism: the emergence of the oral language

Shifts in focus of "linguistic science," both diachronic and synchronic, thus entailed a shift from logocentrism to phonocentrism. Françoise Gadet's chapter "La langue française au XXe siècle" in Chaurand's new history of the French language begins by noting as a primary effect "the emergence of oral language." Lanson and Bédier notwithstanding, she remarks, the long reign of the literary text as paragon came to an end and was replaced by "spontaneous production/speech":

> L'oral—que d'ailleurs on a longtemps connu fort peu—devait constituer le
> seul espace vrai où s'inscrivit la langue. On pouvait croire auparavant qu'il

n'y avait de bonne prononciation, de bon usage de la grammaire, que dans
un seul type de discours. Selon une conception élargie, si la langue
académique est toujours appréciée dans des situations déterminées, elle
n'est pas à sa place hors de celles-ci. Des différences de niveau de registre
ont été reconnues et ont fini par entrer jusque dans l'enseignement du
français. (Gadet 1999: 583)

The elitist status of "academic discourse" (and the prescriptive grammar it
infers) was not entirely compromised as such, but its domain was sharply
reduced. A holistic approach emerged that privileged speech as it occurs. As
a consequence, for example, historical phonetics gave way to the science of
the production, transmission, and reception of speech, or "phonetics," which
in France, given the challenges of the French sound system, has come to
mean "the descriptive or synchronic study of sound" (Pei 1966: 205).
Technical advances facilitated study and analysis. Recordings from around
France allowed comparisons of regional and ethnic pronunciations; models
or norms were adopted for the continued standardization program within
the schools and for teaching French across the globe.

On the social front the heightened migration from the country to the
city after World War II further stigmatized rural speech and fostered new biases
beyond the chronic problems of unemployment and cultural displacement.
The awareness of speech differences led to new sociolinguistic classifications
within Paris itself, usually pejorative or marginalizing to one degree or
another. Accents from the popular quarters of the outer reaches of the city
attracted new designations as the capital expanded: *boulevardier* becomes
faubourien, which in turn becomes *banlieusard* as the suburbs develop. The
advent of radio, an urban production centered in Paris, challenged the primacy
of print media and brought both popular and "professionally trained voices"
into households. Soon even students of French outside France could identify
a "Parisian accent" and could explain how it deviated from norms posited
by phoneticians such as André Martinet or Pierre Delattre (Gadet 587–91).

5.4.6 The French language in the twentieth century

The French language, of course, has continued to evolve. Rampant
innovation in science and technology in the twentieth century as well as
drastic changes in demographics and socio-economics (especially since the
Second World War) have posed a greater lexical and phonological challenge

for European languages than ever before. Numerous acoustical changes in the French idiom identified at the midpoint of the century appear to be continuing at present, although some of them in altered form.[9] The "e caduc" or schwa [ə] remains in a state of flux; its pronunciation at the end of words has persisted (somewhat attenuated) as a regional characteristic in the Midi and, more recently, has cropped up in urban settings in the form of schwa-tagging.[10] The palatal or rolled *r* remains a common feature in the south. Regional pronunciations of nasals (nasal consonant plus nasal vowel as opposed to nasal vowel alone) has endured. Vocalic conflation, underway for decades, has heightened. The dichotomy "open e" [ɛ]/"closed e" [e] or "elongated e" [ɛ:] has generally disappeared in favor of the former ([ɛ]) in words such as mettre/maître; the dichotomy pâte [ɑ]/patte [a] has declined in favor of the latter; closed e [e] has come to dominate in both *j'irai* and *j'irais*. The nasal vowel [œ̃] (as in *lundi*) has generally given way to [ɛ̃]. Similar tendencies or fluctuations have been discerned sporadically across the social spectrum: [œ] (*œuvre*) is often pronounced [ø] as in *eux*; and there is confusion of *pomme* [ɔ] and *paume* [o], *blanc* [ã] and *blond* [õ], and so on.

---

[9] André Martinet's 1945 questionnaire published in his *La prononciation du français contemporain* is the primary source for documenting these changes. Gadet reproduces the questionnaire as an appendix (668–70). The choice is perfectly justified, despite the date of the survey, for more recent studies have confirmed a continuation of the general tendencies and phonetic reductionism Martinet outlined in his findings. Nigel Armstrong has contributed a useful study of variations and "levelling" in spoken French. His distinction of "standardization" (hierarchical) and "levelling" (horizontal or non-hierarchical) diminution of differences in language varieties is essential for understanding the dynamics of reductionism. Many of the present-day variations and trends in both the spoken and written language and their sociolinguistic environments are fully documented in the authoritative *Histoire de la langue française 1945–2000* edited by Gérald Antoine and Bernard Cerquiglini and published by CNRS in 2000. For an absolutely up-to-date description of the French sound system, see Part 2 of *The French Language Today* (Battye, Adrian, et al.): "The Sound System of French" (51–118).

[10] Schwa-tagging is defined as the pronunciation of a schwa at the end of a word whether or not there is an orthographic basis for it: cf. Pierre/bonjour (neither of them standard). Interestingly, at present this variation has been found to be especially prevalent among young, urban women. This and similar variations have prompted Fernand Carton and others to wonder whether French might not be in the midst of a radical change in accentuation, from "oxytonism" (*accent final: mardi*) to "barytonism" (*accent non final: mardi*). If the question remains unresolved at present, there is evidence that "oxytonism" has become less prevalent (Carton 46).

Consonants attest to related variations or fluctuations: [t], [k], and [g] continue to be palatalized ([t'], [k'], [g']) as they have been in popular register for a very long time. There is a marked instability of [ɲ] which is often rendered [nj]. The velar [ŋ] derivative of the English *-ing* has taken its place on the sound charts. The pronunciation of final consonants that add "substance" to certain words, especially monosyllables, has become increasingly common: aoû<u>t</u>, bu<u>t</u>, mœur<u>s</u>, fai<u>t</u>, jadi<u>s</u>. Assimilation colors or reduces certain consonant pairs: *ch'parle, ch'ai* pas. Truncation or reduction occurs frequently—*v'là, menfin* (*mais enfin*), *chtement* (*justement*)—and suppresses liquid consonants at the end of words: *ronfle* > [ʀɔ̃f] and *genre* > [ʒɑ̃]. Apheresis reduces words such as *adulte* to [dylt] and aphesis eliminates a word or words completely: (*il ne*) *faut pas*. Hiatus is now commonly used to underscore the importance of certain words: *quelque chose d<u>e</u> irresistible, un<u>e</u> faute*. The number of liaisons (even in "careful speech") has decreased. The primary victims at all levels, as might be expected, are the "liaisons facultatives," the "optional liaisons" that in the past tended to identify register (e.g., *nous avon<u>s</u> insisté*). Exceptions to this trend are readily observable in didactic speech or political discourse where emphasis often "energizes" key syllables: *il es <u>t</u>essentiel que, il es <u>t</u>indispensable que*, the *que* frequently pronounced [kø] followed by a pause for added emphasis.

Certain tenses have experienced a significant decline in usage: the imperfect and pluperfect subjunctives, the passé simple, and especially the passé surcomposé, which is now used by only the most careful speakers. The pleonastic "ne" ("avant qu'il *ne* parte") has became more rarified; apocope has multiplied, even in the case of proper nouns: *stylo, apéro, porno, photo, prof, vélo, télé, cinéma* (*ciné*), *fac, sympa, pub, rétro, d'ac, Science Po, Boul(e) Mich(e)*. The suppleness of oral syntax has influenced written syntax along the way, due in large part to journalistic style where sentence fragments abound and the historical present (another of Voltaire's contributions) may appear virtually out of nowhere. Interrogative inversions replaced by intonation in the oral language have tended to give way to "est-ce que" plus declarative order in writing. Further modifications of diverse character are documented by Gadet: neologisms, professionalisms, "particularisms" such as "argot," acronyms, class and gender differentiations, and so on.

As for the array of developments and variations noted above (and there are many others), Nigel Armstrong in his comparative study of French and English comes to the conclusion that with regard to the "oïl" phonetic inventory both the consonant system and the vowel system have remained "relatively stable" over the last half century. His findings, supported by convincing statistical analysis, indicate that variations are noteworthy but do not constitute radical change. André Goosse, having surveyed the current state of French syntax in both the written language and the oral language, hesitates to characterize the numerous anomalies he lists as being indicative of permanent change. He writes: "Pour constater les grands mouvements, s'il y en a, il faudrait un recul, ne pas être à l'intérieur du train." He feels confident identifying no more than three unquestionably permanent alterations, two of them belonging to the oral register and already discernable in 1945: 1) the disappearance of the passé simple and 2) the replacement of *de* by *du, de la, des* when a noun is preceded by an adjective. As for the written language he confirms only the disappearance of "mots outils" of the sort *bas coton, la pensée-Foucault,* or les *relations parents-enfants,* in which the preposition has disappeared very much like the English *cotton stockings* or *child-parent relations* (131, 141).

Goosse's hesitancies reflect the problem of determining how and to what degree the language is changing at present. The dynamics—especially given the incursions of English in commerce, popular culture, the media, and the internet, as well as the demographics of immigrant populations (both first and subsequent generations), the increasing cultural and market influence of *ados* and their *français des jeunes* or *le nouveau français,* and the new identities of the post-colonial era—appear more disparate than ever. Moreover, the sophisticated technical means of gathering samples and generating data today were unavailable in the past, thereby rendering base information less authoritative than it was heretofore believed. In order to at least gauge the enormity of the question, Etienne Brunet (in "Ce que disent les chiffres") judiciously turned to the "meilleure base de données linguistiques au monde: *Frantext,*" which has made available online the entire corpus of the recently completed, multi-volume *Trésor de la langue française* and has digitized 3000 literary texts. Another database, FRANCIL, provides him the source for spoken French throughout Francophonia. Brunet presents statistical table after statistical table and diagram after diagram relevant to various periods, levels, and types of discourse. Conclusions, given the vastness of the project, remain indeterminant. Yet Brunet notes the resilience of the French language over time. Its failure to compete with English in the current linguistic arena may be seen as a triumph for the French language, he asserts, a guarantor for the future; for in order to compete it would have had to "denature" itself; it would have had to sacrifice along with its difficulties and unwieldy conjugations the precious assets of subtlety and nuance, both inherently germane to French culture (727).

Its attributes notwithstanding, it is clear that after a lengthy tenure acknowledgment of French as THE LANGUAGE of diplomacy has come to an end. Although still recognized as a principal, it now coexists with other idioms as an official language of the United Nations, NATO, and UNESCO. This erosion of status has come to pass despite the continued efforts of the central authority to control the national idiom. Myriad associations and a growing language bureaucracy have executed various charges according to the mandates of the administration in office. The Academy published its *Grammaire de l'Académie Française* in 1932. The Office de la Langue Française was instituted in 1937 and was succeeded by the Office du Vocabulaire Français in 1957. Eight years later, in 1966, the Haut Comité de la Langue Française was organized, only to be replaced by three separate committees in the 1980s: Délégation Générale de la Langue Française, Conseil Supérieur de la Langue Française, and Haut Conseil de la Francophonie. If the resolve has been enduring, results have been mixed. The latest in the long series of endeavors to reform orthography fell short once again as the new millennium approached.

Although French orthography is not non-systematic, it is cumbersome, at best. The language's 36 phonemes (37 if *ng* is included) are transcribed by 130 graphic units or graphemes which themselves are compounded by the use of diacritics (Gruaz 64). As has been documented in previous chapters, evolution in orthography has been a common, irresistible—if grudgingly sporadic—feature of the French language. The need for meaningful reform was articulated once again as early as 1965 in the Beslais report. In response, two organizations embarked on a simplifation project that stretched into the 1980s: the Association pour l'Information et la Recherche sur les Orthographes et les Systèmes d'Ecritures and HESO (Histoire et Structure des Orthographes et Systèmes d'Ecriture), the latter an arm of the CNRS. Orthographic reform had been conducted in Germany, Belgium, and elsewhere. The list of so-called "rectifications" was published in toto in 1990. Immediately, outcries of protest were heard from the public at large as well as from academicians. It was as though something sacred had been disturbed, if not desecrated. In the end the Academy retained only 30% of the "rectifications," many of them listed only as variants in tome I of the new *Dictionnaire*.

The majority of the mainline dictionaries were even less welcoming. Proposed simplifications may be categorized as follows: 1) the elimination of the hyphen in compound words where phonetic integrity is not at risk: *extrasensoriel, ultramoderne*, but not *extra-utérin* in which the *au* might be pronounced [o]; 2) the elimination of the circumflex if it has no phonetic or morphological function: *flute, maitre, naitre*, but not *évêque, rôle, sûr, eût*, etc.; 3) the addition of accents to reflect pronunciation, especially in foreign words: *caméraman, allégro*; 4) the use of *è* to reflect the pronunciation of *évènement* and to replace the double consonant in the case of verbs ending in *eler* and *eter* and based on *j'achète*: *je ruissèle, j'étiquète*, etc.; 5) the displacement of the diaeresis (tréma) to indicate the vowel pronounced: *ambigüe, aigüe*.[11]

Beyond the atavistic regional and minority language policies previously discussed, two other polarizing language issues have sparked controversy and concern in France during the final decades of the twentieth century: the increasingly pervasive government measures to stem the tide of Anglicisms that preservationists fear are overwhelming the national idiom and the polarizing drive to feminize titles, ranks, and professions.

---

[11] For a succinct overview of the policies and polemics in context, see Rodney Ball's insightful article: "La réforme de l'orthographe en France et en Allemagne" and Nina Catach's "The Reform of the Writing System" in *French Today* (Carol Sanders, ed.).

6

Enemy at the Gates:
Parlez-vous franglais? Evitez le franglais!

PARLEZ-VOUS FRANGLAIS?, the title of the provocative book authored by
(René) Etiemble in 1964, stands out as an initial volley in the ongoing
French campaign to protect the national idiom (and culture) from Anglo-
Saxon incursions. Etiemble's publication and its success was not his first foray
into the language conflict theater. The Sorbonne professor's humanistic goal
of fostering a holistic cultural construct for the future included a healthy role
for France and a revitalized French language. To those ends, beginning as
early as 1946, he published a series of articles in reaction to what he perceived
as untoward "yanqui" cultural influences.[1] In 1964 he put his thoughts
together in stunning fashion. As it gained in notoriety, *Parlez-vous franglais?*
became widely endorsed as a new "Défense de la langue française." For a
government rededicated to the time-honored policy of promoting national
interests through language, it would attain the status of manifesto.

6.1 Etiemble: the Anglo-American invasion

Politically, France's policies promoting independence from U.S.
foreign policy following WW II had taken on an increasingly antagonistic
face: the Suez crisis, France's nuclear designs, the Bay of Pigs, the recognition
of China, disagreements within NATO and France's impending withdrawal

---

[1] Salient titles published between 1946 and 1961 reflect Etiemble's concerns: "Le
français langue universelle ou parler moribond" (1946); "Nouvelle défense (mais non point
illustration) de la langue française" (1950); "Les américanismes dans le français contemporain"
(1961). Trescases (139–40). Trescases's study brings statistical accountability to Etiemble's claims.

from the pact all contributed to the anti-American atmosphere that surrounded de Gaulle. Squabbles between France and Britain over Common Market entry did nothing to relieve tensions. Culturally, the manifestation of Anglo-American popular influence had not reached anything like the epidemic proportions of today. There were no McDonalds or Harry Potters. French and European films and filmmakers dominated the market: Godard, Truffaut, Bertolucci, Fellini. Only front-line American and English films found their way systematically into cinemas, although small specialty houses ran westerns (mostly John Wayne titles and *High Noon/Le train sifflera trois fois*), Jerry Lewis features, and *Gone with the Wind/Autant en emporte le vent*. Johnny Holliday, Georges Brassens, Charles Aznavour, Mireille Mathieu, and Françoise Hardy starred as perennial headliners at the Olympia and elsewhere. American jazz had long been esteemed by French *amateurs*, but primarily as an intellectual pursuit. In Paris one could be sure to find an Anglo-American hamburger only at a lone Wimpy's restaurant (an English chain whose name derives from a Popeye cartoon character) where Parisians came in elegant attire to dine on the exotic fare knife and fork in hand. A strained version of the "hot dog" could be found as well: a lengthy sausage stuffed into the center of a portion of baguette and surrounded with French mustard. An American inspired fantasy institution, le Drugstore, attracted students, tourists, and people of "*standing*," but it resembled nothing in the U.S. or the UK.

Beneath the surface, however, the cultural "invasion" had truly begun. French teens looked abroad as an escape from a culture out of step with the youth movements in England and the U.S. In lycées throughout France the *assistants d'anglais* from the UK were soon hounded by students smitten with *Beatlemania*; their American counterparts struggled to decipher the entangled lyrics of the Beach Boys for wide-eyed youngsters bent on becoming initiates of *le surfing*. As the sixties wore on in de Gaulle's tedious Paris, the French-disheveled Flower Children packed a Montparnasse club called *Le Week-End* on rue de la Gaité and hung out there until all hours of the morning; and the City of Light finally acquired *le soul* when James Brown's European tour came to town and his *show* (an Anglicism documented as early as the late-nineteenth century) dazzled audiences night after night.

Signs such as "pizza américaine" and "heures joyeuses" ("happy hour") belonged to the future. Yet Madame de Gaulle, who shared Etiemble's sensibilities, was not amused by the English phrases she observed cropping up in and about Paris. She waged a mini campaign that was amply covered by the press. The public at large attributed her designs to the same regal *snobisme* (an aged Anglicism favored by Maupassant) that had become her husband's trademark. Her concern changed nothing. *Oléoduc* was not about to replace *pipeline* in popular parlance; and the proprietors of *les night clubs* (already in use in the thirties) and sex shops (*le sex-shop* would not appear until the early-seventies) around the Place Pigalle and along rue Saint Denis could not be expected to take down of their own accord placards reading *strip-tease or films hard(s)*.

The first chapter of *Parlez-vous franglais?* bears the title "Histoire pas drôle." It consists of a humorous text laced with Anglicisms that, while exaggerated, conveys an ominous potential beyond its lexical borrowings. It begins thus:

> Je vais d'abord vous conter une manière de *short story*. Elle advint à l'un de mes *pals*, un de mes potes, quoi, tantôt chargé *full-time*, tantôt chargé *part-time* dans une institution mondialement connue, le C. N. R. S. Comme ce n'est ni un *businessman*, ni le fils naturel d'un *boss* de la City et de la plus *glamorous ballet-dancer in the world*, il n'a point pâti du *krach* qui naguère inquiétait *Wall Street*; mais il n'a non plus aucune chance de bénéficier du *boom* dont le *Stock Exchange* espère qu'il fera bientôt monter en flèche la cote des valeurs. Vous *réalisez* que ce n'est pas un *crack*, mon copain. (13, emphasis added)

Now the business and commercial terminology dominating the passage might be attributed to France's longstanding (and envious) denigration of England as a venal, commercializing society (and culture), a status inherited and enhanced by the upstart Yankees in the nineteenth century and labeled the cult of the "almighty dollar." In reality British and American products—from toothpaste to laundry detergents—were becoming increasingly prevalent in France in the 1960s. Indeed, the American "alien corporation" Procter and Gamble enjoyed the reputation of being the largest company in the country; and IBM and its British counterpart, BULL, competed for the spoils of the nascent computer industry while French companies looked on in awe.

Etiemble's apprehensions, he makes it clear throughout the text, extended far beyond linguistic window dressing or business concerns. To his mind the very essence of France was at stake. He pointed to Quebec as a prime example of a culture and a language in the process of being absorbed by the "greater" Anglophone community.[2] In the conclusion to the second edition (1973), he took to task *The New York Herald Tribune*, the newspaper whose Paris offices produced the daily copy read religiously by Americans in France: "Ces gens sont francs," he wrote. "Ils ne nous cachent pas leurs intentions prochaines: parlez franglais, ou disparaissez comme nation. Ce qui revient à dire: disparaissez comme nation et comme culture; ou disparaissez comme culture et comme nation." And that is exactly what will happen in final analysis, he added, "si le gouvernement ne fait pas son devoir" (356–57).

6.1.1 Servan-Schreiber: the government responds

The French government did intervene, but not before another writer, the political analyst and founder of *L'Express* Jean-Jacques Servan-Schreiber, produced a best-selling essay that sent shock waves throughout the country: *Le défi américain* (1967). De Gaulle's pull out from NATO and the creation of the Force de Frappe notwithstanding, Servan-Schreiber urged France and Europe to take decisive measures to combat the increasing economic and technological dominance of American enterprises. He carried his message to lecture halls and public forums in France and other "Common Market" countries. He decried the shortfalls in European research and funding that could only be overcome, he reasoned, through multi-level cooperation in the form of the establishment of collective economic and political policies and a common currency. The widely translated book and its fiery author provided a boost to a foundering European Union beset with British recalcitrance and rekindled the hope of a revitalized and decentralized France. The denunciation made it all the easier for the French to reject de Gaulle and to reformulate policies in the aftermath of the "Vive le Québec libre" fiasco and the tumultuous events of 1968.

By 1973 a good deal had changed in France. New political and economic directions had been undertaken, including an updated version of

---

[2] In reality Quebeckers had already come to the same realization and had begun a program of language control that would ultimately serve as a model for France. It was not until the1970s and the success of the Parti Québécois, however, that meaningful results were produced. The separatist agenda was able to establish French as the province's official language and to enact legislation to mandate and monitor its use in a broad spectrum of affairs: business, education, medicine, juridical matters, and so on. The legislation included stringent enforcement measures and provided for the personnel to enact them.

language reform. If Etiemble still had reason for concern, he could point to progress in the battle against what he now defined as "l'impérialisme yanqui":

> Moins de dix ans après la première édition de *Parlez-vous franglais?* le gouvernement a pris plusieurs des mesures que je préconisais pour lutter contre le fléau qui nous livre à *l'impérialisme yanqui*. Voici enfin que le *Journal Officiel* du 18 janvier 1973 publie une liste de plusieurs centaines de mots et tours franglais qui sont déconseillés ou bannis de nos vocabulaires techniques. (Etiemble 1973:11, emphasis added)

In effect this was the first in a lengthy record of government measures that would be catalogued in the *Journal Officiel* in the coming decades. Historically, of course, precedents dated back to the Renaissance and François I. Theoretically, given the country's socialistic institutions and practices, as well as its administrative centralization, such measures could be more pervasive and could be monitored more effectively than in more federated systems. Just as the Villers-Cotterêts ordonnance had been enforced in the King's *parlements*, approved technical terminology could be required in government documents, contracts, and government controlled radio and television.

6.1.2 *Le franglais vingt ans après*: statistical realities, cultural concerns

The list to which Etiemble refers resulted from political maneuvers following the publication of the first edition of his book, beginning in March 1966 with the establishment of the Haut Comité pour la Défense et l'Expansion de la Langue Française. In 1972 a hands-on approach was facilitated by the creation of individual ministerial committees, each of them charged with the oversight of particular lexical corpuses. Beyond the initial list and after three years of deliberations, in December 1975 legislation relative to the "défense de la langue française" was voted into law specifically mandating the use of French in the audio-visual industry as well as certain business, work, and employment procedures. Seven years later, in 1982, Pierre Trescases authored the book *Le franglais vingt ans après* in which he conjectured that if the1975 law was promoted as a continuation of the "croisade contre le franglais" (9), the breadth of the measures served another purpose: suppression of regional and minority languages. Trescases argued that in reality such measures were designed to discourage all forms of "bilingualism," domestic as well as foreign.

In his initial chapter, "Les faits," he wrote the following concerning government attempts to standardize the national idiom:

> Ces mesures linguistiques prises par le pouvoir central ne sont-elles pas en effet comme les actions individuelles dirigées, de manière plus ou moins directe et consciente, contre des influences étrangères, c'est-à-dire non indigènes aussi bien que non nationales? Entendons par là: non seulement toute autre langue dite de civilisation mais aussi ce qu'on nomme aujourd'hui les langues régionales [...] En un mot, les autres idiomes de l'Hexagone ne finissent-ils pas, et ce n'est pas toujours sûr qu'ils ne soient les premiers visés, par être les principales victimes de ces manifestations du nationalisme linguistique français? (9)

In order to put such questions into perspective, Trescases proposed to analyze quantitatively and qualitatively (lexically, morphologically, phonologically, syntactically) the impact of Anglo-American borrowings on the French language following World War II. The findings are of paramount interest. Having amassed the relevant data from both general and specialized dictionaries (neologisms, Anglicisms, contemporary speech), other related sources (cinema lexis, the press, etc.), and prior studies, he came to several conclusions concerning the most visible of the categories, the lexical category. Despite conflicting data emanating from the various emphases of the sources consulted, he determined that since 1945 several hundred Anglo-Americanisms had found their way into general dictionaries but that their number, statistically, represented no more than 2.5% of the neologisms created between 1949 and 1960 and an even lesser percentage between 1960 and 1979. Moreover, their usage, as determined by studies focusing on the press (*Le Monde, Le Figaro, L'Humanité*), actually had decreased to fall below 1% overall, although a slightly higher percentage was found for advertisements in *Le Monde*, for example (1.5%), and a significantly higher percentage for highly specialized vocabulary in the same newspaper (4%).

In matters of technical and scientific vocabulary, however, an entirely different picture emerged: "c'est par milliers que les emprunts à la langue anglaise ont déferlé dans les vocabulaires techniques et scientifiques." Trescases points to that state of affairs as an international phenomenon, rather than a purely French concern. Internationally, by 1980, "American supremacy" in science and technology had produced an Anglo-American lexical majority of 65% whereas the French language contributions had experienced a decline of from 5.2% in 1961 to a mere 2% twenty years later. Furthermore, over the same period in France the percentage of scientific and technological studies published in French had decreased from 90% to 47%, the remainder, ostensibly, in English.[3]

Quantitatively, these data tend to substantiate the premise that as of the early-1980s Anglo-American lexical borrowings, in the public sector, posed no real threat to the integrity of the French language. Continued intervention by the French government (lists were updated regularly after 1975) targeted "specialized" areas of lexical incursion that had little to do with matters of general culture. Perceptions to the contrary related to visibility. American and British television programs, though dubbed, could be seen with increasing regularity in France (*Dallas* was truly an international phenomenon; it spawned similar home grown productions throughout Europe, including France); British and American music (including country music) made new inroads on the airways (once again across Europe). An increasing number of slick, glitzy, but otherwise mediocre American films appeared at name-line cinemas. Franchises of American fast food and pizza restaurants proliferated, giving birth to French renditions and changing the iconography along urban streets. Esthetes complained that gastronomy itself was imperiled, owing to these influences and the influx of tourists who could not tell a sole from a *limande* (a lesser, hybrid version of the coveted fish). French wines were being forced from their pinnacle and having to make room for the California upstarts. Clearly, French culture was in transition. Understandably, traditionalists (language purists prominent among them) reacted negatively, lamented the loss, and supported further government measures. Their stance derived from qualitative concerns. The quality of French life was endangered in their view, and with it the very language-linked identity that had been cultivated since the seventeenth century.

6.1.3 Lexicogenesis: the dreaded neologism or creative neology?

Linguistically, what was also involved was the traditional aversion to neologisms that, regardless of their origin or form, had long been a hallmark of the "guardians of the French language." In the general scheme of things

---

[3] Trescases (14). The statistics were drawn from an analysis of vocabulary in *Chemical Abstracts* whose results were published in *Le Monde* in September of 1981.

and for a number of reasons, then, adverse reactions to Anglo-Americanisms hardly seem out of the ordinary. Yet the rapidly changing socio-economic, technical, and scientific landscape after 1945 imposed constant innovation and necessitated a change in attitude. Neology/lexicogenesis became a more pressing fact of life than ever before. The question of how to differentiate between the vicissitudes of Anglicisms, on the one hand, and the dynamics of creative neology on the other does not have an easy answer. In *Anglicisms, Neologisms and Dynamic French*—a revision of his 1987 doctoral dissertation (written in French at the Sorbonne)—Michael D. Picone presents perceptively the parameters of the problem:

> To say that *week-end* in French is an Anglicism is uncontroversial. But what of *station-service*, whose elements are French? Plainly, it is a semantic calque in imitation of English *service station*. But is it also a partial semantic calque, in that no particle is provided to define the link between the two component nouns? Does the existence of the same apparently innovative structure in other binomial constructions, such as *assurance-vie*, "life insurance," but without benefit of any known link to English, attest to the spread of a structural Anglicism? Or does it provide evidence for an opposite conclusion: that English influence reinforces but does not create this kind of structural innovation, which is being sourced primarily in some other neological dynamic in the language? (1)

Picone divides the problem along the lines that Trescases had established. His taxonomy includes seven categories that provide for semantic and morphological mutation over time (quoted verbatim 4–8):

1. Integral borrowing: This is when a new word, morpheme or locution of Anglophone confection accompanies a new entity or concept into the recipient French language: *scanner* (n.), *week-end, un self-service, un self.*

2. Semantic borrowing (semantic calque): This is when a preexisting French word, morpheme or locution shifts in meaning or becomes more extended or more restricted in meaning due to imitative language contact with English: *réaliser.*

3. Structural borrowing (structural calque): This is when morphosyntactic structural innovation is attributable to language contact with English resulting in its imitation in French: *tour-opérateur.*

4. Pseudo-Anglicism: This is when a neologism of French confection but composed of English constituents mimics an integral borrowing: *new look, tennisman.*

5. Hybrid: This is when a neologism of French confection combines elements of English with French, Latin or Greek: *top-niveau,* meaning "top level or quality."

6. Graphological borrowing: This is when a graphic or graphemic element of English is replicated or when a preexistent element of the French writing system is assigned a new function in French usage due to contact with English (especially in advertising): *modern Hôtel, Rapid Service,* [makdo] for McDonald's.

7. Phonological borrowing: This is when a phone, a sequence of phones or a phoneme is introduced into French primarily due to contact with English: the velar nasal *-ing* in *parking* and *footing.*

Picone readily admits that not all examples fall into a particular category. His exhaustive probings also allow for such phenomena as code mixing (an English phrase within a French song, for example), analyticity, syntheticity, normativity, derivation and compounding, and so on. The overwhelming documentation he provides is, frankly, overwhelming. His conclusions merit close attention. He emphasizes the creativity of the process, "the synthetic nature of the new terms," their success in "encoding semantic complexity with concision," their efficacy in responding to "the requirements and dispositions of a changed ambient culture" (366). In other words, he shares the same optimism that Brunet has expressed in "Ce que disent les chiffres." If he readily admits that significant alterations in the language have occurred, he has confidence in the resilience and adaptability of both the language and its inherent culture.[4]

6.2 The "Loi Toubon" of 1994: a language police

Picone's book appeared in 1996, the bulk of his research having been completed prior to 1994; only a handful of titles dating from that year are

---

[4] A very different conclusion was reached by Maurice Pergnier in his *Les anglicismes. Danger ou enrichissement pour la langue française?* (1989). Indeed, his "postface" depicts the French as abdicating in the face of American linguistic imperialism. He issues a challenge and a call to rally against the incursion, to "prendre acte" (208). As in the past, the French government was poised to do just that.

referenced in his extensive bibliography, and none after it.[5] The time frame is significant, for the controversial "Loi Toubon" enlarging and extending the 1975 language legislation dates from the summer of 1994. The law, so called for Jacques Toubon, the Minister of Culture who pushed it through administrative and legislative channels, stirred political division and drew vociferous criticism from several academics. The Conseil Constitutionnel (the high court of France) was called into the fray on July 1, 1994 to examine its constitutionality. Whereas the Conseil's decision of July 29 upheld its overall constitutionality, two provisions were found to be contrary to the freedom of thought and expression clauses contained in article 11 of the Déclaration des droits de l'homme et du citoyen (see below).

The constitutionality of the law drew on article 2 of the Constitution which had been approved only in June of 1992 and according to which "la langue de la République est le français." The administrative responsibility for language oversight was established by decree (April 16, 1993), placing the charge in the hands of the Ministre de la Culture et de la Francophonie and the Délégation Générale à la Langue Française et aux Langues de France (the D.G.L.F). The D.G.L.F. defines and defends its charge on its web page. The Délégation, specifically, has the responsibility of elaborating "la politique linguistique du Gouvernement en liaison avec les autres départements ministériels." Owing to the coming of age of the European Union and the dynamics of globalization, it is claimed that

> les pouvoirs publics sont appelés à réaffirmer une politique de la langue qui, tout en veillant à *garantir la primauté du français sur le territoire national*, participe à l'effort de cohésion sociale et contribue à la promotion de la diversité culturelle en Europe et dans le monde.[6]

In final form the law of August 4, 1994 contained twenty-four articles, each of them emanating from the first, which reads:

---

[5] Picone's bibliography is essential for anyone wishing to do further research on this question. He lists the following titles among the primary reference works: *Dictionnaire ethnologique et historique des anglicismes* (Paris: Delagrave, 1929); *Dictionnaire des anglicismes* (Paris: Le Robert 1980/1990); *Dictionnaire de franglais* (Paris: Guy le Prat, 1980); and *Dictionnaire des anglicismes* (Paris: Larousse, 1982). Manfred Görlach's *A Dictionary of Anglicisms in Sixteen European Languages*, of course, would not appear until 2001.

[6] http://www.culture.gouv.fr:80/culture/dglf/accueil.htm, emphasis added. This politically correct contextualization of safeguarding the "primacy of the French language" in France is written to include both "plurilinguisme" and the promotion of the French language

Langue de la République en vertu de la Constitution: la langue française
est un élément fondamental de la personnalité et du patrimoine de la
France. Elle est la langue de l'enseignement, du travail, des échanges et des
services publics. Elle est le lien privilégié des Etats constituant la communauté
de la francophonie.

As straightforward as it may appear, this and subsequent provisions provide
the legal basis for denying regional languages and LSF primary status in the
classroom, a point of contention that persists more than a decade later. The
new law also exceeds the purview of the 1975 statute in employment, financial, trade, publicity, and audio-visual related controls. Product descriptions,
labels, and operating instructions are among the more obvious and least controversial targets. Other areas appear more tenuous. The concern cited by
Trescases regarding the falling number of research projects conducted in
French is the focus of two provisions. Article 6 stipulates that, unless the
event concerns foreigners exclusively or foreign commerce, 1) any participant in a demonstration, colloquium, or congress in France has the inherent
right to use the French language; 2) all documents relating to said programs
must be written in French (translations may be supplied, additionally); 3)
presentations and their publication may be in a foreign tongue, but synopses
in French must be provided. Article 7 invokes the same synopsis requirement
for the publication of public service documents or documents that are publicly funded. The Conseil Constitutionnel voided two provisions: one requir-
ing teachers and researchers receiving public funding to either publish their
findings in French or to provide translations in French, another mandating
the use of "officially approved terminology" anytime the French language is
legally required. For all the categories of infractions remaining in effect, it
should be added, the law provided for penalties and sanctions, thus, in effect,
criminalizing non-French language usage. It should also be added that,
according to polls, a significant majority of the French people favored the
legislation.[7]

"comme langue de communication internationale." The "plurilingualism" stance thus has
more to do with Anglocentrism and the threat of English language proliferation than with
nurturing diversity or multiculturism.

[7] In his article titled "Linguistic Purification, the French Nation-State and the
Linguist," Jacques Durand is careful to distinguish the intent of the "Loi Toubon" from the
oppressive language policies of the former Yugoslavia, Nazi Germany, Franco's Spain, among

6.2.1 Academics object

Across the Atlantic in March of 1994, while the controversial law was still in the making, the annual French Literature Conference at the University of South Carolina had assembled a distinguished group of sixteen scholars from the United States and France. The theme that year was "Values in French literature." Given the venue and the topic, it is not surprising that Franco-American polarities should surface. The keynote address, delivered in English by the late Naomi Schor, reviewed the literary, cultural, and historical relations of the two countries in terms of two "universalisms," that is to say two contrasting, narcissistic world-views. Other presentations, in French or English and without benefit of synopses, treated various aspects of the question relating to authors as diverse as Pascal, Corneille, Diderot, Flaubert, George Sand, Marguerite Duras, and Roland Barthes. Jean-Jacques Thomas's paper, "Les hommes de paroles"—much anticipated owing to its focus—zeroed in on the "Loi Toubon."[8] Concern arose because of the presence of a representative of the French government who had come to preside at a Palmes Académiques ceremony involving a university professor. Opposition in intellectual circles in France had been keen, and Thomas's incisive observations held no promise that the visiting dignitary would be amused. A solution was found by contriving an impromptu tour of the azalea and magnolia adorned campus at precisely the time Thomas was to speak. Potential "misunderstandings" were thus avoided.

Of course Thomas's presentation could be read in published essay form in the annual *FLS* volume. But that would be after the fact, publication being some months away. Readers of the text could not mistake Thomas's

---

others (the Kurds of Turkey could be added to his list). Durand cites the long history of centralization in France and efforts to standardize the national idiom as contextualizing elements. He is right to do so, of course. He is also right in the following assessment, an obvious motivating factor: "The status of French as a major world-language and especially as the language of diplomacy has clearly been in decline throughout the twentieth century. The economic, military and cultural power of the United States combined with a widespread use of English throughout the former British empire have led to a situation where English has become the *koine* of the modern world. Even within the EU, the presence of Britain and of countries with a strong anglophile tradition such as Denmark has weakened the role of French as a working language" (82).

[8] Thomas's title derives from a book by Claude Hagège: *L'homme de Parole*. Both Thomas and Schor were teaching at Duke University at the time.

position on the Law, however, nor his views on language values in general. With regard to the French language, he expressed dismay. "La langue française," he wrote, "n'est plus le havre de paix œcuménique où l'on sent à l'aise et chez soi." The French language, he continued, is involved in

une guerre [...] qui date du moins du temps du brûlot d'Etiemble sur le franglais. Chaque année, depuis, semble nous apporter un écho de batailles livrées épisodiquement. Que l'on se souvienne, il y a deux ans, des démarches et contre-marches à propos de la réforme de l'orthographe; aujourd'hui c'est Michel Serres [of the Académie Française] qui apporte son soutien à la loi ultra-nationaliste dite "De l'usage du Français en France" (adopteé par le Sénat en première lecture le 14 avril 1994). [...] Cette nouvelle tentative dogmatique de purifier et de faire de la langue française un monopole d'usage, va tout à fait à l'encontre d'un modèle pluraliste et multiculturel fondé sur un relativisme des valeurs consensuelles. Contre le "plurilinguisme" qui semble la formule adaptée à l'Europe et seule capable de ne pas éliminer la France des grandes conférences scientifiques et technologiques internationales. (12)

For Thomas, beyond the political expediency relating to impending elections, the measure reflected the very narcissism noted by Schor and, for all its pretense, could only be counterproductive with regard to the goal of maintaining the French language as a viable vehicle of international communication. French linguists, he pointed out, had voiced their support of "plurilingualism" and their faith in "les hommes de paroles" in contrast to what might be termed a misguided "neo-Chomskyism" that reduced language to an abstraction to be manipulated as though it existed ipso facto and devoid of human medium.

Thomas's admonition concerning the risk France was running by legislating a "linguistic monopoly" goes beyond concern for minority and regional languages. Since 1958 the European Union's Council of Ministers has followed a policy of granting official (and working) status to the languages of all member countries: Dutch, French, German, and Italian as of that year. Other languages were added as membership grew: Danish and English (1973), Greek (1981), Portuguese and Spanish (1986), Finnish and Swedish (1995). As membership has increased since then, the dynamics and costs of translation and dissemination have increased commensurately, prohibitively according to some. As Leigh Oakes explains, the United Nations operates with only six official languages for 189 countries (Arabic, Chinese, English, French, Russian, Spanish) and the Council of Europe functions with only two languages for 43 countries (English and French). As a consequence a movement to limit the EU's official working languages has gained some momentum. "English is often claimed to be best suited to the role of EU's official working language," Oakes continues, "either alone or in addition to one or two other languages. Much to the indignation of the French, it has already taken over as the main language used by young Eurocrats" (133). Given the reductive character of the provisions of the Loi Toubon, France's objections to similar EU measures (which might not include French at all) could prove politically inauspicious, to say the least.

6.2.2 The statistics

Law number 94-665 of August 4, 1994 went into full effect September 7, 1995, allowing the various agencies and organizations under its jurisdiction the time to make appropriate adjustments. Owing to their complexity, regulations for the international transport sector were not in place until July 1, 1998. Whereas the 1975 law did not stipulate specific penalties or sanctions, an impediment to its effectiveness and enforcement, the new law brought infractions under existing consumer and fraudulent activity codes. The law also provided for the participation of designated language associations in court proceedings in the interest of maintaining civil rights and mandated that, in the public interest, a report be filed by the Government by September 15 of each year, its contents to be published via internet by the D.G.L.F.

Statistics for the years 1990 to 2000 published in the 2002 report document the increased number of investigations, infractions, adjudications, and convictions resulting from the new law. Already, under the 1975 law, vigilance had intensified (see table). Fines for the 80 convictions of the year 2000 totaled 40,540 euros or an average of approximately 500 euros per conviction.

Another table in the 2002 report lists the particular products and services involved in investigations and adjudications for the year 2000. The primary target of investigations and the highest number of adjudications befell industries producing furniture, jewelry, music, sporting goods, games, toys, and souvenirs. Of the 6584 total investigations, 1962 were conducted

Year	Number of Investigations	Infractions	Warnings Issued	Adjudications	Convictions
1990	796	186 (23%)	101	85	—
1991	1077	205 (19%)	95	110	—
1992	1080	216 (20%)	100	116	22
1993	1888	356 (19%)	191	165	22
1994	1918	308 (16%)	201	107	N.A.
1995	2576	390 (15%)	246	144	32
1996	6258	1091 (17%)	725	366	56
1997	7783	1103 (14%)	713	390	127
1998	7824	913 (12%)	658	255	124
1999	9573	1007 (11%)	725	282	98
2000	6584	826 (13%)	608	218	80

in this general category, 64 (out of a grand total of 218) resulting in adjudications. The largest ratio of adjudications to investigations was logged by the agricultural, fish and food products category, 55 adjudications out of a total of 784 investigations. For those concerned about educational and cultural matters, it may be comforting to know that the education category (including continuing education and driving schools) attracted only 11 investigations and resulted in 0 warnings and 0 adjudications; and the recreation, culture, and sports category attracted 64 investigations resulting in just 8 warnings and 0 adjudications. (Such statistics may not tell the entire story, but the fears of government persecution in such areas appear unfounded.)

The report details the activities of the Bureau de Vérification de la Publicité. Between May 1, 2000 and April 30, 2001, the BVP reviewed 11,481 television commercials, finding all but 607 in compliance with regulations. Of those not in compliance, a mere 20 cases merited a "do not broadcast" verdict, and only 4 were required to cease and desist after the fact. Grammarians may take heart that several investigations were undertaken for faulty spelling and solecisms of varying descriptions. English language incursions continued to be a focus: translations were demanded for such terms as *lubricants, very good boy, roots, aquadrink, the fashion album, the best of electromusic, freat, feat, kid, houseboat bonus track, employee self service, web design, software, handware, stock options, only by, a group company, connect you to the future techno sound, you tell your friends about, the TDK mediactive kids connection, robotic invention system, vision command,* among others. Translations from languages other than English, if any were required, are not recorded.[9]

6.3 *Evitez le franglais, parlez français!*

It is noteworthy that no other language receives such attention in the report. Indeed, the use of English in France has continued to spark controversy and concern into the new millennium. Members of the Institute express conflicting attitudes toward the inroads English has made in France and elsewhere. For the historical linguist Gérald Antoine the die has been cast. Speaking before the Association Curturelle des Administrations Financières in 2000, he had this to say about the current status of the English language:

> Soyons plus précis: le français n'est plus la langue de communication partout entendue et reconnue, y compris dans les domaines des sciences, des techniques, de l'économie—c'est à dire les secteurs-clés de la civilisation moderne. Il a cédé la place à l'anglais.

Antoine added that the transition had been underway for some time and that France needed to face up to the reality and make the necessary adjustments and accommodations. Michel Serres, who favored the protectionism of the 1994 law, had a different view as late as 1996. In an interview published in *Contemporary French Civilization*, he contested the "alarmism" of some of his French colleagues and members of the press:

> L'anglais tel que les journaux français le parlent est un anglais faux. Lorsque tel journal dit tel mot et que je le fais voir à mes collègues américains, ils ne comprennent pas. Donc ce n'est pas l'anglais qui est introduit en France, c'est le latin de Molière. Le latin de Molière n'était pas du latin; c'était une langue spéciale pour faire croire aux ignorants qu'on est plus fort qu'eux. (Giusti 116)

Perhaps so, but either because of such reasoning or in spite of it, there remains a viable market for French language self-help books in the tradition

---

[9] *Rapport au Parlement. La Politique linguistique conduite au niveau national. L'information des consommateurs,* available on the DGLF web site.

of the corrective grammars of the early-nineteenth century and the *franglais* texts of Etiemble and Trescases. The latest contribution belongs to Yves Laroche-Claire: *Evitez le franglais, parlez français!* (2004). Bernard Pivot makes the following statement in the "Préface":

> Voici le premier dictionnaire franglais-français. C'est un événement, parce que son auteur, Yves Laroche-Claire, a fait œuvre utile en proposant pour chaque anglo-américanisme un ou plusieurs équivalents français, en provenance soit des commissions *ad hoc* chargées précisément de substituer au mot "yankee" un terme qui sonne français, soit de sa propre imagination. (5)

Directly or indirectly, Pivot's remarks raise several points of interest. First, the fact that Laroche-Claire contributes solutions of "his own imagination" places the work in a tenuous linguistic category and fuels suspicions that underlying (and perhaps commercial) motivations may have more to do with public or popular perceptions than with linguistic realities. Second, the word *événement* is spelled in the traditional manner, rather than the recently reformed and widely accepted *évènement*, suggesting a conservative stance reminiscent of the dictates of the Academy's dictionary. Third, if the term "anglo-américanisme" designates both British and American usage, the term "yankee," used as a synonym, reflects the increasingly held notion (already documented by Trescases in 1982 [58–60] and used by Etiemble before him) that America (the USA) is the culprit and that, somehow, the British have been absolved. As the preface develops, Anglicisms are associated with "colonialism" and "cultural mutation." They have arrived by the boatload, Pivot observes, many of them technical terms "shipped from California." To write a preface for another author is to accept a measure of complicity, of course. It should not entail an abandonment of integrity, however. To his credit, Pivot saves his integrity in the final paragraph:

> A chacun son franglais. Rejeter tous les mots recensés par Yves Laroche-Claire serait déraisonnable. Les accepter tous, même les inutiles, les prétentieux, serait irréfléchi et ridicule. L'un des mérites de cet ouvrage est de nous obliger à prendre conscience d'un phénomène de société, d'une dérive grandissante de la langue. (8)

Yet the final sentence of that same paragraph returns to the promotional emphasis of the rest of the text: "Car ce dictionnaire est sûrement, hélas! appelé à grossir..." The suspension points say it all: the present volume does not suffice, it will need to be enlarged or joined by other volumes, thereby promising a lucrative future for author and publisher alike.

Laroche-Claire's "Introduction" follows the preface. In it he issues a "call to action" ("le temps n'est plus au discours mais à l'action" [9]), as though the French government had not been actively involved for more than thirty years. His rhetoric and recriminations translate hyperbolically as an impassioned call to revolt against oppression, treachery, and dictatorship:

> L'usage quotidien d'une langue française anglicisée à l'excès, relayé par les médias et la publicité, lamine inexorablement et insidieusement notre vocabulaire, mettant en péril des centaines de mots bien français. Nous sommes soumis à la dictature des *bodybuilding, brushing, casting, dumping, fixing, footing, forcing, holding, jogging, meeting, training*, etc. [...] C'est bien de notre culture commune qu'il s'agit; de la langue que nous partageons avec une communauté francophone riche de quelque cent vingt-neuf millions d'âmes. (9–10)

One hundred twenty-nine million "souls" (not people) from around the Francophone world, it is no longer a mere question of Metropolitan French. The statistic and the trope in tandem intimate a quasi-religious conflict of global proportions. Laroche-Claire appeals to the power of the people, because "official" efforts at "refrancisation," that is to say, "reclamation," of the French language have failed. And the means to victory? This little red book (actually, it is white): "Le présent ouvrage, unique dans son genre (as though scores had not been written following the Revolution), est conçu pour offrir à tous ceux désireux de refranciser leur vocabulaire un outil pratique les aidant dans leur démarche" (14).

All of this is not to say that Laroche-Claire's contribution has no instructional value. To the contrary, despite the fact that no sources are referenced, its nearly three hundred pages provide an up-to-date panorama of Anglicized words and phrases. It promotes an awareness and proposes potential remedies for those interested in speaking and writing a sounder, more authentic French. Teachers of French and their students, in both French speaking and English speaking environments, stand to benefit. In fact the 1048 entries offer a wealth of significant information as well as remedies and "official recommendations": etymologies, "glissements de sens" (shifts in meaning from English to French), synonyms, antonyms, historical and cultural contextualizations. Phonetic transcription would be useful in some instances:

the pronunciation of the term *débuger*, for example—meaning to "debug" (a computer or computer program)—defies the imagination. The terms themselves may surprise or mystify the Anglophone unfamiliar with the forces at work in the process. In addition to the pseudo Anglicism *tennisman* (drawn analogically from words such as *barman* and *sportsman*), the sport of tennis has added the verb *débreaker*, not meaning to "debreak," but rather to "break back." Other entries that catch the eye include: *hardcore gamer* (Ce logiciel de jeu a pour cible les *joueurs invétérés*); *pool* (*groupe bancaire or piscine privée*); *speedé* (*surexcité, hyperactif*); *tag* (*graffitis*); *truster* (*monopoliser, s'approprier*); *déstresser* ([*se*] *décontracter, détendre*); *lock-out* (*interdire de travail*); *megastore* (*grand magasin, grande galerie*); *must* (*indispensable, immanquable*); *sponsoriser* (*financer, patronner*).

6.4 Language cultures, language sensibilities

As brief as it is, this list helps understand why conscientious individuals may be offended by the proliferation and concerned about the integrity of the former universal language of Europe. It also serves to demonstrate how the dynamics of the process exceed mere lexical appropriation. If the English language provides the source in each instance, the product very often remains distinctively French. The terms *speedé* and *truster* result from a morphological (re)structuring foreign to English which produces an accompanying semantic alteration. They thus tend to support Picone's findings to the effect that rather than being an isolated phenomenon and despite their common origin, "English borrowings [...] are entering the French lexicon as part of the response to the neological challenge"; lexicogenisis accomplishes its task "in ways that are clearly not English but rather of native French inspiration, and it also does so in ways that conform to the synthetic pressures that are operating in the language generally" (365).

French is hardly the sole language affected. Aware of the expanse of the proliferation throughout Europe, Manfred Görlach set about determining its magnitude by calling together an international team of twenty-two lexicographers who accepted the challenge of producing a comparative dictionary. The result, *A Dictionary of Anglicisms in Sixteen European Languages*, was published by Oxford University Press in 2001. It examines and lists terms in Germanic (Icelandic, Norwegian, Dutch, German), Slavic (Russian, Polish, Croatian, Bulgarian), Romance (French, Spanish, Italian, Romanian), and other European languages (Finnish, Hungarian, Albanian, Greek). The listings, documented through the early 1990s, total in the thousands. Holistic comparisons are difficult to make at this stage, for the volume lacks tables and statistics, understood to be forthcoming following digitization. The dictionary does provide 837 readily interpretable grids of terms selected, it would appear, at random. The grids may not be totally representative, but statistics derived from them provide at least some insight as to the proliferation of Anglicisms in individual languages. Statistical analysis of French, German, and Spanish (Anglicisms known in the latter two languages as Germish/ Denglisch and Spanglish) reveal the following: of the 837 lexical entries characterized by the grids, German has the highest number of listings, 734 or 88%; French ranks as second at 566 or 68%; and Spanish is a close third with 519 or 61%. What these figures convey, if they are at all representative, is that the French language is not unduly "victimized" in the grand scheme of things and in comparison with the country's European neighbors. At the very least and beyond national prerogatives, the fact that neither Germany nor Spain has mounted the sort of anti-Anglicism campaign underway in France for more than a quarter century speaks to the variance and range of sensibilities inherent in individual European language cultures.

7

A House Divided:
Madame la/le Ministre

L'OBÈLE, A FIRST NOVEL WRITTEN by Martine Mairal, presents itself as a literary hybrid. A subtle blend of first-person fictional narrative and scholarly (auto)biography, it draws on the French "new autobiography" of an Alain Robbe-Grillet and the "autofiction" of a Serge Doubrovsky.[1] Unlike its predecessors, however, Mairal's 2003 work, published by the well-known Editions Flammarion, contains footnotes, a bibliography, and information relative to recent colloquia devoted to the figure she portrays. The novel begins thus:

> La peste soit de l'Académie et des Académiciens! Aussi soumis à la voix de Richelieu que fille transie à son galant. Docte assemblée des plus prudents lettrés de France, réunis pour sa gloire et par sa volonté, ils ne le contredisent jamais. Le pouvoir et l'amour font également perdre le sens commun à cette sorte d'hommes. Fâcheux état à qui prétend en dicter les termes et en régler la définition! Il faut les voir façonner leur dictionnaire de la langue française à coups de serpe, déclarant hérétique l'usage des plus vieux mots de notre langue. (11)

---

[1] Fictionalized "autobiography" has the advantage of being non-definitive and thus renewable. Robbe-Grillet's trilogy (*Le miroir qui revient* [1984], *Angélique ou l'enchantement* [1986], *Les derniers jours de Corinthe* [1994]) kept the ink flowing for a full decade. The last title's eponymous Henri de Corinthe emerges as a blatant fabrication. Doubrovsky's elaboration of his controversial theory of "autofiction" has found perpetual rejuvenation in a series of self-centered Lacanian musings dating back to the 1969 publication of *La dispersion*. Mairal's contribution falls into the category of pseudo-autobiography.

The recriminations directed against the incipient Academy become more pointed in the pages that follow. They assail the decision to allow no women to participate in the great language debate despite the fact that it was mothers and nurses who taught its appointees to speak in the first place:

> A-t-on jamais parlé de langue paternelle? […] La vérité, c'est que Monsieur de Richelieu m'a volé mon cercle particulier d'amis érudits et l'a versé d'un trait de plume au rôle de son Académie. (13)

7.1 The stolen fire: Marie de Gournay speaks out (again)

The voice belongs to Marie de Gournay who accuses Richelieu of stealing away the members of the language circle she had brought together only to deny her the right to sit with them because she is a woman. The accusation of male-dominant power politics and sexism thus accompanies the very formation of the Academy, the novel contends.

Historically, Marie articulated her women's rights stance in two works that have drawn increasing critical attention in recent years: *Egalité des hommes et des femmes* (1622) and *Grief des dames* (1626), the first title predating the establishment of the Academy by more than a decade. These writings defend the intellectual capacities of women who, Marie insists, only appear to be inferior because society has not granted them equal access to education. For those women who have somehow managed to overcome that obstacle (as she had), she argues forcefully for parity—especially for writers such as herself who are so often summarily dismissed as unworthy pretenders to a masculine calling. Marie's egalitarian appeal was not new. It originated in the early-fifteenth century with Christine de Pisan and by the seventeenth century had become a recognized literary form accessible to females alongside epistolary writing. Marie's notoriety and voice owe their resilience to a male, however, Michel de Montaigne, whose works she edited and to whose well-being she devoted her life. *L'obèle*, the novel's title, signifies a proofreading symbol indicating marginalia to be added to the body of the text. If Marie is a willing accomplice to the great essayist, she is compelled, literally—as she readily admits in the narrative—to live her life in the margins of his writings.

Mairal's novel brings both persona and period language to the fore. As the initial lines of the novel attest, the narrative resuscitates the color and vibrance of the "preclassical" French that Richelieu's reformers, bent on bringing the language under control, would decry as aberrations. New millennium readers cannot fail to recognize the relevance of this restorative revoicing (surely a factor in Flammarion's decision to publish an unknown writer). The emphases have changed, but the setting, principals, and conflict remain the same: four centuries later and despite government efforts to mediate, the language controversy pitting women against the Academy persists amidst renewed accusations of politicization and sexism.

7.2 Gautier and *La Gazette des Femmes*: defending the *genre masculin*[2]

For the perceptive reader a second book, published in 2005, sounds a related a note of irony. *Gautier et l'Allemagne*, edited by Wolfgang Drost and Marie Hélène Girard, is a collection of critical essays that examine Théophile Gautier's relationship with German writers and culture. It is a worthy volume containing contributions by leading Gautier scholars. As such, it has nothing to do with feminism or the Academy, but the final section listing the names and credentials of the contributors bears the title "Autrices et Auteurs." The term "autrice" may surprise certain readers, not so much because it is "feminized," but because it is the "approved" Swiss signifier rather than the recently recognized French (une) "auteur" or (une) "auteure." The German site of the colloquium from which the collection derives and its German publisher (Universität Siegen) explain the preference. The Gautier connection with the feminized forms of "auteur"—and the irony—stems from the columns he penned anonymously for the *Figaro* (sometimes in collaboration with Nerval) at the beginning of his long career as journalist.

---

[2] Gautier's views on grammatical gender may be placed in historical perspective by consulting Saint-Gérand's penetrating article on the "sexuisemblance des noms": "Dans un *Littré* classique, les genres sont-ils la propriété qu'ont les noms de représenter en langue les sexes, et—dans certaines—leur absence?" Saint-Gérand divides the question into four parts: "Dictionnairique," "Stéréotypes," "Idéologie grammaticale," "Langue et linguistique." After having underscored the incoherence on the subject reflected in the opinions of various writers, lexicographers, grammarians, and linguists, he notes across the nineteenth century a movement toward representational ambiguity issue of an evolving social construct of desire, on the one hand, countered by the need for distinct representational finality imposed by an increasingly scientifically oriented and objectifying society, on the other hand. Gautier, both a hard-line "gender grammarian" and the author of *Mademoiselle de Maupin*, may be seen as embodying the two.

His reputation as esthete, semanticist, and consummate master of the technical vocabulary germane to the performing, plastic, and decorative arts was matched only by the esteem in which editors held the cheerful bantering that endeared him to a broad range of readers and boosted sales. Gautier was no misogynist (a title long associated with his friend and admirer Charles Baudelaire), but should his column call for it, he could assume the role as ardent chauvinist. When controversy arose concerning the publishers of *La Gazette des Femmes*, he seized the opportunity to display the full array of his humoristic arsenal.

The catalog of the Bibliothèque Nationale in Paris provides basic information concerning the *La Gazette des Femmes*. The full title of the publication reads: *Journal de Législation et de Jurisprudence, Littéraire, Théâtral, Commercial, Judiciaire, de Musique et des Modes. Rédigé par une société de femmes et d'hommes.* Its fifteen issues date from July 1836 to April 1838. The library's holdings on microfiche include only nine issues—the numbers six through eleven of volume two are missing. The name Madame Marie-Madeleine Poutret de Mauchamps appears as owner and "rédacteure en cheffe." From the outset the journal publicizes itself as an organ of political activism in the interest of women's rights. Its specific agenda is announced as seeking to bring to the Charter of 1830 a series of amendments establishing "l'égalité des sexes devant la loi." To that end the initial issue highlights a petition to rewrite the laws governing the press to allow *La Gazette de Femmes* to begin publication as a daily newspaper without having to comply with the stipulation that it be owned and directed by a male of legal age.

The editors took their task seriously. Their goals were wide-ranging. They sought to enlist the support of the bourgeoisie at a time of great economic and political expansion for the middle class. Their arguments exceeded the usual egalitarian appeals by going to the heart of bourgeois values and demonstrating that women were a vital—indeed indispensable—part of the economy. Women, they emphasized, had thus "earned" the entitlements of legal and social parity; hence they should be allowed to bear witness in matters pertaining to civil law; they should be allowed equal access to education and the professions; they should be spared the obedience clause in the marriage contract, and—a cause that would test emotions for generations to come— they should be granted the option to divorce. Needless to say, controversy and opposition arose. *La Gazette des Femmes* held its own for a time. It was the most effective and best-informed "feminist" publication of the day and might well have served as a model for subsequent endeavors had scandal not put a premature end to it after a run of only two years. The "propriétaire-gérante" of the journal, Marie-Madeleine Poutret de Mauchamps, was discovered to be a figurehead for the real editor: her paramour, a certain Frédéric Herbinot, a jurisconsult and former fashion journalist for trendy women's magazines. If readers felt deceived by the masquerade, they were appalled when in 1838 both were arrested and convicted on charges of moral corruption involving a minor. The general press feasted on their misfortune, of course; the couple's marriage as inmates in Saint-Lazare prison in October of 1838 brought the matter to a dramatic end.[3]

Gautier's journalistic interest in the affair grew out of the masquerade. He had already written *Mademoiselle de Maupin* whose eponymous protagonist had disguised herself as a man and, in so doing, had displayed courage, intelligence, and acumen. Gautier qua journalist was addressing another audience. In several articles published in 1836 and 1837, he mocked the would-be editor. He equated Marie-Madeleine with George Sand, claiming the two had been sighted recently in "compromising" attire: Sand dressed as a woman and Marie-Madeleine as a man. As the articles unfold, hyperbole makes it difficult to determine how Gautier really felt about the journal's political agenda. With regard to culture and language, however, there is little doubt: Gautier had no sympathy for the Journal's proposed language reform that, in support of parity for women in the professions, targeted the domination of the "genre masculin." His sense of lexical decorum suffered at the sight of the journal's feminized designations—"rédacteure," "cheffe," "avocate," "professeure," "docteure," "auteure," écrivaine," among others. He associated the reform with the bourgeois concept of Progress that, to his mind, was undermining aesthetic good taste and leading civilization down the path to venal pragmatism. As a consequence, these "semantic improprieties" moved him to take aim at the very basis of the journal's existence, the goal of attaining parity for women. In the March 18, 1837 issue of the *Figaro*, he wrote that the "Rédacteure en Cheffe" was requesting that "Louis Philippe soit considéré non-seulement comme Roi des Français, mais encore Roi des Françaises." The notion that the masculine plural could not serve as a gender neutral

---

[3] For further details pertaining to the journalistic "saga" of *La Gazette des Femmes*, see Abensour (212–14), Albistur and Armgathe (286–90), Henry (1994 and 2001), and especially Sullerot (191–209).

collective gives rise to a flippant diatribe that culminates with a question. What will such women want next, Gautrier asks, the "théâtre français" and the "théâtre française"? Gautier sees feminized nomenclature as solecisms and infers that such aberrations surely bode ill for the journal's entire program. In the same article he writes:

> Il est certain que si les femmes arrivent, suivant sa courageuse logique, aux grades de *députées*, de *ministresses*, de *soldates*, d'*électeures*, de *jurées*, etc., il demeure dans le langage politique des formules absurdes, des fautes grammaticales qu'il devient urgent de corriger.

Derisive accusation follows reproof. The article concludes with a warning of the impositions in store should the reform take hold. Everything will have to be rewritten in order to accommodate the so-called gender parity in language: patriotic songs, poetry, speeches, soliloquies.

> On chantera désormais:
>> Peuple français, et *française*, peuple de braves!
>> La liberté rouvre ses bras;
>> On nous disait, soyez esclaves,
>> Nous avons dit, soyons soldats et *soldates*.
>
> On déclamera pareillement sur un air connu:
>> Ah! Qu'on est fier d'être Français et *Françaises*
>> Quand on regarde la colonne.
>
> De même, on fredonnera:
>> Non, non, jamais
>> Le soldat français et *la soldate française*
>> Ne doute du succès.

7.3 Feminization: the failed attempt of 1984

It is curious to discover that one hundred seventy years later the same question continues to be debated in virtually the same terms as in the 1830s. Indeed, Gautier's reaction does not seem out of place today, given recent events and renewed polarities. While France forged ahead with legislation to counteract the threat of an Anglo-American language invasion, little attention was paid to renewed appeals to feminize the French language in recognition of the gains women had made and in support of those that remained to be

accomplished. If "feminization" had not become a national priority, it was
due in part to the status of French feminism. By the mid-1970s French
feminists had succeeded in attaining an international audience. Hélène
Cixous, Luce Irigaray, and Julia Kristeva were widely read and translated.
They were especially valued for their theories on the female voice, language,
and psyche. Therein lay the impediment: unlike their Anglo-American
counterparts, Toril Moi points out in her seminal *Sexual/Textual Politics*
(1985), they had not mobilized politically. Rather than operating at the "level
of politics," the impact of French feminist writers was "found to be at the
level of theory or methodology"; they "preferred to work on problems of
textual, linguistic, semiotic, or psychological theory, or to produce texts
where poetry and theory intermingle" (97). The dichotomy is an old one that
often crops up simplistically in discussions pertaining to essential differences
in Anglo-American/French culture and mentalities: theory and aesthetics
versus pragmatism, argumentation versus action, and so on. What is clear is
that the radicalization and politicization of the feminist movement that had
taken place in the United States had yet to come to France. The ensuing
years would witness a turnaround and with it, along with newly concerted
efforts to bridge the male-female gap across a broad spectrum of disparities,
the establishment of a reprioritized agenda that included a drive for official
recognition of feminized terms relating to professions, titles, ranks, and
functions. Moreover, it is accurate to say, the drive for linguistic parity would
become the most visible and openly contentious of those efforts.

    Bureaucratic mechanisms potentially capable of implementing
initiatives were not lacking. But a lengthy and evolving series of offices and
titles points to uncertainty and confusion. In 1965 the Comité du Travail
Féminin was instituted under the auspices of the Ministre du Travail. In
1974 that committee was upgraded to the Secrétariat d'Etat à la Condition
Féminine and rehoused within the office of Prime Minister. Two years later
the Délégation Nationale de la Condition Féminine, still under the Prime
Minister, opened its doors in Lyon. In 1978 The Secrétariat d'Etat à l'Emploi
Féminin came into being within the Ministère du Travail. That same year
the Prime Minister created the position of Ministre Délégué à la Condition
Féminine. The year 1981 saw the advent of yet another office, that of the
Ministre Délégué des Droits de la Femme (responsible to the Prime Minister).
In 1985 that position was upgraded to full ministerial rank and consolidated
the various other offices. The title has since undergone several alterations

and relocations, the latest version (2005) being an appointment within the Ministère de l'Emploi, de la Cohésion Sociale et du Logement. The appointment of Yvette Roudy as Ministre Délégué des Droits de la Femme and her promotion to full-fledged minister in 1985 was a turning point of sorts. Roudy had been in close contact with American feminists and had translated several of their works. Her own *La femme en marge* (1975) and *A cause d'elles* (1985) placed her alongside Marina Yaguello (*Les mots et les femmes*, 1978) as proponent of the elimination of sexism in language (and society) and solidified her position as spokesperson. Highly esteemed by both President Mitterrand and Prime Minister Laurent Fabius, she was able to arrange the appointment in 1984 of a Commission de Terminologie charged with reinstating or creating an official "feminized" terminology that would assimilate grammatical gender and natural gender.

The Commission, under the direction of "la Ministre des Droits de la Femme"[4] (Roudy), met with an immediate, negative response from the Academy in June of that year. Its declaration of opposition was drafted by Claude Lévi-Strauss, the celebrated ethnologist, professor at the Collège de France, and member of the Academy for over a decade. Lévi-Strauss defended "accepted" usage based on the Indo-European origins of French, a language family that makes no distinction between grammatical gender and natural gender. Moreover, he insisted, since French recognizes no true neuter (as some Indo-European languages do), the masculine serves without prejudice as the non-marked form and applies to mixed groups. The controversy had begun.[5] In July Benoîte Groult—journalist, biographer of French feminists such as Olympe de Gouges, author of the essay "le féminin au masculin," and "Présidente" of the Commission de Terminologie—replied in *Le Monde*. She herself had lobbied hard for the project and she minced no words; she accused the Academy of power mongering and nothing short of "verbal terrorism." A month later, in the September 7–13, 1984 issue of *Le Nouvel*

---

[4] Such was the title as Roudy understood it. When the decree legitimizing the Commission was published, she was dismayed to find that her title was listed as Madame *le* Ministre. The portent was all too obvious.

[5] The accounts found in Claudie Baudino's *Politique de la langue et différence sexuelle* (2001) have been extremely useful in establishing the chronology and tenor of events outlined in this chapter. Indeed, her study is nothing short of remarkable both for its abundant documentation and for its evenhanded thoroughness. It is essential reading for those drawn to the question of "gender politics" in France.

Observateur, Georges Dumézil, the Academy's renowned philologist and expert in Indo-European civilization, published a rebuttal with the derisive title "Mme Mitterrande, Mme Fabia." In addition to maintaining that the use of traditional titles such as *Madame le maire* sufficed to mark the gender of the title holder and was perfectly appropriate and justified within the domain of the Indo-European language community, he also submitted that the use of the masculine as a non-marked form did nothing to abuse the "opposite sex" but, rather, resulted in the loss of masculine identity, thereby representing—one is to infer—a willing sacrifice on the part of males in the interest of egalitarian, linguistic abstraction. Lines had been drawn and polarizing bifurcations had been imposed, harbingers of things to come: grammatical gender versus natural gender in language, sexism in language versus sexism in society, the Academy versus feminists, the Academy versus the French Government.

In addition to feminists such as Groult and Michelle Coquillat, the Commission recruited lexicographers and general linguists alike, the popular phonologist André Martinet the most broadly recognized of the group. Despite its composition the Commission faced an uphill battle; the polemics were stifling. The accusations and counter-accusations made it impossible to remove the project from the political arena. The media feasted. Cartoonists reveled. The Commission vacillated in the face of the Academy's standing and an adverse public that opposed orthographic reform and had come to view the feminization project as an attempt to commandeer the national idiom in the name of ideology. After numerous closed-door meetings, a report was produced supporting the use of the feminine form of the determinant (*une/la*) and the option of either the masculine form of the substantive or a form feminized according to the conservative guidelines recommended by the Commission: (*agent/agente*, for example), the use of the controversial Quebecois -*eur* solution (*auteure, professeure*) to be determined by usage (Baudino 245). As moderate as the report was, political maneuvering at the upper levels of government prevented the measure from becoming policy. The Academy had prevailed—but only for the time being.

7.4 A second attempt: the great divide of 1998

A decade later, March 6, 1998, yet another Prime Minister, Lionel Jospin, intervened. Believing the time had come for definitive action, he issued a circular mandating that two separate administrative bodies undertake the task of providing official guidelines for the feminization of terms relating to professions, titles, ranks, and functions. The decision stemmed from a series of events. The European Council had issued a similar circular in 1990 urging member constituencies to eliminate sexist terminology and to recognize fully the autonomy of both sexes. Canada, Belgium, and Switzerland had each produced guidelines recognizing divergent lexicons. Feminized terminology was already gaining headway in the press and elsewhere. *Le Monde* saluted the several feminized designators relating to the professions that appeared in the most recent edition of the Larousse dictionary. Other pressures and legislative prerogatives made the move both expedient and necessary. The proposed law on (sexual) parity modifying article 3 of Title I and article 4 of the Constitution was being shaped and readied for debate in the National Assembly and the Senate (it would be adopted in joint session in June of the following year [1999]).[6] Furthermore and most compellingly, five new ministers in Jospin's government insisted that their offices be designated by the feminine form—"Madame *la* Ministre" or "Madame *la* Garde des Sceaux," etc. (Groult 72).

The Academy, once again, was quick to respond and quick to condemn. Members contacted Jacques Chirac personally to express their dismay. The renewed "Querelle des Femmes" (also categorized as "la querelle du neutre" by Marc Fumaroli [*Le Monde*, 31 July 1998]) was set for center stage. The appointment of two separate bodies corresponded to the two sides of the question. Their composition could not have been more disparate. The first, the Commission Générale de Terminologie et de Néologie is a permanent board operating under the direct auspices of the Prime Minister. The second, the Institut National de la Langue Française, is the independent unit functioning as an arm of the CNRS (Centre Nationale de la Recherche Scientifique) charged with producing the *Trésor de la langue française*. The Commission Générale de Terminologie et Néologie, chaired by Gabriel de Broglie of the Académie des Sciences Morales et Politiques and the Conseil d'Etat, was composed of nineteen members, all of them prominent: six belonged to one of the Institute's academies, six were university professors, three held various ranking government titles, two were career diplomats, one a magistrate, and one an editor—only three were women. The Institut National

---

6 For a succinct discussion and history of the parity law, see Fauré.

de la Langue Française committee consisted of six work-a-day scholars very much abreast of recent developments in French language and culture, five of them women. It was obvious to informed onlookers that, in the end, these committees were sure to present Jospin with divergent recommendations.

7.4.1 The report of the Commission Générale de Terminologie et Néologie: a rejection

In tone and in substance the fifty-four page report of the Commission Générale de Terminologie et Néologie (electronic version) reads like an indictment rather than an objective evaluation. Its text alternates between blatant confrontation and pointed innuendo. Dated October 1998, it begins by reviewing the Commission's original mandate and chronicling the events leading to its current charge. From the outset the legitimacy of producing the guideline is placed in question. The very first sentence posits institutionalized language as the restrictive juridical rock upon which the French Nation is built: "Les compétences du pouvoir politique sont limitées par le statut de la langue, expression de la souveraineté nationale et de la liberté individuelle, et par l'autorité de l'usage qui restreint la portée de toute terminologie officielle obligatoire" (2). Previous efforts to feminize the French language— both in France and in other Francophone countries—are cast in dubious hue and have the sole "virtue" of revealing "les impasses à éviter." It is implied that the Prime Minister is ill-advised and that present efforts are an exercise in futility and a waste of time; the 1984 Commission failed in its task, one reads, owing to a lack of consensus on the legitimacy of the project and social outcry ("résistances du corps social à toute tentative autoritaire de diriger l'usage de la langue"[2]). Moreover, feminization is depicted as posing a grave danger to the Republic: on the one hand it purports to neutralize sexual difference in language, on the other hand it prevents, paradoxically, "toute désignation claire du sujet juridique" and thus places at risk the "principe républicain qui fonde nos institutions" (15) and the (abstract) citizen whose very existence and well-being depend on statutory language (2).

The last point is not to be taken lightly. Whereas some may see just another example of Chomskyism in this pronouncement, it is undeniable that the French language does not possess a neuter. Non-discriminatory referencing must utilize other means: as in other Romance languages the masculine form fulfills that function. Alternate means would need to delineate with at least the same clarity cases involving the "juridical subject." That tenet of the Commission's report appears unassailable. Too, the report recognizes that the French language does not benefit from a single universally feminizing suffix—unlike German—and that feminization, as it exists, has entailed a complex linguistic process determined by usage. As a language, French thus possesses within its very nature the capacity to feminize, and has done so according to need. Accordingly, there is no reason that the language itself should constitute a linguistic obstacle to feminization. In fact usage, the report also recognizes, has brought numerous feminizations to the professions (métiers) "where identification between individuals and their activities is complete" (witness the recent Larousse dictionary and several listings in the Academy's own dictionary). But as for the designation of functions, titles, and ranks, which as a matter of law are open to males and females alike and which do not equate individuals and activities, the report insists, the neutrality and "impersonality" of the masculine form inherent in Indo-European culture is essential. In other words, the designation "Madame *la* Ministre," for example, is thereby both deviant and illegitimate. Ultimately, the "laissez-faire" opinion of the 1998 Commission is diametrically opposed to the pro-active position taken by the government in the case of the Loi Toubon:

> Le bon sens demande d'admettre que nous sommes inscrits dans un mouvement de transformation de la société qui entraîne sans conteste des conséquences linguistiques. Cependant, il nous faut reconnaître que le langage est aussi une réalité objective qui a des règles de fonctionnement propres. Il n'est ni possible, ni souhaitable de les modifier d'une manière générale et mécanique, autoritaire et instantanée. (14–15)

If that stance was readily predictable, given the Commission's makeup, the form and terms of the argumentation reveal competing, surrogate agendas. The Commission expressed unequivocally its support of the proposed parity law: "La légitimité de cet objectif n'est pas contestable. Pour autant, l'écart entre le droit et la pratique n'est pas comblé. L'égalité de droit entre les hommes et les femmes exige une traduction concrète qui tarde à se manifester dans les faits" (11). Relevant statistics are cited in a footnote: a majority (53%) of low-level bureaucratic positions are occupied by women; yet only a small minority (10%) of the directorships in the central administration are exercised by women; 13% in the government as a whole; 3% at the prefect level; and a mere 2% in the diplomatic corps. But for all that, the report asserts emphatically: "il ne va pas de soi que cet objectif ait nécessairement une implication linguistique et que la parité doive se traduire dans la langue." Furthermore, the argument continues, making feminization of the French language a priority would run the risk of artificially inserting it as a fulcrum in a purely social conflict and thereby distorting the outcome. Language as such, the report holds, in order to retain its inherent value, must remain independent from social and political relativities: "Non seulement il n'est pas démontré que le langage soit une oppression, mais surtout il est dangereux de lutter contre une idéologie par une autre idéologie. Les phénomènes sociaux ou politiques évoluent et le langage reste." (11) To endeavor to modify language for such reasons is patently "absurd" and "vain" (10); the results in the end can only rival the "interprétations grammaticales arbitraires et hautement fantaisistes" of the *Dictionnaire féminin-masculin* published recently in Geneva and according to which the terms *la pondeuse, la couveuse, la balayeuse, la raboteuse, la moissonneuse* can only be feminine because they designate robotic, no-brainer tasks. Likewise, those who maintain that Medieval French accommodated feminizations more readily and in a healthier way than modern French are accused of being retrogressive, so many trogdolytes desirous of returning to the chaos from which the Renaissance of François I and subsequent policies of language control rescued civilization.

"Social or political phenomena evolve and language remains." The claim is worthy of a Rivarol, only the elegance of style and the power of metaphor are lacking. Language of course evolves, most often owing to political and/or social developments. The Commission has temporarily suppressed from memory the French Revolution and its enduring effects on semantics. Temporarily. Only two pages later the report asserts the contrary only to reject the premise upon which the feminization project resides. "Il n'est pas anormal," one reads, "que le langage traduise les changements de société et coïncide avec eux. La féminisation des titres est un phénomène social avant d'être un phénomène linguistique" (13). The argument only disintegrates further from there. The following page exploits the hyperbole used by Gautier a century and a half before. It is maintained that feminization endangers the very structure of the French language and would lead to the "feminine appropriation" of inflections, agreements such as "les garçons et les filles sont également *fortes* en maths" (14). Feminization is thus characterized as a putsch, a linguistic occurrence of political consequence. The report, an obvious rhetorical shell game, relies on the dynamics of empowerment. Whatever the validity of the Swiss hypothesis, for example, it is taken out of context and used for derisive purposes. Belittlement in the face of the prestige of the Academy and the mandate of the Commission translates as arrogant coercion. It is a successful strategy. It worked in 1984. Why not in 1998? But there were other fish to fry—the redoubtable ones, the nemeses from across the Channel and across the Atlantic.

In addition to the confusion emanating from conflicting French language feminization guides and practices adopted by Quebec, Belgium, and especially Switzerland where prerogatives were left to each canton, the Commission branded efforts to eradicate sexist language from English linguistically incompatible with the present project. Indeed, the endeavors to institute and require "politically correct English" are depicted as belonging to the social rather than the linguistic stratum. Since English is inherently gender neutral, the report states, "les débats ont lieu sur un plan autre que linguistique dans les pays anglo-saxons. Ainsi, aucune des dispositions législatives réunies dans le Sex Discrimination Act, qui vise à assurer l'égalité entre les sexes, ne porte sur cette question" (28). "Anglo-Saxon" legislation and non-sexist terminology such as "salesperson" rather than "salesman" or "saleswoman," or even "humankind" do not apply. If the Commission recognizes a certain ambiguity in the generic use of "homme," it cites a potentially antagonizing phrase to document it ("un homme sur deux est une femme") and defends its use by citing the Littré dictionary which defines the term as "l'être qui, dans l'espèce humaine appartient au sexe mâle" only in its eleventh entry, the ten others being asexual ("asexuées") (31–32). In addition, it calls into the play the prestigious historical linguist Ferdinand Brunot who is quoted as stating that many women seek complete assimilation in society, including titles: "Elles veulent porter tout crus des titres d'hommes" (35). The underlying notion, although somewhat evolved, can be reduced to the atavistic "women who want to be men."

In matters of titles, the Commission asserts repeatedly, the republican ideal mandates that individualizing terminology must yield to function. Etymology is conveniently summoned: "*Res publica* n'est rien d'autre que la chose publique, l'espace public par opposition à la vie privée." Once again Anglo-Saxon culture is presented as antagonist. The French Republic "ne conçoit pas le corps social, contrairement aux démocraties anglo-saxonnes, comme une juxtaposition d'individus ou de communautés dont chacune pourrait revendiquer, au nom de la spécificité, un traitement différencié" (44). Such contrary thinking adopted by feminist activists in the United States, it is implied, has led to clamors for a quota system, the logical political and social consequence of good intentions gone awry. In the interest of the Republic, the report concludes, the Commission restricts its approval of feminized terms to "noms de métier," and then only in texts of non-juridical, non-regulatory status. Texts regulating professions by statute are excluded. As for functions, ranks, and titles, current official practices (meaning the generic masculine) should prevail (hence Mme *le* Ministre). The framers of the report could not resist a parting volley. Those determinations are accompanied by a denial and a veiled accusation. "La langue n'est pas un complot ourdi dans les coulisses du pouvoir contre les femmes," the report reads. "Il ne faut pas voir derrière chaque mot une arrière-pensée et derrière chaque règle de grammaire un piège" (50). In another context the fear factor cited here would be construed as paranoia. In this highly polemical document critical of feminization and feminism alike, it connotes a misogynic pathology: the inherently female stereotypical affliction known as *hysteria*.

7.4.2 *Femme, j'écris ton nom*: the difficulties of conciliation

In the interim, led by Annie Becquer, the Institut National de la Langue Française committee (Comité de Féminisation) had also gone about its work and produced a very different report fashioned strictly according to the terms of its charge and based on the findings of the 1984 Commission. In published form, it would include three initial sections examining historical and morphological factors, delineating impediments to across-the-board feminization germane to modern French, and positing rules of formation; a section outlining the bases of the selection process; a section devoted to the role of the adjective in terminology related to the professions; a conclusion followed by bibliographical references (French and Francophone, including the Commission report); and, finally, the "guide d'aide" itself containing more than two thousand entries. The conclusion stresses the interest the subject had generated over the decades and the emotions it had stirred alongside other language initiatives such as the Loi Toubon and orthographic reform. It marvels at the passion with which the French view their language and the scores of articles devoted to it that find their way into newspapers and magazines. If language politics create polarities, the committee infers, rather than being a divisive issue in a cultural sense, it remains the cohesive element that François I envisioned. The final paragraph emphasizes conciliation:

> Cet attachement profond des citoyens à leur langue paraît à beaucoup une spécificité française. Quels qu'en puissent être le fondement et les raisons externes (l'histoire, la centralisation, l'enseignement, le génie de la langue), il est révélateur du puissant facteur d'identité fédératrice et culturelle que constitue la langue française. (56)

This was music to Jospin's ears. He accepted the guidelines generated by the INaLF and published subsequently in 1999 under the title *Femme, j'écris ton nom. Guide d'aide à la féminisation des noms de métiers, titres, grades et fonctions*. On the all-important question of natural gender versus grammatical gender the INaLF committee agreed with the Commission that the masculine should remain the neutralizing form for mixed groups and for the singular in statutory/regulatory texts. However, contrary to the Commission, it found that anytime the function is personalized, the sexual specificity (natural gender) of the individual shall obtain. Therefore in a juridical text one would find, for example, "le ministre de la Culture dans ses attributions," whereas in a text which designates a person, "singulière et spécifique," one would find, for example, "Mme X est la ministre de la culture"; or "Mme Y est nommée directrice de l'administration centrale"; or "Mme Z, inspectrice générale des bibliothèques, présidera la réunion" (38). The guide is especially useful because it also lists numerous variants adopted by Belgium, Quebec, or Switzerland (cf. Fr. un/une auteur(e), Sw. un auteur/une autrice; Fr. annonceur/ annonceuse, Qu. annonceure; Fr. un, une clerc, Bel. Clerc/clercque, Sw. clerc/clergesse).

Government recognition of the guidelines drew less attention than one would suppose. The parity law was being hotly contested at the time in both the National Assembly and the Senate. The opposition in the latter chamber, led by the socialist majority leader Robert Badinter, fashioned its case in virtually the same terms the 1998 Commission had used to oppose the feminization of language: the French universal Republic cannot be divided in half (into male and female entities) without subjecting it to the perils of division that have been the undoing of its predecessors. Once the law was in place, language concerns arose again. As much of an improvement as the new guidelines were, they still excluded specific female representation in official juridical language, thereby reinstituting the very inequity many proponents had sought to overcome. Furthermore, according to the guidelines, feminine designations are limited to "singulière et spécifique," in other words women cannot be referenced collectively, in the plural. Their collective existence as members of humanity, let alone citizens of the Republic, detractors lamented, cannot therefore be recognized.

Even the title of the new guidelines soon came under scrutiny. "Femme, j'écris ton nom" derives from a poem, "Liberté," written by Paul Eluard. Eluard, who had suffered from a gas attack in World War I, became an active *résistant* in World War II. Several of his poems were dropped as leaflets from Allied aircraft over occupied France. "Liberté" has survived as the most heralded of them. It is known to all school children and is frequently used in induction ceremonies for honorary and philanthropic societies. Its refrain, "J'écris ton nom," is repeated twenty times before, at the end of the final stanza, the term "Liberté" is revealed as referent (Eluard 1: 1105–07). At first glance the association with "liberation" seems obvious and appropriate. Certainly that was the intent. But, as Baudino emphasizes in the very first paragraph of her elucidating study, there is also something very much out of place about it:

> *Femme, j'écris ton nom*...est une paraphrase d'un vers célèbre de Paul Eluard. Ecrits en 1942, ce vers et le poème tout entier ont représenté un véritable hymne à la résistance. En intitulant ainsi le *Guide d'aide à la féminisation des noms de métiers, titres, grades et fonctions*, il semble que les pouvoirs publics aient voulu affirmer le pouvoir de libération des mots et engager les femmes à poursuivre leur lutte dans la langue. D'un autre côté, il faut reconnaître que la femme n'est pas le sujet de la phrase et, surtout, que ce titre ne sonne pas comme celui d'un rapport officiel. En le choisissant les pouvoirs publics ont donné à cette question une connotation poétique qui rappelle la récurrence de l'interrogation sur son statut politique et les limites de sa concrétisation. (9)

Conceptually for Baudino, then, this title tends to reinforce the perception of the issue of "la femme" as a matter of aesthetics (as Moi had observed), rather than a bona fide political and social concern and an injustice to be righted. Taking her logic a step further, the unannounced subject— which she equates to "les pouvoirs publics"—also creates a dichotomy, woman as subservient other: "I" ("the powers that be") write your name either condescendingly or because you cannot write it yourself. It is little wonder that when Thérèse Moreau ("écrivaine, docteure ès lettres") published the revised version of the Geneva guidelines (*Le nouveau dictionnaire féminin-masculin des professions, des titres et des fonctions* [1999]) the year following the filing of both reports, she minced no words. She showed no tolerance for the use of the masculine as generic in juridical or other texts. She took to task, vituperatively, academies, commissions, and committees alike:

> De fait, ce masculin que l'on dit neutre, est discriminatoire envers toutes les femmes: reflétant la position inférieure des femmes, il véhicule la misogynie et le sexisme ordinaires. Il convient donc de lutter contre cette injustice et de rendre aux femmes la place sociale et symbolique qui devrait être la leur par une féminisation systématique conforme aux règles des grammaires francophones, afin de répondre à l'attente de celles et ceux qui s'inquiètent de la correction de la langue. (19)

Three years later Edwige Khaznadar, "professeure de Lettres honoraire, docteure en linguistique et docteure ès-lettres," published *Le féminin à la française. Académisme et langue française* (2002) which gleans some 5000 masculine/feminine entries from dictionaries. If she is reluctant to condemn the "generic masculine" as blatantly prejudicial, she finds no linguistic defense for its usage. "Pour la dénomination de l'être humain, nous avons le choix entre d'une part le français académique, ou plutôt académiste [. . .] et d'autre part: le français vivant." The practice, she insists, is non-linguistic in character; it is rather a socio-political phenomenon: "la norme de 'l'homme' générique et du masculin dominant dans le langage," Khaznadar insists, "c'est la société avec son idéologie qui la produit" (226).

7.5 Gender in the world language community: why the fuss in France?

According to this line of thinking, masculine gender dominance in language arises from male dominance in society. If that is true—and it may seem obvious to many—it becomes essential to explore its historical bases, on the one hand, and also to endeavor to discover why it has acquired such importance in France and other French-speaking countries (or regions such as the cantons of Switzerland) on the other hand. After all, as the adverse Commission report emphasizes, women's issues have also been thoroughly debated in Italy and have spawned equal rights legislation there. But there has been no such language controversy in the very country whose vernacular dominated Europe before French attained "universal" status. Surveys conducted in Italy indicate that Italians, males and females alike, are not very interested in the question (28–29). The Commission (qua Academy) found no satisfactory explanation for the heightened feelings in France. Of course it did not look very hard. The early institutionalization of the language and politicized controls recognized by Marie de Gournay are not cited in the report, nor are the draconian measures used to curtail Anglo-American language incursions. Beyond the fact that both grammar and lexicography in France have been and continue to be male-dominated, the report also fails (conveniently) to recognize that the controversy has two sides: male and female, both equally adamant, both equally sensitive to gender usage. Gender in the French language, it can be inferred, has attained a special, polarizing status within the modern "Indo-European language community." That status begs two questions: first, are there reasons for it beyond the scope of the present debate; and, second, is there a polarizing agent, something linguistically inherent in the French language—in the way it has evolved and differentiated itself from other Indo-European languages—that contributes to the intensity of the discord?

Defined basically and broadly, genders "are classes of nouns reflected in the behavior of associated words" (Hackett 231). Gender marking is a common practice throughout the world language community. It is so varied, however, that linguists and anthropologists alike are at pains both to understand its logic and to explain the particular forms gender has taken in various tongues. Greville G. Corbett, in the introduction to his consummate study titled, simply, *Gender*, has this to say:

> Gender is the most puzzling of the grammatical categories. It is a topic which interests non-linguistis as well as linguists and it becomes more fascinating the more it is investigated. In some languages gender is central and pervasive, while in others it is totally absent. [...] The classification frequently corresponds to a real-world distinction of sex, at least in part, but often it does not. (1)

Modern Indo-European languages themselves attest to the variance. Some of them have a three-gender grammatical gender system, some a two-gender system, a few have no grammatical gender system at all (Uralic, Hungarian, Finnish, Estonian), others still continue to invent subgenders (the Slavonic group, for example); and the thirty-odd languages of the Caucasus differ markedly from their Indo-European cousins. Elsewhere languages belonging to virtually all the world's language families feature some sort of gender marking.[7] If gender assignment always has a semantic basis, whatever the language, that basis may differ greatly from language to language in the same way that either word structure and/or sound structure may differ as markers even within a single language family.

Corbett divides the various systems of gender assignment into three categories: strict semantic systems, predominantly semantic systems, and formal systems. Strict systems or natural gender systems are not very common. Tamil and other Dravidian languages fall into this category, as do Diyari (the Australian aboriginal language), Defaka (Africani of the Niger Delta), and English, whose pronominal gender system (he, she, it/his, her, its) has as exceptions only affective or metaphorical usage (ship/she). Gender in such languages is almost always predictable. In Tamil and other Dravidian languages, for example, god(s) and male humans are predictably masculine, goddess(es) and female humans are predictably feminine. All else is neuter, including animals, although both metaphor and affective usage do exist. Predominantly semantic systems contain a significant number of non-conforming occurrences. Zand (Zaire and the Sudan), Dyirbal (north-east Queensland of Australia), and Ket (Siberia) are of this sort, as are Ojibwa and other Algonquin languages. Zand has four gender classes: 1) male humans, 2) female humans, 3) other animates (animals), and 4) the inanimate (neuter). However, a significant number of inanimates have been assigned the animal gender, as have small children. Formal systems contain a large number of occurrences that do not conform to semantic assignment paradigms. These occurrences are of two sorts: morphological and phonological. Morphological gender assignment involves at least two (and usually more) forms—Latin's first declension in which nouns are masculine, for example. Phonological gender assignment involves a single form—Romance nouns ending in -ion(e) which are typically feminine, for example.

---

[7] Corbett confirms that a two-gender system is especially prevalent in the Afro-Asiatic family, that ⅔ of the 600 African languages are gendered languages, and that in the thousand or so languages of New Guinea gender is common. An anomaly can be observed with regard to the Americas where gender is rare, Algonquin's two-gender system being an exception (2–6). Corbett's observations and documentation are essential to the development of the present chapter. His study merits full credit.

7.6 *Les mots et les femmes*: French feminist theories

Gender systems in the world's languages exhibit myriad complexities and incongruities; often they defy efforts to discover how and why gender assignments were made. Corbett (32) points to the role of world view in the process, a mythology whose origins and chronology are frequently lost in the mists of pre-history or covered over by migrations, invasions, conversions, and the like. French feminists have contributed theories that may provide clues pertaining to the formation process and to modern male-female gender system sensibilities. Both biological and cultural in character, these theories relate to languages in general, Western culture in particular, and the development of gender systems in Indo-European languages.

In 1974 Annie Leclerc published *Parole de femme*. Complemented by other texts of similar ilk produced that same year for special issues of the leading periodicals *Tel Quel* and *Quinzaine Littéraire*, Leclerc's theory introduced a new way of perceiving women's relationship with language that would influence French feminist thinking for years to come. Leclerc maintained that owing to their particular biological makeup, women develop a discrete world view and, therefore, experience language in a manner essentially different from men. The exclusively female life events of menstrual cycles, sex and fertilization, pregnancy, labor and childbirth thus constitute both a physiological and a psychological uniqueness around which language develops and evolves. The isolation of women within early societies and the taboos of male invention arising from their necessary lack of experiencing and therefore understanding the "female condition" exacerbated the process, condemned male discourse to silence on such matters, and, ultimately, left men without the linguistic and psychological wherewithal to appreciate meaningfully the "difference," let alone identify with it (Cremonese 18–19). Women, on the other hand, in their social and linguistic isolation and in response to their biological makeup of rhythmic cycles and sexual gratification followed by birth, come to view nature as an essentially benevolent construct in which death has its (rightful) place as does "jouissance," the "joyous" non-competitive, gratuitous pleasure factor unknown to males.

Of course, as the theory developed, the adopted gurus of the period (Marx, Freud, Derrida, Foucault, Lacan, and others) were drawn into the mix. Each feminist writer added her own mark to the growing list: Kristeva's notion of the shattering of language to the benefit of the unadulterated joy of words; Cixous's *écriture féminine*, Irigaray's *parler-femme*, and so on. The theory inspired an effusion of texts, both theoretical and creative, in Quebec. Nicole Brossard, Madeleine Gagnon, Louky Bersianik, and France Théoret brought Canadian writers to the fore in their efforts to retrieve (the written) language for women after centuries of hoarding by men (Gould 36).

Marina Yaguello's *Les mots et les femmes* (1978) owes its theoretical foundations to W. Labov's seminal *Sociolinguistic Patterns* (1972). Paraphrasing Labov's findings, Yaguello writes in her introduction:

> Une langue n'est pas un tout homogène et monolithique. Dans une même communauté linguistique coexistent des variantes sociales et régionales; registres, niveaux de langue, dialectes, argots, jargons s'entrecroisent et se superposent. [...] La langue est un système symbolique engagé dans des rapports sociaux; aussi faut-il rejeter l'idée d'une langue "neutre" et souligner les rapports conflictuels. [...] Parmi les paramètres de la variation, classe sociale, groupe ethnique, âge, profession, région, etc., il convient de faire sa place à la différence sexuelle. (7–8)

As she develops her thought Yaguello is careful to cite relevant studies other than the theories of the aforementioned feminists and cohorts such as Xavière Gauthier and Marie Cardinal. Her approach relocates the discussion from philosophy to sociolinguistics and ethnology where objective data occupy a prominent position. Her originality stems from her integrated view of sexual difference. As discriminatory as sexual difference is in society, she believes, it cannot be isolated as a social phenomenon. Women in society are more than sexual creatures; they are subject to the numerous other social incongruities that are not gender related: class, ethnicity, religion, and so on. Anthropologists have long been interested in the question of male versus female language and speech, she recognizes, but only as a curiosity. As a consequence they have sought out primitive or "exotic" societies where they have documented significant differences in vocabulary, semantics, and speech patterns. They have pointed to biological or physical differences such as voice, pitch, and intonation, but have determined that most differences originate from cultural factors associated with social roles: woman as caretaker and man as provider, woman as consoler and man as protector, etc.

Despite the insights these studies have provided, Yaguello laments, Western languages (and societies) have been neglected. *Les mots et les femmes* is a serious attempt to fill that gap. Yaguello's premise is that in Western society male dominance is ingrained in the "common language," a superiority factor that relegates feminine discourse to inferior position and exacerbates other devaluating *social* factors. Systematically, she documents the devaluating characteristics inherent in French and other languages: the number of pejoratives applicable to females, which by far exceed those applicable to males; the devaluating stereotypical terms relevant to female (as opposed to male) psychology; the use of the feminine to designate the spouse of a man of social or professional worth; and, especially, the absorption of the feminine gender by the masculine—a phenomenon she attributes to many languages around the world where sexism prevails. She notes progress and hope in the strides Anglo-American women had made in combating sexism in language. She encourages French women to follow suit.[8] There is no doubt that Yaguello's ideas anticipated and nurtured the debate that would take place in the 1980s and 1990s. The documentation is convincing. The insights are numerous and the thesis compelling: the social reality of the "common language" imposed on women as a means of continued sex-based oppression. But, as probing as her analyses are, they do not explain *linguistically* why the language gender question in France and in French-speaking regions of Europe should be so extraordinarily polarizing when similar sociolinguistic conditions exist across the continent.

7.6.1 Revising the theory: Proto-Indo-European foundations

The Journal of Indo-European Studies, as the title projects, is the scholarly periodical in which one would expect to find the most recent theories and observations concerning the origins, evolution, and derivations of the languages of modern Europe. In subsequent issues in 1982 two separate articles by Paul W. Brosman, Jr. appeared in its pages that would provide the bases for another theory relating gender in the Indo-European language family to world view. The first, "Designation of Females in Hittite," was published in the Spring/Summer issue. The abstract reads as follows:

> The only Hittite derivational suffix denoting females appears not to have been productive. Since Hittite did not possess a feminine gender, one must apparently conclude that the use of lexically distinct forms was the only

---

[8] In 1989 Yaguello added her small, but controversial dictionary, *Le sexe des mots*, illustrating the bias of the "fonctionnement du genre en français." It appeared at a crucial point and helped keep alive interest in taking up the feminization project again.

means of designating females employed in Hittite. Moreover, for similar
reasons it seems probable that the Hittite method of specifying sex was
largely, if not entirely, inherited. (65)

What this means is that Hittite possessed no working "grammatical gender"
system; its two genders were all-inclusive: common (or animate) and neuter
(or inanimate); its only means of referencing males and females depended
on a "natural gender" (lexical) system. As Brosman explains, the sole feminine
derivational suffix (-sara) was used exclusively to designate human or divine
females and was limited to six instances: "queen," "mistress," "virgin,"
"female slave," and two divine names. These forms are found in written texts.
Brosman infers that because of the extreme rarity of these specific terms in
the entirety of Hittite speech production, they would have disappeared from
the spoken language (66). If this feature was "largely inherited," it also means
that, in addition to Hittite's continuing the practice of its predecessor(s), the
feature was in all likelihood common to the other languages of the Anatolian
group (the oldest attested group of Indo-European languages): Luwian, Lydian,
and Lycian, for which there exist no written texts. Although falling outside
the immediate parameters of his study, Brosman—without emphasizing the
point—related the rise of an Indo-European feminine gender to a subsequent
occurrence. His concluding sentence reads: "If the view that the feminine
arose as a third gender following the separation of Anatolian is correct, it is
apparently under these circumstances that the semantic association of the
new gender with females began to develop" (69).

The second article, "The Development of the Feminine"—with
expanded parameters—appeared a few months later. The abstract reads in part:

It is held that shortly after the separation of Anatolian sex was designated
in Indo-European by lexical, rather than inflectional or derivational,
means. Since the inherited o-stems and recently arisen a-stems were then of
slight numerical significance, the bulk of nouns referring to females, as
well as those denoting males and other referents, animate and inanimate,
belonged to non-vocalic declensions. As many of these nouns were
thematicized during the expansion of the o- and a-stems, a few stems
which had come to denote females caused words with female referents to
tend to enter the a- rather than the o- stems through an analogical process
[. . .] Before the resultant association of females with the a-stems became
firmly established, hesitation as to gender on the part of several nouns with

animate referents produced doublets in *-o* and *-a* which were susceptible to later interpretation as representing the corresponding female and non-female of the same species and thus provided the basis for motion among nouns. Subsequently the use of the *a*-stem form of sustantivized o-stem adjectives to refer to females led to the employment of *a*-stem adjectival forms with words for females under other circumstances. (253)

Brosman thus theorizes as to how gender inflections arose (analogically) in Indo-European and how they evolved, proliferated, and expanded in usage and function. Progressively, a semantic shift occurred that altered the inherited system: "once it had taken place the *a*-stems with animate referents would have belonged to two categories: agent nouns (regardless of sex) and females (in general)." Hence the animate universe becomes divided into gendered grammatical paradigms: "the contrast that emerged was not between males and females but between females and non-females"; "the [asymmetric] process ultimately responsible for it had nothing to do with sex" (266–67). Thus the progressive development of a third gender (arbitrary and feminine) completed the three-gender system (masculine, feminine, neuter) common to reconstructions of Proto-Indo-European (PIE).

7.6.2 Reconstructing Old Europe: the civilization of the Goddess

This information and pertinent radiocarbon-dated archeological documentation are crucial to a related (feminist) theoretical reconstruction found in Marija Gimbutas's *The Civilization of the Goddess: The World of Old Europe* (1991). Gimbutas combines history, comparative Indo-European linguistics, and mythology in a systematic endeavor to reconstitute Old European culture—that is to say a horseless, agricultural culture that existed prior to the invasions of the horse-riding Kurgans of the 5th and 4th centuries B.C.E. and that was extremely similar to if not a product of Anatolian culture:

The Anatolian Neolithic was a goddess civilization characterized by the dominance of the worship of the Goddess imbued with mysterious generative power, the importance of temples that functioned as social foci and catalysts for creativity in arts and religious expression, and by balanced matrilineal social structure. From around 6500 B.C., the same features of culture are found in southeastern Europe and later in most of Europe up to the time of the demise of this civilization, between 4500 and 2500 B.C. (9)

The Kurgan invasions, she observes, brought two contrasting societies/cultures into conflict: the patriarchal, patrilineal Kurgan culture of the Volga forest-steppe and the matrilineal/matricentric culture of the "indigenous" Old Europeans.

Old European culture was endogamic. Governance was shared by the clan's female elder (Great Mother) and her brother or her uncle, along with a council of women. Religion centered on the worship of the Goddess (Mother Earth) for whom temples were built and finely crafted artifacts (sculptures, urns, altars, etc. have been unearthed). The Goddess, a self-generating, parthenogenetic deity, was the sole source of life. Male gods exercised minor duties or served purely metaphorical purposes. Religious symbolism reflected a world view based on renewal in nature. Old Europeans celebrated the mysterious cycles of birth, death, and rebirth. Symbols were drawn from fertile, nurturing nature: springs, wells, the moon, the sun, animals, plants, the earth itself. Tombs were thought of as wombs, graves often took the form of eggs or of the anthropomorphic Goddess. Old European culture accepted life and celebrated it symbiotically. Indo-European culture, on the other hand, in addition to being patriarchal, patrilineal, and patrilocal, was exogamic, bellicose, and dominated socially by a class of male warriors. The male sun god reigned, but a pantheon of male gods reflected the social hierarchy: warrior-gods at the top, subsumed by lesser gods drawn from agricultural and economic practices. The warrior-gods were often depicted on horseback with weapon in hand. Female gods existed, but only as spouses of male gods. Artifacts include scepters in the form of horse heads and solar motifs. In lieu of a celebration of nature and life, this culture sanctified war, martyrdom, and a very different view of death. "The frightening black God of Death and the Underworld," Gimbutas writes, "marked the warrior for death with the touch of a spear tip, glorifying him as a fallen hero" (399).

This clash of cultures produced marked demographic consequences, Gimbutas maintains. The Old Europeans who remained were overcome; they and their descendants were absorbed by the "trading and raiding" society where women were treated as chattels. Those who fled relocated farther to the west where they continued to live and worship as before until they too were overtaken and absorbed by the marauding, male dominant Indo-European culture. Evidence of the matrilineal society has been uncovered from the Baltic to Spain and northward through France, Germany, Britain, and into

Scandinavia. Particular cultural pockets have been of great interest to anthropologists and historians. The ancient Iberians of coastal Spain worshiped the Goddess in contrast with the inland Iberians. The Picts of northern Britain survived as a matrilineal culture until they merged politically with the Scots in the ninth century. Linguistic evidence is lacking in these areas, however; indigenous signs have been absorbed by the language community at large and irretrievably lost. The Basques present a different case.

7.6.3 The extraordinary Basques and their "genderless" language

Gimbutas's argument gains particular strength from Basque history and culture. The Basques, of the western Pyrenees of northern Spain, are a unique people. DNA tests separate them from the general European population. Sociologically, Gimbutas adds, "they are the great exception to all the laws of European political and cultural history"; their language is "the only indigenous language to survive the invasions and cultural influences of the last 3000 years"; the Basques are "living Old Europeans" (348). Once again she relies on the authority of the *Journal of Indo-European Studies*: T. Wilbur's "Indo-Europeanization of the western Pyrenees" published in 1980. From this and other sources she pieces together a convincing line of reasoning: 1) The Basques exhibit the physical characteristics of the Cro-Magnon sort; 2) worship of the Goddess, a lunar calendar, matrilineage and other remnants of a gynaecocratic society subsisted until the early-twentieth century; 3) women continue to hold high ranking in law codes and to be used as judges and arbiters; 4) in the French Basque region total equality of the sexes exists in matters of inheritance.

None of this is to say that sexism has not come to the Basque country. Women's organizations are active there. And although Gimbutas does not say so, the Basque Academy of Letters, responsible since 1918 for creating and overseeing the standards for a unified Basque language (Euskara Batua), has joined with concerned groups in an effort to preserve the language's *genderless* status. Basque, it is well known and very much like Hittite, is "gender-free." It has no grammatical gender system. It uses lexical means or "natural gender" to designate males and females of all species: e.g., *ama* (mother); *aita* (father); *guraso* (parent); *oilo* (hen); *oilar* (cock); *behi* (cow); *zezen* (bull), and so on. Gimbutas makes no effort to compare Basque and Hittite or to link the two other than culturally. There is no need, conceptually speaking, since an essential tenet of feminist theory holds that sexism in language and the oppression of women are parallel and culture-bound.

It is easy to see how Gimbutas's interpretation of the Kurgan invasions and cultural proliferations—especially as they relate to the Aryans by way of the Iranian plateau—fits into the broader context of feminist ideology.[9] Sexism in the West, one is induced to infer, is a socio-political phenomenon of cultural origin whose traces remain in the gender systems of language. It is associated with patriarchy qua phallocracy, violence and aggression, commerce and productivity. Of course other, competing theories exist that do not recognize the westward migration of tribes to become the Picts, the Iberians, or the Basques. Whereas it would be beyond the scope of this study to examine them here, it is clear that, whatever the validity of Gimbutas's hypotheses—as enticing as they may be—they shed no particular light on the gender system of the French language and the hypersensitive attitude of many "indigenous" speakers toward it. If there are archetypal remnants of these events in the psyche of modern European females (and males, one would have to assume), they would be generalized throughout Europe and the speakers of the many European languages. As a consequence it becomes necessary to seek answers elsewhere, to return to the French language itself.

7.7 French gender-marking anxiety: a psycho-phonological phenomenon

Any student who has endeavored to learn French as a second language is abundantly aware of the obstacle that gender assignment poses. Pronunciation may be difficult owing to the buccal tension and constricted aspiration that articulation requires. Open syllabification challenges the ear to a greater degree than the more staccato languages: words run together phonetically and comprehension depends on being able to discern patterns, much as one needs to discern phrasing in order to recognize (and appreciate) music. Intonation, too, has its own, unique register. The grammar, however, while not without impediments (agreement of the past participle, the subjunctive, pleonasms, and the like), does not rank with that of the most demanding

---

[9] Cixous's *Vivre l'orange* laments the fate of the women of Iran during the revolt against the Shah, a reenactment of the Aryan invasion that evicted a matrilineal society (and, ostensibly, Cixous's Promethea) from the Iranian Plateau. See R. Ghirshman (28) and Henry (2004: 242–44).

languages; and the syntax, by all standards, appears controlled and largely consistent in comparison with "synthetic" languages and other Romance languages. Orthography is a problem. But even spelling has its own logic; it is a question of learning a manageable number of graphic paradigms as they relate to the sound system. But gender, there seem to be so many exceptions, so many epicenes (words that have the same form for both the masculine and the feminine). How do native speakers manage so well? Even French children rattle off sentence after sentence without an error. When confronted with a new word, they seem to know instinctively what the gender is. A closer look at their "innate" ability produces both "linguistic" explanations and—somewhat surprisingly—provides insight into the polarities of recent gender debates.

An awareness of the pedagogical, linguistic, and psychological import of discovering the means by which "native/indigenous" speakers internalize and anticipate gender usage in French led a team of researchers from McGill University (two psychologists and a linguist) to conduct a thorough investigation in the 1970s. G. R. Tucker, W. E. Lambert, and A. A. Rigault soon found that most of the French speakers interviewed were not at all cognizant of the process and could offer no explanation for their mastery; those who did offer explanations were either inconsistent or completely misguided. Now there is nothing derogatory in this finding. Most speakers simply do not think about their language analytically. (Grammarians themselves have not effectively puzzled out the problem.) Nevertheless, this initial determination shaped the investigation to the extent that in order to obtain pertinent results the team needed to devise an experimental approach utilizing a "non-introspective" methodology. That approach entailed testing subjects by using rarely occurring real nouns (study 1), invented nouns (study 2), nonsense nouns (study 3), endings in isolation (study 4), and, finally, by testing connotative/emotional reactions linking sound to meaning (study 5)—all in an effort to substantiate paradigms and measure predictability. Drawn from diverse Montreal educational institutions and of varied social class and achievement levels, the study's 1125 subjects were children (all native speakers of French) ranging from seven to seventeen years of age. Testing design and format benefited from the participation of phoneticians; content was derived based on the 31,619 nouns of the *Petit Larousse*.

The stunning results of the inquiry were published in 1977 under the title *The French Speaker's Skill with Grammatical Gender: An Example of*

Rule-Governed Behavior. The sub-title is all-important: it posits a predictable regularization that, heretofore, had not been completely discerned or understood. Accordingly, the extent to which gender paradigms operate systematically across the language is at the root of the speaker's mastery and ability to predict. The type of paradigm and the means by which gender acquisition occurs, however, tell a good deal more: these aspects produce an unconscious awareness and expectation, a "gender sensitivity" that may carry over into other cognitive or emotive areas.

Corbett's taxonomy proves useful in interpreting the data provided by Tucker et al. Corbett's division of formal systems into morphological systems and phonological systems is a primary factor. "French," Corbett says, "is often regarded as having one of the most opaque gender systems" (unlike other Romance systems such as the "more straightforward system of Spanish") (57). Essentially, it is a binary (masculine/feminine) phonological system. Like all systems, French has a basic semantic core: "sex-differentiable nouns denoting males" and "sex-differentiable nouns denoting females": *homme/femme.* Morphological assignment is limited to one sort: compound nouns formed from a verb plus another element are masculine: *porte-monnaie* ([change] purse), *pare-brise* (windshield), *garde-boue* (fender). Other seeming morphological occurrences are really phonological: the *-ation* suffix, which is invariably feminine (*inondation, datation*) for example, appears to be formed from a verb (*inonder/dater*). But *nation,* feminine as well, is not formed in that way. Like examples abound, as the many charts and statistics produced by Tucker et al. confirm. The determinant, therefore, is not the suffix as such, but rather the interplay of syllables, regardless of their origin or how they may have been derived. In other words, there is no overarching morphological assignment rule other than the one pertaining to the compounds noted. As for other formal assignments, although there is some morphological overlapping, the overwhelming majority of assignments are phonological in character. This fact, coupled with the knowledge that deaf children never master the gender assignment system in French, points to "aurality" and the acoustical environment of the individual speaker as keys (Tucker et al. 59, Corbett 61). The findings of the McGill team's study support the following conclusions:

1. Native speakers are sensitive to gender-marking recurrences of nouns and develop a schema to making gender assignments based on prior experience.

2. Non-native speakers do not develop this sensitivity owing to lack of exposure.

3. The degree of this decoding skill depends on the degree of linguistic experience; the greater the linguistic experience (linguistic sophistication), the greater the sensitivity to gender marking recurrences and the higher the degree of decoding skill.

4. Native speakers process nouns from their termination back toward their beginning; they scan back to front until they recognize a gender specific paradigm.

5. In some cases, though more rarely, native speakers are able to make gender assignments based on initial syllables by processing from front to back.

Corbett marvels at the rate of predictability of French as confirmed by the McGill team. The data provided by Tucker et al. measure predictability beyond final phone cues (eighteen consonant cues and twelve vowel cues). Penultimate and even antepenultimate phones provide added cues. Corbett cites a pertinent example: "While nouns ending in /e/ may be masculine or feminine, the majority of those ending in /te/, in fact 924 out of 997, or 92.6 per cent, are feminine. Once these are separated out, the prediction about remaining nouns in /e/ improves considerably: 1,325 out of 1,794, or 73.9 per cent, are masculine" (60). Hence native speakers of French, virtually automatically, will correctly assign the masculine gender to a word such as *le dérivé*, even if it is being encountered for the first time.[10]

These observations indicate that, psychologically, native speakers of French, males and females alike, are conditioned to maintain a constant, acute—if unconscious—awareness of the gender assignment process. Based on hundreds of thousands of occurrences as the child grows to adulthood, the skill and the gender expectations of the speaker become part and parcel of language itself. The process, flowing from back to front, mirrors French syntax. Adjectives, attributives, and appositions usually follow the noun or pronoun: *la maison blanche*; *le cheval est blanc*; *Marie est une étudiante supérieure*. The fact that certain sounds at the beginning of words also trigger the process (e.g., the predominately feminine *flor-* and the predominately

---

[10] For similar observations, see also Marie-Marthe Gervais's "Gender and Language in French" in *French Today*.

masculine *coup-*) attests both to its pervasiveness and to the acuity of the speaker's perceptibility. In order to be able to ascertain gender, the mind must be keyed not only to scan, but also to anticipate. There must exist as a consequence—it is reasonable to assume—a certain gender-marking anxiety. That may explain in part why native French speakers are quicker than others to raise an eyebrow or offer an uninvited correction when a non-native makes a mistake in gender. That same anxiety, when combined with a socially, politically, or sexually motivated ideology, may explain—at least in part— why the dispute over *Madame le/la Ministre* has been so divisive and of such lengthy duration.

8

Conclusions

8.1 France: a nation in crisis or in transition?

THE ANSWER TO THE ABOVE QUESTION DEPENDS on where and how one looks. For Timothy B. Smith, author of the 2004 book *France in Crisis: Welfare, Inequality, and Globalization since 1980*, the outlook is bleak. His chapter titles constitute a veritable indictment: "The 'treason of the intellectuals': globalization as the big excuse for France's economic and social problems"; "Persisting inequalities"; "The protected people"; "The excluded: immigrants, youth, women"; "The French exception." The last chapter outlines the French proclivity for believing that, as a nation, France is not subject to the same socio-economic exigencies as other countries. The thirty-five hour week, rising salaries and increased public spending, an enormous social welfare entitlement and bureaucracy, these factors and many more lead Smith to conclude that reform is the only answer, a reform that, if properly instituted, could revitalize the nation's eroded solidarity—a reform, he laments, that is not forthcoming.

Smith's call for reform is but the latest in a series of warnings sounded initially within France by Servan-Schreiber in 1967 and echoed a dozen years later by Michel Crozier in his *On ne change pas la société par décret* (1979). Crozier's Soviet-era view of the situation involved "the crisis of Western society" and within it the "the real French disease," meaning the vertical power structure, the inertia that extreme centralization had induced, and an overwhelming, self-perpetuating bureaucracy. He called for new attitudes across the board to revitalize French resolve and competitiveness. Smith's observations a quarter of a century later serve to underscore the persistence of such concerns.

Another recently published study broadens the perspective: *France at the Dawn of the Twenty-First Century: Trends and Transformations* (2000). The work of a team of nineteen scholars (including Alain Kimmel of the Centre International d'Etudes Pédagogiques and editor of *Echos*, a journal of contemporary French life) directed by Marie-Christine Weidmann Koop, its essays in both French and English survey a vast landscape: politics, social issues, identity, culture, cross-culture. (It is of note that economics does not figure in the headings.) The subtitle of this collection of essays suggests a more temperate interpretation. Yet at virtually every turn apprehensions arise anew to indicate that France finds itself at a crossroads. At the core is French identity both within the European Union—with its shifting populations—and globally. Edward C. Knox sounds a positive note. He points to the euphoria of France's World Cup triumph (1998) and the "multicultural lovefest inspired by the victory of the so-called 'Black-Blanc-Beur' World Cup team" (138). Knox sees in that event and the two-month period of self-examination and reconciliation that followed a potential for an expanded ideology that would "integrate" France's various ethnic, social, and regional identities. Unfortunately, of course, those two months have come and gone, and two succeeding World Cups have produced other results.

Jacqueline Thomas, puzzled by the ebbing "sense of identity" she encountered in France at the end of the 1990s, prior to the Cup victory, turned to the national image presented in six newspapers: *Le Monde, Le Figaro, Libération, La Croix, L'Humanité,* and *France-Soir.* For the period February 1997 to July 1998 she found "threats to Frenchness" and "further threats to Frenchness" headlined in the press: 1) Celebrated heroes of the Resistance Lucie and Raymond Aubrac became the center of controversy when they could not answer detailed questions to the satisfaction of a panel of historians; 2) the trial of Maurice Papon, former Vichy administrator, led to debilitating journalistic speculation about France's complicity (and guilt) in the deportation of Jews; 3) the uncovering of Mitterrand's relationship with René Bousquet, "the murderous Vichy police chief," generated further suspicion; 4) the need for sweeping social and economic restructuring in the face of global competition continued to be a topic of priority; 5) encroachment on national prerogatives by the European Union and the switch to the euro caused widespread concern; 6) the "immigration problem" and Jean-Marie Le Pen's inflammatory rhetoric were covered continuously by all the papers. Thomas does quote a sage voice in all of this, François Léotard, who was the leader of the UDF (Union pour la Démocratie Française) at the time. Léotard's remarks were published in *Le Monde* of 22 February 1997. While addressing the turmoil surrounding the immigration issue, he urged the French to reassert their identity and to believe in France as "un grand pays, fier de sa langue, assuré de son destin et attaché au respect de ses lois" (qtd. in Jacqueline Thomas 151).

8.2 French: a language in crisis or in transition?

It is revealing that Léotard should list "linguistic pride" as the first attribute of a "great country." Perhaps, if questioned, he would rearrange the terms. Perhaps not. For the phraseology reflects the fact that the very notion of French national identity is inextricably linked to pride in the national idiom. Léotard's counsel emanates from an awareness of the losses the French language has suffered over the last century. As Antoine, Durand, and others have pointed out, its role as diplomatic medium has diminished; other languages have moved in to assume greater responsibilities in the international arena. Economic growth has enhanced the prospects of Chinese. The Spanish language has gained numbers—especially in the US but also elsewhere—owing to immigration policies and demographics. English, of course, has risen to the virtual status of *lingua franca*. Today many students who would have looked to French in the past are acquiring English language competencies. Prior to 9/11 and subsequent Middle-Eastern developments, inroads had even been made in areas of the former French dominion such as Tunisia and Morocco. ESL (English as a second language) has become a mega-business. Textbooks and self-help instruments abound. Proprietary agencies and public institutions alike are able to market their product through home-based programs in the UK and the US and by means of on-site, outreach programs for which lucrative contracts are concluded. (Indeed, founded in 1985 and located in the heart of the French capital, the American Business School in Paris offers American-styled English-language programs leading to both a bachelor of business administration degree and a master of international business degree.) ESL and related programs are commercially oriented; they are market driven just as their clients are moved by the desire to climb the economic scale. In that sense, they are not unlike their French counterparts of the past. The commercialization of the French language following the Revolution—with its highly competitive and sometimes ruthless practices—

was similarly motivated. But there are essential differences. The French version also included a social esteem that today's English-language movement seems to lack. The social prestige and upward social mobility that careful speakers of French could expect to enjoy, economic factors aside, were a result of a longstanding policy and ideology that granted stature and status to the national idiom. The Bescherelle brothers' national dictionary and national grammar appealed ideologically to a deep-running patriotic vein, the same vein that prompted concerned citizens to form the Alliance Française in the 1880s amidst what was perceived as a period of extreme crisis. The question remains, then, to what degree is that ideology in jeopardy today?

8.3 Hegemonic imperatives: from concord to fracture

The French government has taken an active role in the determination and execution of language policies. From François I onward its institutions have fought to stave off foreign incursions and domestic infelicities at every turn: Latin in the sixteenth century, indigenous amorphism in the seventeenth century, regionalisms beginning with the Revolution and running to World War I, artificial languages at the end of the nineteenth century, and English today. For many years planned intervention tended to strengthen the idiom. Indeed, elitism and the fixity promoted by the Academy served the nation so well that French became the vehicular language of Europe and the culture it carried across much of the globe reigned as virtual archetype. But the modern nation-state is a complex phenomenon. As early as the nineteenth century, as Hélène Merlin-Kajman explains, the very term "académique" acquired a pejorative meaning, the "antonyme du plaisir et de la singularité" (187); thus even as government geared up to disseminate the French language throughout the countryside, the Academy's policies were increasingly viewed as adversarial, oppressive, detrimental to the idiom's vitality. Moreover, an unexpected antagonism had begun to develop. Despite the prestige that the Academy continues to enjoy to this day (what author does not wish to be honored beneath "la Coupole"?), circumstances have placed government at odds with the venerable institution. Language legislation and a bureaucracy to implement and enforce it have taken their place within the gigantic French bureaucratic machine. Members of the Academy, who may be consulted or even asked to serve on select committees, remain largely in the margins and are compelled to make their case in the media.

The years preceding Y2K witnessed a flurry of language-related hegemonic maneuvers: the aborted orthographic reform of the early-1990s; the 1992 amendment to the Constitution making French the official language of the Nation; the 1994 "Loi Toubon" written primarily to protect the national idiom from the English language and under which thousands of infractions are investigated annually; the two reports of 1998 reflecting divergent attitudes toward feminization of the French language; the subsequent mediation conducted by the Office of the Prime Minister and published in 1999 in the form of the *Guide d'aide à la féminisation des noms de métiers, titres, grades et fonctions*; Jacques Chirac's decision (May 16, 1999) to sign the European Charter for Regional and Minority Languages in order to put it to a constitutional test; the Conseil d'Etat's declaration (June 15, 1999) that the Charter contradicts anti-discrimination clauses of the French Constitution and conflicts with its recognition of the French language as the national idiom, thereby blocking ratification of the Charter until such time that the Constitution is amended to accommodate its provisions, a procedure that does not appear to be in the offing. As of 2004 the Charter had been ratified by seventeen countries; France was not—and is still not, as of this writing—among them.

These acts have left significant numbers of constituents disconcerted. In addition to the discord stemming from the feminization dispute, regional language communities and the deaf community have felt particularly affected. Dominique Breillat, a professor of public law at the University of Poitiers, has examined in detail France's position on the Charter. Having traced minority language policies back to Grégoire, he turns to issues and attitudes that have characterized the various governments since the Fourth Republic. Breillat discerns a relaxation of policy beginning in the 1950s, the Deixonne Act of 1951 for example that permitted Breton, Basque, Catalan and Corsican to be taught in primary and secondary schools (those languages not considered languages of another state or country). The 1975 Haby Act added regional cultures to the list of potential curricular offerings. The 1984 Higher Education Act urged the promotion of regional languages and cultures alongside the national idiom. The 1992 recognition of French as the official (and sole) national idiom signaled a hardened position. The Charter, then, whose preamble recognizes as inalienable the right to use a regional or minority language in both private and public life, became untenable for "constitutionalists" (Breillat 8–10).

There is reason for France's deaf community to feel even more disaffected. In December 2001 the European Union of the Deaf met at the European Parliament in Brussels to voice its opposition to the Charter's exclusion of sign languages from the Charter. The E.U.D. resolved to argue its case forcefully before the Council of Europe in an effort to gain recognition in the European Community as a whole and in individual states. Two years later the European Parliamentary Assembly recommended inclusion of sign languages in the Charter (Recommendation 1598, 2003). If that recommendation has not been formally incorporated into the Charter, individual member states have been encouraged to extend recognition to the various sign languages as minority languages. Several states have done so: Finland, Germany, Czechoslovakia, and Portugal, for instance. France remains among the many that have not.[1]

8.4 French language and culture in perspective

Multiculturalism, on a linguistic plane, has never been a French hallmark. The French people themselves have never been known as avid foreign language learners, unlike the Germans and the Scandinavians. The French share this linguistic insularism with other cultures, of course: Americans (to be sure) and Russians (if to a lesser degree), for example. Such attitudes have been fashioned according to need. France, from the seventeenth century onward, has not felt the collective need to internalize the idioms of other cultures or subcultures, be they foreign or located on French soil. The prestige and authority of the national idiom have determined another course. If the German members of the Berlin Academy of Frederick the Great found much to admire in French culture in general and the French language in particular, they complained bitterly about the linguistic snobbism of their francophone cohorts. Yet they did admire French language and culture, to the point of envy in many instances. In the Prussian Academy's 1782–1784 essay competition whose topic was the future of French as the universal language of Europe, supporters based their position on metalinguistic or epilinguistic properties. The "aesthetics" of its acoustics or sound system, the "regularity" of its syntax, the "fixity" of its vocabulary point at least to aspects

---

[1] For an overview of the factors contributing to this lack of status, see Branson and Miller's *Damned for their Difference*.

generally identifiable as linguistic phenomena. But others prove to be quite distant: French literature, theater, and the arts; taste, manners, and style; Huguenot industriousness; national politics; international commerce; the French Academy; achievement in the sciences; and notable monarchs (François I and Louis XIV, in particular).

Of course prior to the competition Voltaire claimed that France was already living on its laurels, that "les bons auteurs" and leaders of the eighteenth century could not measure up to those of the seventeenth century—in short, that France, politically and culturally, was in a state of decline, a state of crisis. Such perceptions are cyclical; historically, the cycles in France have been all too evident. They have been so because they have often entailed violent upheaval and because France has enjoyed such a prestigious position in the history of modern Western civilization. France today finds itself in yet another of these cycles. It is not merely a matter politics or language (French or English). The shift from formal or high culture to popular culture is in part to blame. Too, "les bons auteurs," on whom France has staked its cultural reputation and prestige, appear to be more lacking today than in recent memory. In the first half of the twentieth century the names of Proust, Gide, Sartre, Camus, and Beauvoir became universal. Later, the New Novel received international attention. If it was not widely imitated, it was believed that only the French had the intellectual wherewithal and readership to support such an extraordinary literary phenomenon. (One might make a similar observation with regard to cinema.) Intellectually, France became the nucleus for the entry of "theory" into the academic mainstream: Lévi-Strauss, Starobinski, Barthes, Bourdieu, Foucault, Deleuze, Derrida, Lyotard, and Lacan led the way. Today they are all either deceased or over eighty years of age. France's front-line feminists of the 1970s, those who combined such creative talent and intellectual acumen—Irigaray, Kristeva, Cixous—are themselves "gray panthers." Who has emerged or is emerging to carry the torch?

Denise Brahimi, professor of literature at the University of Paris VII, finds contemporary French writers out of touch with the "mutations vécues par la France dans les dernières décennies du vingtième siècle et au tournant du siècle nouveau" (185). Those mutations, she emphasizes, are demographic, political, and cultural. She singles out three interrelated occurrences of magnitude: 1) the absorption of traditional peasant culture into urbanized society, 2) the demystification of revolutionary movements and philosophies following 1968 (and the subsequent demise of the Soviet Union), 3) the end both of France as a colonial power and the preeminence of its language and culture. The last occurrence has been particularly difficult to accept. Brahimi finds little willingness on the part of present writers to address that "mutation." Her observations put one in mind of the *débâcle* of 1870–1871 that was avoided so systematically and for so long by all but a handful of writers. One author she does not mention warrants consideration: Jean Rolin. Rolin, author of a dozen novels, depicts a post-colonial guilt-ridden France stripped of its inherent nationalism and imperialistic grandeur and fallen into ghettoized dysfunction. Many of his Parisian characters, as in *La clôture* (2002), are itinerants, squatters, prostitutes, drug traffickers, and the like, come from foreign lands, especially Eastern Europe and Africa. Others are peripherals, nomads passing through French ports on their way elsewhere, such as many of the dockhands and sailors of *Terminal Frigo* (2005). Rolin reveals a society in the throes of cataclysmic change, adapting poorly to its loss of identity and not knowing where to begin to construct a new one based on an alien theory: "le métissage." The portrayal is grim, and yet the beauty and power of the French language are everywhere evident, the following passage from *La clôture*, for instance:

> Trois heures du matin: des éclairs zèbrent le ciel au-dessus des trois tours de la rue Jean-Cocteau; puis la porte de Clignancourt, ses quelques passants tardifs, ses prostituées, ses dealers de crack enkystés toute la nuit dans l'étroit passage entre la grille du collège Utrillo et la palissade de travaux, tout cela est en un instant noyé sous des trombes d'eau. (97)

Amidst the buoyant phrasing that captivates eye and ear, unlikely terms commingle in concert: an Anglicism, a medical term ("enkysté") used metaphorically, two prominent representatives of French cultural history commemorated by the capital's official nomenclature. The great city's inhabitants—the unfortunates of Baudelaire's Paris, one is tempted to say—rub shoulders in a still shot, all of them equally subject to the nuisance of a sudden downpour. Whatever the future holds for France, the French language, and French culture, it is obvious that the national idiom remains a splendid vehicle for the skillful hand—a welcome note of optimism, to say the least.

That optimism permeates the final chapter of the second edition of Peter Rickard's *A History of the French Language* (1993). The chapter titled "The Defence of French" makes a number of salient points that are worth retaining. First, he cites strength in numbers. French "is the native language of some ninety million people," Rickard writes, "and [...] as a second language it reaches some two hundred million more."[2] Second, he notes the continued "interest of educated French people in linguistic questions" as documented by the number of "semi-popular articles on questions of language which have long been a feature of national journals and newspapers" (158). Third, he praises the hundreds of chapters of the Alliance Française world-wide that impart French language and culture to thousands of students annually. Fourth, he has this to say about competition from the English language:

> French will be doing itself a disservice if it misguidedly resists the need to adapt itself to the ever-changing requirements of a highly technical and industrialized society; it will only place itself at an even greater disadvantage in relation to English. Fortunately this is widely realised, and it is also fortunate that the French language today shows itself to be more resilient and adaptable than it has been at any time since the sixteenth century. (160)

Jean-Benoît Nadeau and Julie Barlow, authors of the scintillating narrative *The Story of French* just released, share Rickard's optimism—tempered with reservations. Their optimism derives from the positive dynamics they observe in the language, culture, and demographics outside of France, from French Polynesia to Quebec to Africa and the Orient. Their reservations stem from the uncertainties of geopolitics and the development of sub-Saharan Africa as well as concerns about France itself. "France is both the greatest strength and the worst weakness of French," they write, "its backbone and its Achilles' heel. What the French do, how they understand the world and how

---

[2] Rickard's figures correspond generally to those compiled for the French government's 1999 report titled *Etat de la francophonie dans le monde* and which listed the following statistics for speakers of French worldwide: French as a first or second language and used on a daily basis (112,660,000); French in bilingual or multilingual societies and used on an occasional basis (60,612,000); French as a foreign language and used sporadically (100,000,000–110,000,000). The total thus approaches three hundred million speakers. Although specific data may not be completely reliable, it is estimated that French currently ranks "in tenth or eleventh position behind Chinese, English, Hindi, Spanish, Russian, Arabic, Bengali, Portuguese, Malay, and possibly Japanese" (Battye et al. 2, statistics and rank). When geography is taken into account, however, the influence of the language and the culture it conveys broadens considerably. The maps and tables provided by Naudeau and Barlow (x–xi, 451–60) document the pervasiveness and breadth of the language as well as the numbers of speakers and students it continues to attract worldwide.

the world understands them, will continue to weigh heavily on the future of the French language" (443–44). Indeed, how will France react? Will future policies be based on the proverbial cup half empty or half full? In assessments of this sort it is always wise to look to the past. Four and a half centuries of history cannot be disregarded. In matters of language, milestones in Western civilization were reached in France: the Académie Française, the *Dictionnaire*, the *Encyclopédie*, Braille, LSF, the *Dictionnaire universel*, the Société de Linguistique de Paris. The cast of characters is of epic proportions. Their names are known far and wide: Du Bellay, Montaigne, Richelieu, Descartes, Pascal, Condillac, Voltaire, Rivarol, Rousseau, Diderot, Bréal, Saussure, to mention a few. Others find their way into more specialized dominions: Marie de Gournay, Grégoire, the Bescherelles, Louis Braille, Etienne de Fay, abbé de L'Epée, abbé Sicard, Laurent Clerc, Jean-François and Joséphine Sudre, Martinet.

It is difficult to imagine that, after all this time, such a tradition will not find a way to survive—and thrive—in the years to come.

Works Cited

Abensour, Léon. (1979) *Histoire générale du féminisme*. Paris/Geneva: Slatkine.

Abraham, Claude K. (1971) *Enfin Malherbe: The Influence of Malherbe on French Lyric Prosody, 1605–1674*. Lexington, Kentucky: University of Kentucky Press.

Adams, Mark B., ed. (1990) *The Wellborn Science: Eugenics in Germany, France, Brazil, and Russia*. Oxford: Oxford University Press.

Ager, Dennis. (1990) *Sociolinguistics and Contemporary French*. Cambridge: Cambridge University Press.

Albertini, Pierre. (1998) *L'école en France, XIXe–XXe siècle*. Paris: Hachette.

Albistur, Maïté, and Daniel Armogathe. (1977) *Histoire du féminisme français du moyen âge à nos jours*. Paris: des femmes.

Anon. (1847) "Notice biographique sur M. Bescherelle aîné." *Extrait de La Revue des Contemporains*. Paris: Gallot: 1–8.

Antoine, Gérald. (2000) "La langue française face aux défis de la modernité." *Revue de l'Association des Membres de l'Ordre des Palmes Académiques* 148 (2e trimestre): http://www.amopa.assoc.fr.

Antoine, Gérald, and Bernard Cerquiglini, eds. (2000) *Histoire de la langue française 1945–2000*. Paris: CNRS.

Aristotle. (1986) *History of Animals*. London: Penguin.

Armstrong, David, Michael A. Karchmer, and John Vickrey Van Cleve, eds. (2002) *The Study of Signed Languages: Essays in Honor of William C. Stokoe*. Washington, D.C.: Gallaudet University Press.

Armstrong, Nigel. (2001) *Social and Stylistic Variation in Spoken French: A Comparative Approach*. Amsterdam/Philadelphia: John Benjamins.

Arnauld, Antoine, and Claude Lancelot. (1660) *Grammaire générale et raisonnée contenant Les fondemens de l'art de parler; expliquez d'une manière Claire & naturelle; Les raisons de ce qui est commun à toutes les langues, & des principales differences qui s'y rencontrent; Et plusieurs remarques nouvelles sur la Langue Françoise*. Paris: Pierre Le Petit.

Arnauld, Antoine, and Pierre Nicole. (1981) *La logique ou l'art de penser contenant, outre les règles communes, plusieurs observations nouvelles propres à former le iugement*. Edition critique. Ed. Pierre Clair and François Girbal. Paris: Vrin.

Auroux, Sylvain. (1983) "La première société de linguistique—Paris 1837?" *Historiographia Linguistica* 10.3: 241–65.

Ayers-Bennett, Wendy. (1987) *Vaugelas and the Development of the French Language*. London: Modern Humanities Research Association.

Ball, Rodney. (1999) "La réforme de l'orthographe en France et en Allemagne: attitudes et réactions." *Current Issues in Language & Society* 6.3–4: 270–75.

Barère, Bertrand (de Vieuzac). *Rapport du Comité de Salut Public sur les idiomes*. Certeau et al. *Une politique de la langue. La Révolution française et les patois: l'enquête de Grégoire*: 291–99.

Barral, Pierre. (1998) "Depuis quand les paysans se sentent-ils français?" *Ruralia* 3:1–33. Online: http://ruralia. Revues.org/document53.html (1 January 2003): 1–12.

Battye, Adrian, Marie-Anne Hintze, and Paul Rowlett. (2000) *The French Language Today: A Linguistic Introduction*. 2nd ed. London/New York: Routledge.

Baudino, Claudie. (2001) *Politique de la langue et différence sexuelle. La politisation du genre des noms de métier*. Paris: L'Harmattan.

Baynton, Douglas C. (1993) "'Savages and Deaf-Mutes': Evolutionary Theory and the Campaign Against Sign Language in the Nineteenth Century." Van Cleve, ed. *Deaf History Unveiled*: 92–112.

Beaken, Mike. (1996) *The Making of Language*. Edinburgh: Edinburgh University Press.

Bébian, Roch A. (1817) *Essai sur les sourds-muets et sur le langage naturel*. Paris: Dentu.

———. (1825) *Mimographie, ou essai d'écriture mimique propre à régulariser le langage des sourds-muets*. Paris: Colas.

Becquer, Annie, Bernard Cerquiglini, Nicole Cholewka, Martine Coutier, Josette Frécher, and Marie-Josèphe Mathieu (Comité de féminisation). (1999) *Femme, j'écris ton nom. Guide d'aide à la féminisation des noms de métiers, titres, grades et fonctions*. Paris: CNRS-InaLF.

Bell, David A., ed. (1999) *La recherche dix-huitiémiste. Raison universelle et culture nationale au siècle des Lumières*. Paris: Champion.

———. (2001) *The Cult of Nation in France: Inventing Nationalism, 1680–1800*. Cambridge, MA: Harvard University Press.

Bellay, Joachim du. (1950) *La deffence et illustration de la langue françoyse*. Fac-similé de l'édition originale de 1549. Geneva: Droz/Lille: Giard.

Benveniste, Emile. (1971) "Allocution." *Bulletin de la Société de Linguistique de Paris* 66. 1: 73–81.

Benjamin, Walter. (1974) *Charles Baudelaire. Le poète lyrique à l'apogée du capitalisme*. Trans. Jean Lacoste. Paris: Payot.

Bergounioux, Gabriel. (1994) *Aux origines de la linguistique française*. Paris: Agora.

———. (1996) "Aux origines de la Société de Linguistique de Paris (1864–1876)." *Bulletin de la Société de Linguistique de Paris* 91.1: 1–36.

———. (1997) "La Société de Linguistique de Paris (1876–1914)." *Bulletin de la Société de Linguistique de Paris* 92.1: 1–25.

Berthier, Ferdinand. (1852) *L'abbé de L'Epée, sa vie, son apostolat, ses travaux et ses succès*. Paris: Michel Lévy frères.

_____. (1873) *L'abbé Sicard. Célèbre instituteur des sourds-muets, successeur immédiat de l'abbé de L'Epée.* Paris: Douniol.

Bertin, Fabrice. (2003) "Intégration scolaire des élèves sourds et éducation bilingue (français-LSF): des objectifs contradictoires ?" *La Nouvelle Revue de l'AIS* 21.1: www.cnefei.fr.

Bescherelle, Louis-Nicolas, Henri-Honoré Bescherelle, and Litais de Gaux. (1835–36) *Grammaire nationale.* Paris: Bourgeois-Maze.

Bézagu-Deluy, Maryse. (1990) *L'abbé de L'Epée: Instituteur des sourds et muets 1712–1789.* Paris: Seghers.

_____. (1993) "Personalities in the Worlds of Deaf Mutes in 18th Century Paris." Fischer, Renate, and Harlan Lane, eds. *Looking Back: A Reader on the History of Deaf Communities and their Sign Languages*: 25–42.

Bogart, Darleen, Tim V. Cranmer, and Joseph E. Sullivan. (2000) "Unifying the Braille Codes." Dixon, Judith M., ed. *Braille into the Next Millennium*: 161–81.

Bonet, Juan Pablo. (1620) *Reduction* [sic] *de las letras y arte para enseñar a los mudos.* Madrid: Francisco Abarca de Angula.

Boulad-Ayoub, Josiane. (2005) *L'abbé Grégoire apologète de la république.* Paris: Champion.

Boulton, Marjorie. (1960) *Zamenhof, Creator of Esperanto.* London: Routledge.

Brahimi, Denise. (2006) "Roman et société dans la France contemporaine." *Civilization in French and Francophone Literature.* Day, James, and Buford Norman, eds. French Literature Series 33. Amsterdam/New York: 185–93.

Branson, Jan, and Don Miller. (2002) *Damned for their Difference: The Cultural Construction of Deaf People as Disabled.* Washington, D.C: Gallaudet University Press.

Breillat, Dominique. (2006) "The European Charter for Regional or Minority Languages." http://www.abo.fi/fak/hf/folklore/projekt/migration/TheFrench Case.pdf#search=%22The%20European%20Charter%20for%20Regional%20 or%20Minority%20Languages%3A%20The%20French%20Case%22: 1–10.

Bridoux, André. (1953) "Introduction." Descartes. *Œuvres et lettres*: 9–23.

Broc, Numa. (1976) "Patrimoine, régionalisme et géographie: Pierre Foncin." *L'Information Historique* 39: 30–33.

Brosman, Paul W., Jr. (1982) "Designation of Females in Hittite." *Journal of Indo-European Studies* 10.1–2: 65–70.

_____. (1982) "The Development of the PIE Feminine." *Journal of Indo-European Studies* 10.3–4: 253–72.

Bruézière, Maurice. (1983) *L'Alliance Française: histoire d'une institution.* Paris: Hachette.

Brunet, Etienne. (1999) "La langue française au XXe siècle. Ce que disent les chiffres." Chaurand, Jacques, ed. *Nouvelle histoire de la langue française*: 673–728.

Brunot, Ferdinand. (1966-1972) *Histoire de la langue française.* 13 vols. Paris: Armand Colin.

Buroker, Jill Vance. (1996) "Introduction." Arnauld, Antoine, and Pierre Nicole. *Logic or the Art of Thinking*. Cambridge: Cambridge University Press: ix–xxx.

Cannon, Garland. (1990) *The Life and Mind of Oriental Jones: Sir William Jones, the Father of Modern Linguistics*. Cambridge: Cambridge University Press.

Cannon, Garland, and Kevin R. Brine, eds. (1995) *Objects of Enquiry: The life, Contributions, and Influences of Sir William Jones (1746–1794)*. New York: New York University Press.

Canut, Cécile. (2000) "Subjectivité, imaginaires et fanatismes des langues: la mise en discours 'épilinguistique.'" *Langage et Société* 93 (September): 71–97.

Carroll, Cathryn, and Harlan Lane. (1991) *Laurent Clerc: The Story of His Early Years*. Washington, D.C.: Gallaudet University Press.

Carton, Fernand. (2000) "La prononciation." Antoine and Cerquiglini, eds. *Histoire de la langue française 1945–2000*: 25–60.

Catach, Nina. (1993) "The Reform of the Writing System." Sanders, Carol, ed. *French Today*: 139–54.

Célestin, Roger, Eliane Dalmolin, and Isabelle de Courtivron, eds. (2003) *Beyond French Feminisms. Debates on Women, Politics, and Culture in France, 1981–2001*. New York: Palgrave Macmillan.

Certeau, Michel de, Julia Dominique, and Jacques Revel. (1975) *Une politique de la langue. La Révolution française et les patois: l'enquête de Grégoire*. Paris: Gallimard.

Chaline, Jean-Pierre. (1998) *Sociabilité et érudition: les sociétés savantes en France, XIXe–XXe siècles*. Paris: Editions du C.T.H.S.

Chaurand, Jacques, ed. (1999) *Nouvelle histoire de la langue française*. Paris: Seuil.

Chervel, André. (1977) *Histoire de la grammaire scolaire*. Paris: Payot.

———. (1982) *Les grammaires françaises 1800–1914. Répertoire chronologique*. Paris: I.N.R.P.

Chevalier, Jean-Claude. (1993) "Enseignement du français et institutions universitaires: 1789-1989." Saint-Gérand, Jacques Philippe, ed. *Mutations et sclérose de la langue française*: 135–51.

Christiansen, Morten H., and Simon Kirby, eds. (2003) *Language Evolution*. Oxford: Oxford University Press.

Cixous, Hélène. (1979) *Vire l'orange*. Paris, des femmes.

Clark, Linda. (1984) *Social Darwinism in France*. University, Alabama: University of Alabama Press.

Clair, Pierre, and François Girbal. (1981) "Avant-propos." Arnauld and Nicole. *La logique ou l'art de penser*: 1–10.

Clerc, Laurent. (1976) *The Laurent Clerc Papers*. New Haven: Yale University (microfilm).

Clerico, Geneviève. (1999) "Le français au XVI siècle." Chaurand, Jacques, ed. *Nouvelle histoire de la langue française*: 145–224.

Commission Générale de Terminologie et de Néologie. (1998) *Rapport sur la féminisation des noms de métier, fonction, grade ou titre. Journal Officiel*. (October): Electronic version: http://www.culture.gouv.fr/culture/dglf/cogeter/feminisation/sommaire.html

Compagnon, Béatrice, and Anne Thévenin. (1995) *L'école et la société française*. Bruxelles: Complexe.

Condillac, Etienne de. (1998) *Essai sur l'origine des connaissances humaines. Ouvrage où l'on réduit à un seul principe tout ce qui concerne l'entendement humain.* Préface de Michèle Crampe-Casnabet. Paris: Editions Alive.

Conry, Yvette. (1974) *L'introduction du darwinisme en France*. Paris: Vrin.

Corbett, Greville G. (1991) *Gender*. Cambridge: Cambridge University Press.

Corsi, Pietro. (1988) *The Age of Lamarck: Evolutionary Theories in France 1790–1830*. Tr. Jonathan Mandelbaum. Berkeley: University of California Press.

Couturat, Louis, and Léopold Leau. (1979) *Histoire de la langue universelle*. Hildesheim/New York: Georg Olms Verlag.

Crampe-Casnabet, Michèle. (1998) "Préface." Condillac, Etienne de. *Essai sur l'origine des connaissances humaines*: 5–18.

Cremonese, Laura. (1997) *Dialectique du masculin et du féminin dans l'œuvre d'Hélène Cixous*. Fasano/Paris : Schena/Didier.

Crosland, Maurice. (1992) *Science under Control: The French Academy of Sciences 1795–1914*. Cambridge : Cambridge University Press.

Crozier, Michel. (1979) *On ne change pas la société par décret*. Paris: Grasset.

Danesi, Marcel. (1993) *Vico, Metaphor, and the Origin of Language*. Bloomington: Indiana University Press.

Delesalle, Simone, and Jean-Claude Chevalier. (1986) *La linguistique, la grammaire et l'école 1750–1914*. Paris: Armand Colin.

Descartes, René. (1953) *Œuvres et lettres*. Ed. Bridoux, André. Paris: Gallimard/Pléiade.

Dewachter, Michel. (1990) *Champollion: un scribe pour l'Egypte*. Paris: Gallimard.

Dictionnaire du bas-langage ou des manières de parler usitées parmi le peuple; ouvrage dans lequel on a réuni les expressions proverbiales, figurées et triviales; les sobriquets, termes ironiques et facétieux; les barbarismes, solécismes; et généralement les locutions basses et vicieuses que l'on doit rejeter de la bonne conversation. (1808) 2 vols. Paris: Haussmann. Online at the following web site: www.chass.utoronto.ca/epc/langueXIX/hautel

Diderot, Denis. (1964) *Lettre sur les aveugles. Œuvres philosophiques*. Ed. Paul Vernière. Paris: Garnier: 75–146.

———. (1978). *Lettre sur les sourds et muets à l'usage de ceux qui entendent et parlent*. Ed. Jacques Chouillet. *Œuvres complètes*. Ed. Dieckmann, Herbert, et al. Paris: Hermann. 25 vols. 4:108–233.

Dixon, Judith M., ed. (2000) *Braille into the Next Millennium*. Washington, D.C.: Library of Congress/National Library Service for the Blind.

Donzé, Roland. (1967) *La grammaire générale et raisonnée de Port-Royal*. Berne: Editions Francke.

Drost, Wolfgang, and Marie-Hélène Girard, eds. (2005) *Gautier et l'Allemagne*. Siegen, Germany: Universitätsverlag Siegen.

Duchet, Michèle, and Michèle Jalley, eds. (1977) *Langue et langages de Leibniz à l'Encyclopédie. Séminaire de l'Ecole normale Supérieure de Fontenay*. Paris: Union Générale d'Editions.

Durand, Jacques. (1996) "Linguistic Purification, the French Nation-State and the Linguist." Hoffmann, Charlotte, ed. *Language, Culture and Communication in Contemporary Europe*: 75–92.

Eco, Umberto. (1995) *The Search for the Perfect Language*. Tr. James Fentress. Oxford, UK: Blackwell.

Elias, Norbert. (1982) *Power & Civility*. Tr. Edmund Jephcott. 2 vols. New York: Pantheon.

Eluard, Paul. (1997) *Œuvres complètes*. 2 vols. Paris: Gallimard.

Erlanger, Philippe. (1965) *Louis XIV*. Paris: Fayard.

Escalle, Marie-Christine Kok, and Francine Melka, eds. (2001) *Changements politiques et statut des langues. Histoire et épistémologie 1780–1945*. Amsterdam/New York: Rodopi.

Etiemble (René). (1964) *Parlez-vous franglais?* Paris: Gallimard. 2nd edition 1973.

Fauré, Christine. (2003) "Women's History after the Law on Parity." Tr. Lucy McNair. Célestin, Roger, et al., eds. *Beyond French Feminisms*: 39–49.

Fétis, F. J. (1868) *Biographie universelle des musiciens et bibliographie générale de la musique*. 8 vols. Paris: Firmin Dido.

Fischer, Renate. (1993) "Abbé de l'Epée and the Living Dictionary." Van Cleve, John Vickrey, ed. *Deaf History Unveiled*: 13–26.

Fischer, Renate, and Harlan Lane, eds. (1993) *Looking Back: A Reader on the History of Deaf Communities and their Sign Languages*. Hamburg: Signum.

Formey, Jean Henry Samuel. (1750) *Histoire de l'Académie des Sciences et Belles-Lettres depuis son origine jusqu'à présent*. Berlin: Haude et Spener.

Foucault, Michel. (1966) *Les mots et les choses. Une archéologie des sciences humaines*. Paris: Gallimard.

Fragonard, Marie-Madeleine, and Eliane Kotler. (1994) *Introduction à la langue du XVIe siècle*. Paris: Nathan.

Fromilhague, René. (1954) *Malherbe. Technique et création poétique*. Paris: Armand Colin.

Fumaroli, Marc. (2001) *Quand l'Europe parlait français*. Paris: Fallois.

Gadet, Françoise. (1999) "La langue française au XXe siècle. L'émergence de l'oral." Chaurand, Jacques, ed. *Nouvelle histoire de la langue française*: 581–667.

Gajewski, Boleslas. (1902) *Grammaire de Solrésol*. Paris: Librairie du Progrès.

Garat, Jean. (1798) "Discours préliminaire." *Dictionnaire de l'Académie Françoise*. 5e édition. Paris: Académie Française: i–x.

Gautier, Théophile. (March 18, 1837) "Réapparition de Madame Madeleine Poutret de Mauchamps." *Figaro*.

George, Ken. (1993) "Alternative French." Sanders, Carol, ed. *French Today*: 155–70.

Gervais, Marie-Marthe. (1993) "Gender and Language in French." Sanders, Carol, ed. *French Today*: 121–38.

Ghirshman, R. (1961) *Iran*. Baltimore: Penguin Books USA.

Gimbutas, Marija. (1991) *The Civilization of the Goddess: The World of Old Europe*. San Francisco: Harper Collins.

Giusti, Ada. (1996) "L'Académie française et l'évolution de la langue. Entretien avec Michel Serres." *Contemporary French Civilization* 20.1 (Winter/Spring): 106–22.

Girault-Duvivier, Charles-Pierre. (1822) *Grammaire des grammaires, ou Analyse raisonnée des meilleurs traités sur la langue Françoise*. 5e éd. 2 vols. Paris: Janet et Cotelle; (1838) 9e éd. 2 vols. Paris: A. Cotelle; (1853) 15e éd. 2 vols. Paris: A. Cotelle.

Glatigny, Michel. (1998) *Les marques d'usage dans les dictionnaires français monolingues du XIXe siècle*. Tübingen: Max Niemeyer Verlag.

Goosse, André. (2000) "Evolution de la syntaxe." Antoine, Gérald, and Bernard Cerquiglini, eds. *Histoire de la langue française 1945–2000*: 107–45.

Görlach, Manfred, ed. (2001) *A Dictionary of European Anglicisms: A Usage Dictionary of Anglicisms in Sixteen European Languages*. Oxford: Oxford University Press.

Gould, Karen. (1990) *Writing in the Feminine: Feminism and Experimental Writing in Quebec*. Carbondale/Edwardsville: Southern Illinois University Press.

Gournay, Marie Le Jars de. (2002) *Apology for the Woman Writing and Other Works*. Hillman, Richard, and Colette Quesnel (ed./tr.). Chicago: University of Chicago Press.

Grégoire, Henri-Baptiste. (1794) *Rapport sur la nécessité et les moyens d'anéantir les patois, et d'universaliser l'usage de la langue française. Séance du 16 prairal, l'an deuxième de la République*. Paris: Publications de la Convention Nationale.

Groce, Nora Ellen. (1985) *Everyone Here Spoke Sign Language*. Cambridge, MA: Harvard University Press.

Groult, Benoîte. (2000) "The Feminization of Professional Names: An Outrage against Masculinity." Tr. Anne-Marie Smith. Célestin, Roger, et al., eds. *Beyond French Feminisms*: 69–75.

Gruaz, Claude: "L'orthographe en cette fin de siècle." Antoine, Gérald, and Bernard Cerquiglini, eds. *Histoire de la langue française 1945–2000*: 61–70.

Hackett, C. F. (1958) *A Course in Modern Linguistics*. New York: Macmillan.

Hagège, Claude. (1985) *L'homme de parole*. Paris: Fayard.

Hall, Robert A., Jr. (1974) *External History of the Romance Languages*. New York: American Elsevier.

Harrington, Richard K. (2005) *Bibliography of Planned Languages (Excluding Esperanto)*. http://www.geocities.com/Athens/5383/langlab/bibliog.htm/: 1992–1997.

Haßler, Gerda. (2001) "La discussion sur l'universalité de la langue française et la comparaison des langues; une rupture épistémologique." Escalle, Marie-Christine, and Francine Melka, eds. *Changements politiques et statut des langues. Histoire et épistémologie 1780–1945*:15–39.

Hawkins, Roger. (1993) "Regional Variation in France." Sanders, Carol, ed. *French Today*: 55–84.

Henry, Freeman G. (1994) "A Case of Questionable Motives: Théophile Gautier and *La Gazette des Femmes*." *Nineteenth-Century French Studies* 22.3–4: 431–38.

———. (1999): "Anti-Darwinism in France: Science and the Myth of Nation." *Nineteenth-Century French Studies* 27.3–4: 290–304.

_____. (2001) "Gautier, Nerval et Alphonse Karr: Badinage, esprit et parti pris au Figaro." *Bulletin de la Société Théophile Gautier* 23: 275–90.

_____. (2003) "From the First to the Fifth Republic: Antoine de Rivarol, Johann Christoph Schwab, and the Latest *Lingua Franca*. *French Review* 77.2 (December): 312–23.

_____. (2004) "Translating Cixous's 'Orange': Cultural Palimpsest and 'Récriture féminine.'" *Rivista di Letteratura Moderne e Comparate* 57.2: 229–52.

_____. (2005) "Schwab/Robelot/Rivarol: une étude." Schwab, Johann Christoph. *Dissertation sur les causes de l'universalité de la langue française*: 1–57.

_____. (2007) "Rue Cuvier, rue Geoffroy-Saint-Hilaire, rue Lamarck: Politics and Science in the Streets of Paris." *Nineteenth-Century French Studies* 35.3–4: 513–25.

Herie, Euclid J. (2000) "La maison natale de Louis Braille." Dixon, Judith M., ed. *Braille into the Next Millennium*: 72–105.

Hewes, Gordon Winant. (1975) *Language Origins: A Bibliography*. 2 Vols. The Hague: Mouton.

Heylen, Romy. (1993) *Translation, Poetics, and the Stage: Six French Hamlets*. London/New York: Routledge.

Hoffmann, Charlotte, ed. (1996) *Language, Culture and Communication in Contemporary Europe*. Clevedon/Philadelphia/Adelaide: Multilingual Matters.

Huchon, Mireille. (1988) *Le français de la Renaissance*. Paris: Presses Universitaires de France.

Hugo, Victor. (1944) "Réponse à un acte d'accusation." *Les Contemplations. Œuvres poétiques complètes*. Montréal: Valiquette.

_____. (1949) *Préface de Cromwell*. Paris: Larousse.

Institut de France. (1995) *Histoire des cinq académies*. Paris: Librairie Académique Perrin.

Ilsley, Marjorie Henry. (1963) *Marie le Jars de Gournay: Her Life and Works*. The Hague: Mouton.

Johnson, Barbara. (1979) *Défigurations du langage poétique*. Paris: Flammarion.

Jouison, Paul. (1998) *Ecrits sur la langue des signes française*. Ed. Brigitte Garcia. Paris: L'Harmattan.

Kendon, Adam. (2002) "Historical Observations on the Relationship between Research on Sign Languages and Language Origins Theory." Armstrong, David, et al., eds. *The Study of Signed Languages: Essays in Honor of William C. Stokoe*: 35–52.

Khaznadar, Edwige. (2002) *Le féminin à la française: académisme et langue française*. Paris: L'Harmattan.

Kimbrough, Paula. (2006) "How Braille Began." http://www.brailler.com/braillehx. htm.

Knowlson, James. (1975) *Universal Language Schemes in England and France 1600–1800*. Toronto: University of Toronto Press.

Knox, Edward C. (2000) "France in Trouble or in Transition?" Koop, Marie-Christine Weidmann, ed. *France at the Dawn of the Twenty-First Century*: 137–46.

Koop, Marie-Christine Weidmann, ed. (2000) *France at the Dawn of the Twenty-First Century: Trends and Transformations/La France à l'aube du XXIe siècle: tendances et mutations.* Birmingham, Alabama: Summa Publications, Inc.

Labov, William. (1972) *Sociolinguistic Patterns.* Philadelphia: University of Pennsylvania Press.

La Harpe, Jean François de. (1821) *Du fanatisme dans la langue révolutionnaire, ou De la persécution suscitée par les barbares du dix-huitième siècle, contre la religion chrétienne et ses ministres; suivi d'un appendice sur le calendrier républicain.* Paris: Chaumont Jeune.

Lane, Harlan. (1984) *When the Mind Hears: A History of the Deaf.* New York: Random House.

Lang, Harry G. (2003) "Perspectives on the History of Deaf Education." Marschark, Marc, and Patricia Elizabeth Spence, eds. *Deaf Studies, Language, and Education:* 9–20.

Lanson, Gustave. (1951) *Histoire de la littérature française.* Paris: Hachette.

Lanthenas, François. (1793) *Rapport et projet de décret sur l'organisation des écoles primaires.* Tome premier (15 octobre 1792–2 juillet 1793). Paris: Publications de la Convention Nationale.

Laroche-Claire, Yves. (2004) *Evitez le franglais, parlez français!* Paris: Albin Michel.

Larousse, Pierre. (1865–1890) *Grand dictionnaire universel du XIXe siècle français, historique, géographique, biographique, mythologique, bibliographique, littéraire, artistique, scientifique, etc.* 17 vols. Paris: Administration du Grand dictionnaire universel.

Laurent Clerc: Apostle to the Deaf People of the New World. (2006) Gallaudet University electronic publication: http://clercenter.gallaudet.edu/Literacy.

Leclerc, Annie. (1974) *Parole de femme.* Paris: Grasset.

Lee, Penny. (1996) *The Whorf Theory Complex: A Critical Reconstruction.* Amsterdam/Philadelphia: John Benjamins.

Lehning, James R. (1995) *Peasant and French: Cultural Contact in Rural France during the Nineteenth Century.* Cambridge: Cambridge University Press.

L'Epée, abbé de. (1776) *Institution des sourds et muets, par la voie des signes méthodoiques.* Paris: Nyon l'aîné.

_____. (1984) *La véritable manière d'instruire les sourds et muets, confirmée par une longue expérience.* Paris: Fayard.

Lewis, W. H. (1953) *The Splendid Century: Life in the France of Louis XIV.* New York: Doubleday.

Levitt, Jesse. (1968) *The Grammaire des Grammaires of Girault-Duvivier: A Study of Nineteenth-Century French.* The Hague/Paris: Mouton.

Lhomond, Charles-François. (1780) *Elémens de la grammaire Françoise.* Paris: Colas.

Locke, John. (1975) *Essay concerning Human Understanding.* Ed. P. H. Nidditch. Oxford: Oxford University Press.

Lodge, R. Anthony. (1993) *French: From Dialect to Standard.* London/New York: Routledge.

Lorimer, Pamela. (2000) "Origins of Braille." Dixon, Judith M., ed. *Braille into the Next Millennium*: 19–39.

Maat, Jaap. (2004) *Philosophical Languages in the Seventeenth Century: Delgarno, Wilkins, Leibniz.* Dordrecht/Boston/London: Kluwer Academic Publishers.

Mah, Harold. (1994) "The Epistemology of the Sentence: Language, Civility, and Identity in France and Germany, Diderot to Nietzsche." *Representations* 47 (Summer): 64–84.

Mairal, Martine. (2003) *L'obèle.* Paris: Flammarion.

Mallarmé, Stéphane. (1945) "Sur l'évolution littéraire." *Œuvres complètes.* Ed. Mondor, Henri, and G. Jean-Aubry. Paris: Gallimard (Pléiade).

Malmberg, Bertil. (1991) *Histoire de la linguistique de Sumer à Saussure.* Paris: Presses Universitaires de France.

Manichetti, Aldo. (1980) "Romantisme et philologie romane." *Romantisme. Actes du colloque de Sonnenwil 1979.* Fribourg (Switzerland): Editions Universitaires.

Marle aîné. (1828) "Introduction." *Journal Didactique de la Langue Française* 1.1: n.p.

Marschark, Mark, and Patricia Elizabeth Spencer, eds. (2003) *Deaf Studies, Language, and Education.* Oxford: Oxford University Press.

Martinet, André. (1945) *La prononciation du français contemporain.* Geneva: Droz.

Matoré, Georges. (1988) *Le vocabulaire et la société du XVIe siècle.* Paris: Presses Universitaires de France.

Mellor, C. Michael. (2006) *Louis Braille: A Touch of Genius.* Boston: National Braille Press.

Mercier, Louis Sébastien. (1801) *Néologie ou vocabulaire de mots nouveaux, à renouveler, ou pris dans des acceptions nouvelles.* 2 vols. Paris: Moussard/Maradan.

Merlin-Kajman, Hélène. (2001) *L'excentricité académique: littérature, institution, société.* Paris: Les Belles Lettres.

Mirzoeff, Nicholas. (1995) *Silent Poetry: Deafness, Sign, and Visual Culture in Modern France.* Princeton: Princeton University Press.

Moi, Toril. (1985) *Sexual / Textual Politics: Feminist Literary Theory.* London/New York: Methuen.

Montaigne, Michel de. (1962) *Essais.* Ed. Maurice Rat. 2 vols. Paris: Classiques Garnier.

Morçay, Raoul, and Armand Müller. (1960) *La Renaissance.* Paris: del Duca.

Moreau, Thérèse. (1999) *Le nouveau dictionnaire féminin-masculin des professions, des titres et des fonctions.* Geneva: Metropolis.

Morel, B. A. (1976) *Traité des dégénérescences physiques, intellectuelles et morales de l'espèce humaine et des causes qui produisent ces vérités maladives.* Paris: Baillière, 1857; rpt. New York: Arno Press.

Mottez, Bernard. (1993) "The Deaf Mute Banquets and the Birth of the Deaf Movement." Fischer, Renate, and Harlan Lane, eds. *Looking Back: A Reader on the History of Deaf Communities and their Sign Languages*: 143–155.

Nadeau, Jean-Benoît, and Julie Barlow. (2006) *The Story of French.* New York: St. Martin's Press.

Nakam, Géralde. (1996) "Marie Le Jars de Gournay, 'fille d'alliance' de Montaigne. *Marie de Gournay et l'édition de 1595 des Essais de Montaigne.*" Actes du colloque organisé par la Société Internationale des Amis de Montaigne les 9 et 10 juin 1995, en Sorbonne. Réunis par Jean-Claude Arnouls. Paris: Champion.

Neidel, Carol, Judy Kegl, Dawn MacLaughlin, Benjamin Baham, and Robert G. Lee. (2000) *The Syntax of American Sign Language: Functional Categories and Hierarchical Structures.* Cambridge, Massachusetts: MIT Press.

Noël, François, and Charles Chapsal. (1823) *Nouvelle grammaire française.* Paris. Vve Nyon jeune.

Oakes, Leigh. (2001) *Language and National Identity: Comparing France and Sweden.* Amsterdam/Philadelphia: John Benjamins.

Olender, Maurice. (1992) *The Languages of Paradise: Race, Religion, and Philology in the Nineteenth Century.* Tr. Arthur Goldhammer. Cambridge: Harvard University Press.

Padden, Carol A., and Jennifer Rayman. (2002) "The Future of American Sign Language." Armstrong, David, et al. *The Study of Signed Languages: Essays in Honor of William C. Stokoe*: 247–61.

Pécaut, Félix. (n.d.) *Quinze ans d'éducation. Notes écrites au jour le jour.* 2nd ed. 2 vols. Paris: Delagrave.

Pedersen, Holger. (1959) *The Discovery of Language: Linguistic Science in the Nineteenth Century.* Tr. John Webster Spargo. Bloomington: Indiana University press.

Pei, Mario. (1958) *One Language for the World.* New York: Devin-Adair.

———. (1966) *Glossary of Linguistic Terminology.* Garden City, New York: Doubleday.

Pellerey, Roberto. (1993) *La théorie de la construction directe de la phrase. Analyse de la formation d'une idéologie linguistique.* Paris: Larousse.

Pergnier, Maurice. (1989) *Les anglicismes. Danger ou enrichissement pour la langue française?* Paris: Presses Universitaires de France.

Phillipson, Robert. (1992) *Linguistic Imperialism.* Oxford: Oxford University Press.

Picone, Michael D. (1996) *Anglicisms, Neologisms, and Dynamic French.* Amsterdam: John Benjamins.

Plann, Susan. (1993) "Pedro Ponce de León: Myth and Reality." Van Cleve, John Vickery, ed. *Deaf History Unveiled*: 1–12.

Planté, Christine, ed. (1999) *Masculin/féminin dans la poésie et les poétiques du XIXe siècle.* Lyon: Presses Universitaires de Lyon.

Plongeron, Bernard. (1989) *L'abbé Grégoire, ou l'arche de la fraternité.* Paris: Letouzey et Ané.

———. (2001) *L'abbé Grégoire et la république des savants.* Paris: CTHS.

Poliakov, Léon. (1971) *The Aryan Myth: A History of Racist Ideas in Europe.* Tr. Edmund Howard. Sussex: Sussex University Press.

Pollock, Jean-Yves. (1989) "Verb Movement, Universal Grammar, and the Structure of IP." *Linguistic Inquiry* 20: 365–424.

Popkin, Jeremy D., and Richard H. Popkin, eds. (2000) *The Abbé Grégoire and his World.* Dordrecht, Netherlands: Kluwer Academic Publishers.

Pour MM. Simon, et Garnier frères, contre M. Maye. (1858) Folio 4-FM-30183. Bibliothèque Nationale de France (site François Mitterrand).

Presneau, Jean-René. (1993) "The Scholars, the Deaf, and the Language of Signs in France of the 18th Century." Fischer, Renate, and Harlan Lane, eds. *Looking Back: A Reader on the History of Deaf Communities and their Sign Languages*: 413–21.

Renucci, G. (1977) "Notes sur quelques articles de l'*Encyclopédie*." Duchet, Michèle, and Michèle Jalley, eds. *Langue et langages de Leibniz à l'Encyclopédie. Séminaire de l'Ecole normale Supérieure de Fontenay*: 293–304.

Rickard, Peter. (1968) *La langue française au seizième siècle: Etude suivie de textes.* Cambridge: Cambridge University Press.

_____. (1992) *The French Language in the Seventeenth Century: Contemporary Opinion in France.* Cambridge (England): D. S. Brewer.

_____. (1993) *A History of the French Language.* 2nd edition. London: Routledge.

Rivarol, Antoine de. (1797) *De l'universalité de la langue française. Sujet proposé par l'Académie de Berlin, en 1785* [sic.]. Hambourg: P. F. Fauche.

Robins, R. H. (1990) "Jones as General Linguist in the Eighteenth-Century Context." Cannon, Garland, and Kevin R. Brine, eds. *Objects of Enquiry: The life, Contributions, and Influences of Sir William Jones (1746–1794)*: 83–91.

Rolin, Jean. (2002) *La clôture.* Paris: P.O.L.

_____. (2005) *Terminal Frigo.* Paris: P.O.L.

Ronsard, Pierre de. (1950) *Œuvres complètes.* 2 vols. Paris: Gallimard (Pléiade).

Roots, James. (1999) *The Politics of Visual Language.* Ottawa: Carlton University Press.

Rosenfeld, Sophia A. (1999) "Universal Languages during the French Revolution." David A. Bell, ed. *La recherche dix-huitiémiste. Raison universelle et culture nationale au siècle des Lumières*: 119–31.

_____. (2001) *A Revolution in Language: The Problem of Signs in Eighteenth-Century France.* Stanford, California: Stanford University Press.

Ross, Ishbel. (1951) *Journey into Light: The Story of the Education of the Blind.* New York: Appleton-Century-Crofts.

Roudy, Yvette. (1975/1982) *La femme en marge.* Paris: Flammarion.

_____. (1985) *A cause d'elles.* Paris: Albin Michel.

Rousseau, Jean Jacques. (1995) *Essai sur l'origine des langues où il est parlé de la mélodie et de l'imitation musicale. Œuvres complètes.* 5 vols. Paris: Gallimard, 5: 371–429.

Saint-Gérand, Jacques-Philippe. (1981) "Un aspect de l'histoire de la langue française au XIXe siècle: le *Journal grammatical* de 1835 et sa fonction sociolinguistique." *Le Français Moderne* 49: 337–57.

_____. éd. (1993) *Mutations et sclérose: la langue française 1789–1848.* Stuttgart: Franz Steiner Verlag.

_____. (1999a) "Dans un *Littré* classique, les genres sont-ils la propriété qu'ont les noms de représenter en langue les sexes, et—dans certaines—leur absence?" Planté, Christine, ed. *Masculin/féminin dans la poésie et les poétiques du XIXe siècle*: 17–38.

_____. (1999b) "La langue française au XIXe siècle. Scléroses, altérations, mutations. De l'abbé Grégoire aux tolérances de Georges Leygues." Chaurand, Jacques, ed. *Nouvelle histoire de la langue française*: 377–504.

_____. (2000) "Sentiment national, constructions et représentations linguistiques au XIXe siècle: les travaux des frères Bescherelle à l'aune du concept de 'français de référence.'" *Cahiers de l'Institut Linguistique de Louvain* 26.1–4: 55–73.

Sanders, Carol, ed. (1993) *French Today: Language in its Social Context*. Cambridge: Cambridge University Press.

_____. (2004) "The Paris Years." Sanders, Carol, ed. *The Cambridge Companion to Saussure*: 30–44.

Schlieben-Lange, Brigitte. (1996) *Idéologie, révolution et uniformité de langue*. Sprimont (Belgium): Pierre Mardaga.

Schneider, William H. (1990) "The Eugenics Movement in France 1890-1940." Adams, Mark B., ed. *The Wellborn Science*: 69–109.

Schwab, Johann Christoph. (2005) *Dissertation sur les causes de l'universalité de la langue françoise et la durée vraisemblable de son empire*. Tr. Denis Robelot. Etude et présentation des textes par Freeman G. Henry. Amsterdam/New York: Rodopi.

Sepinwall, Alysia. (2005) *The Abbé Grégoire and the French Revolution*. Berkeley: University of California Press.

Servan-Schreiber, Jean-Jacques. (1967) *Le défi américain*. Paris: Denoël.

Shapiro, Fred. R. (1981) "On the Origin of the Term 'Indo-Germanic.'" *Historiographia Linguistica* 8.1: 165–70.

Smith, Timothy B. (2004) *France in Crisis: Welfare, Inequality, and Globalization since 1980*. Cambridge: Cambridge University Press.

Spaëth, Valérie. (2001) "La création de l'Alliance Israélite Universelle, ou la diffusion de la langue française dans le bassin Méditerranéen." Escalle, Marie-Christine Kok, and Francine Melka, eds. *Changements politiques et statut des langues. Histoire et épistémologie 1780–1945*: 103–17.

Spillebout, Gabriel. (1985) *Grammaire de la langue française du XVIIe siècle*. Paris: Picard.

Stojan, Petr E. (1929) *Bibliografio de Internacia Lingvo*. Geneva: Tour de l'Ile.

Storost, Jürgen. (1994) *Langue française—Langue universelle? Die Diskussion über die Universalität des Französischen an der Berliner Akademie der Wissenschaften, zum Geltunganspruch des Deutschen und Französischen im 18. Jarhundert*. Bonn: Romanistischer Verlag.

Sudre, Jean-François. (1866) *Langue musicale universelle inventée par Jean-François Sudre, également inventeur de la téléphonie*. Paris: G. Flaxland and chez la veuve de l'auteur.

Sudre, Marie-Joséphine. (1883) *Théorie et pratique de la langue universelle inventée par Jean-François Sudre*. Tours: Rouillé-Ladevez.

Sullerot, Evelyne. (1966) *Histoire de la presse féminine en France, des origines à 1848*. Paris: Armand Colin.

Sutton, Michael. (1982) *Nationalism, Positivism and Catholicism: The Politics of Charles Maurras and French Catholics (1890–1914).* Cambridge: Cambridge University Press.

Tableau des dépenses et des recettes du Dictionnaire national (1843–1846). Folio-FM-18128. Bibliothèque Nationale (site François Mitterrand).

Thomas, Downing A. (1995) *Music and the Origins of Language: Theories from the Enlightenment.* Cambridge: Cambridge University Press.

Thomas, Jacqueline. (2000) "France's National Identity and the French Press." Koop, Marie-Christine Weidmann, ed. *France at the Dawn of the Twenty-First Century:* 147–56.

Thomas, Jean-Jacques. (1995) "Les hommes de paroles." *Perceptions of Values.* Ed. Freeman G. Henry. The French Literature Series 22. Amsterdam/New York: Rodopi,: 11–24

Tobe, Carol B. (2000) "Embossed Printing in the United States." Dixon, Judith M., ed. *Braille into the Next Millennium*: 40–71.

Trescases, Pierre. (1982) *Le franglais vingt ans après.* Montreal: Guérin.

Truffaut, Bernard. (1993) "Etienne de Fay and the History of the Deaf." Fischer, Renate, and Harlan Lane, eds. *Looking Back: A Reader on the History of Deaf Communities and their Sign Languages*: 13–24.

Tucker, G. R., W. E. Lambert, and A. A. Rigault. (1977) *The French Speakers Skill with Grammatical Gender: An Example of Rule-Governed Behavior.* The Hague/Paris: Mouton.

Valentine, Phyllis. (1993) "Thomas Hopkins Gallaudet: Benevolent Paternalism and the Origins of the American Asylum." Van Cleve, John Vickery, ed. *Deaf History Unveiled*: 53–73.

Van Cleve, John Vickrey, ed. (1993) *Deaf History Unveiled.* Washington, D.C.: Gallaudet University Press.

Van Gennep, Arnold. (1911) *La décadence et la persistance des patois.* Paris: Bureaux de la Revue des Idées.

Vartanian, Aram. (1989) "Derrida, Rousseau, and the Difference." *Studies in Eighteenth-Century Culture* 19: 129–51.

Vendryes, Joseph. (1955) "Première société linguistique. La Société de Linguistique de Paris (1865–1955)." *Orbis* 4.1: 7–21.

Villey, Pierre. (1970) *Les sources italiennes de la "Deffense et illustration de la langue françoise."* New York: Burt Franklin.

Vigny, Alfred de. (1992) *Servitude et grandeur militaires.* Paris: Gallimard (Folio).

Von Wartburg, W. (1971) *Evolution et structure de la langue française.* Bern: Francke.

Weber, Caroline. (2003) *Terror and its Discontents: Suspect Words in Revolutionary France.* Minneapolis: University of Minnesota Press.

Weber, Eugen. (1976) *Peasants into Frenchmen: The Modernization of Rural France1870–1914.* Stanford, California: Stanford University Press.

Weiss, Sheila Faith. (1987) *Race, Hygiene, and National Efficiency: The Eugenics of Wilhelm Schallmayer.* Berkeley: University of California Press.

Wells, G. A. (1987) *The Origin of Language: Aspects of the Discussion from Condillac to Wundt*. La Salle, Illinois: Open Court.

Wilkinson, Lynn R. (1996) *The Dream of an Absolute Language: Emanuel Swedenborg & French Literary Culture*. Albany, NY: State University of New York Press.

Winzer. M. A. (1993) *The History of Special Education: From Isolation to Integration*. Washington, D.C.: Gallaudet University Press.

Yadav, Alok. (2004) *Before the Empire of English: Literature, Provinciality, and Nationalism in Eighteenth-Century Britain*. Palgrave Macmillian: Houndmills (Hampshire), England.

Yaguello, Marina. (1978/2002) *Les mots et les femmes*. Paris: Payot.

_____. (1989) *Le sexe des mots*. Paris: Belfond.

_____. (1991) *Lunatic Lovers of Language*. Tr. Catherine Slater. London: The Athlone Press.

Yates, Frances A. (1968) *The French Academies of the Sixteenth Century*. London: Warburg Institute.

Index

Twenty Years of French Literary Criticism:
FLS, vingt ans après

Edited by Freeman Henry
University of South Carolina

IN THIS RETROSPECTIVE VOLUME which celebrates the memory of Philip A. Wadsworth, a distinguished *dix-septiémiste* who oversaw and nurtured the early stages of *French Literary Series* at the University of South Carolina, editor Freeman Henry has selected twenty-nine representative essays which appeared in *French Literary Series* over a period of twenty years. These articles trace the evolution of critical theory from the rise of structuralism to the post-modernist era at the end of the twentieth century; also included are certain pre-structuralist methodologies that have now come back into vogue. Essays are oriented along the following axes: "Narrative: From Autobiography to Narratology," "Periodization: From the Deffence to Postmodernism," and "Themes and Motifs: From Socratic Irony to Titrologie." Contributors include Benjamin Bart, Serge Bokobza, Patrick Brady, Roland Champagne, Robert Champigny, Lester Crocker, Hugh Davidson, David Ellison, Richard Grant, Robert Gonquist, Ralph Heyndels, Claude Javeau, Philippe Lejeune, Laurent LeSage, Jean-Pol Madou, Bernard Mathias, Edouard Morot-Sir, John Pappas, Christine Planté, Laurence Porter, Gerald Prince, Rima Drell Reck, Laurence Romero, Murray Sachs, Donald Stone, Jr., Pierre Van den Heuvel, Dirk Van der Cruysse, Michel Viegnes, and Philip A. Wadsworth. A lengthy preface by Freeman Henry offers both a summary of the individual articles and an assessment of French critical trends; Wadsworth's career is also reviewed in an extensive biographical and bibliographical essay. "L'introduction de Freeman G. Henry, qui mêle savamment la petite histoire des *FLS* à celle des enjeux théoriques dont ce dernier quart de siècle a débattu, est d'une totale pertinence et d'un constant intérêt."—*Revue d'Histoire littéraire de la France.*
    ISBN 1-883479-02-9, clothbound, 412 pp. $44.95 US

Selected Backlist Titles from Summa Publications, Inc.

Yvonne LeBlanc, *The French Verse Epistle: Va Lettre Va (1400–1550)*
    ISBN 1-883479-04-5, clothbound $41.95 US

Norris Lacy, *Reading Fabliaux* (2nd edition)
    ISBN 1-883479-24-X, perfectbound $29.95 US

Karen Fresco, Wendy Pfeffer, eds., *"Chançon legiere a chanter": Essays on Old French Literature in Honor of Samuel N. Rosenberg*
    ISBN 978-1-883479-54-1, clothbound $59.95 US

Barbara Bowen, *One Hundred Renaissance Jokes: A Critical Anthology*
    ISBN 0-917786-65-3, clothbound, $21.95 US

Elise Noël McMahon, *Classics Incorporated: Cultural Studies and Seventeenth-Century French Literature*
ISBN 1-883479-21-5, clothbound $41.95 US

Buford Norman, *Touched by the Graces: The Libretti of Philippe Quinault in the Context of French Classicism*
ISBN 1-883479-35-5, perfectbound $38.95 US

Nancy O'Connor, *De sa propre main: Recueils de choses morales de Dauphine de Sartre, marquise de Robiac (1634–1685)*
ISBN 1-883479-43-6, clothbound $54.95 US

Philip Wadsworth, *Molière and the Italian Theatrical Tradition* (2nd printing)
ISBN 0-917786-70-X, clothbound $16.95 US

Catherine Montfort, ed., *Literate Women and the French Revolution of 1789*
ISBN 1-883479-07-X, clothbound $45.95 US

Stephen Werner, *The Comic Philosophes: Montesquieu, Voltaire, Diderot, Sade*
ISBN 1-883479-40-1, clothbound $41.95 US

Stephen Werner, *The French Comic Imagination: From Rabelais to Sade*
ISBN 978-1-883479-51-0, clothbound $38.95 US

Richard Bales, *Persuasion in the French Personal Novel: Studies of Chateaubriand, Constant, Balzac, Nerval, and Fromentin*
ISBN 1-883479-16-9, clothbound $34.95 US

Kristof Haavik, *In Mortal Combat: The Conflict of Life and Death in Zola's Rougon-Macquart*
ISBN 1-883479-27-4, clothbound $43.95 US

Robert Godwin-Jones, *Romantic Vision: The Novels of George Sand*
ISBN 1-883479-06-1, clothbound $43.95 US

James Madden, *Weaving Balzac's Web: Spinning Tales and Creating the Whole of La Comédie Humaine*
ISBN 1-883479-41-X, clothbound $48.95 US

Allan Pasco, *Novel Configurations: A Study of French Fiction* (2nd edition)
ISBN 1-883479-00-2, perfectbound $24.95 US

Laurel Cummins, *Colette and the Conquest of Self*
ISBN 1-883479-46-0, clothbound $48.95 US

John Dunaway, *The Double Vocation: Christian Presence in Twentieth-Century French Fiction*
ISBN 1-883479-14-2, clothbound $37.95 US

Yvonne Hsieh, *From Occupation to Revolution: China through the Eyes of Loti, Claudel, Segalen, and Malraux (1895–1933)*
ISBN 1-883479-13-4, clothbound $39.95 US

Pierre Verdaguer, *La séduction policière: Signes de croissance d'un genre réputé mineur: Pierre Magnan, Daniel Pennac et quelques autres*
ISBN 1-883479-25-8, clothbound $51.95 US

Pascal Ifri, *Céline et Proust: Correspondances proustiennes dans l'oeuvre de L.-F. Céline*
ISBN 1-883479-12-6, clothbound $39.95 US

Elizabeth Viti, *Mothers, Madams, and "Lady-like" Men: Proust and the Maternal*
ISBN 1-883479-01-0, clothbound $32.95 US

Paula Ruth Gilbert, *The Literary Vision of Gabrielle Roy* (2nd printing)
ISBN 0-917786-05-X, clothbound $33.95 US

Renée Linkhorn,ed. & trans., *The Prose and Poetry of Andrée Chedid*
ISBN 0-917786-78-5, clothbound $24.95 US

Mary Lou Martin, *The Fables of Marie de France* (English translation)
ISBN 0-917786-34-3, clothbound $23.95 US

James and Nancy Vest, ed. & trans., *The Poetic Works of Maurice de Guérin*
ISBN 0-917786-87-4, clothbound $43.95 US

Joe Johnson, *Once There Were Two True Friends: Idealized Male Friendship in French Narrative from the Middle Ages through the Enlightenment*
ISBN 1-883479-42-8, clothbound $48.95 US

Stamos Metzidakis, ed., *Understanding French Poetry: Essays for a New Millennium* (2nd edition)
ISBN 1-883479-34-7, perfectbound $33.95 US

Clyde Thogmartin, *The National Daily Press of France*
ISBN 1-883479-20-7, clothbound $49.95 US

Anna Norris, *L'écriture du défi: Textes carcéraux féminins du XIXe et du XXe siècles*
ISBN 1-883479-39-3, clothbound $46.95 US

Marie-Christine Koop, ed., *France at the Dawn of the Twenty-First Century* (3rd printing)
ISBN 1-883479-29-0, perfectbound $33.95 US

American Southern Literature:
Critical Studies and Fiction

Shelby Foote, *Tournament*
ISBN 0-917786-56-4, perfectbound $19.95 US

Karl-Heinz Westarp, *Flannery O'Connor: The Growing Craft*
ISBN 0-917786-92-0, perfectbound $26.95 US

James Thomas, *Lyle Saxon: A Critical Biography*
ISBN 0-917786-83-1, perfectbound $23.95 US

For editorial information and ordering procedures, contact:

Summa Publications, Inc.
P.O. Box 660725
Birmingham, AL 35266-0725
USA